I love this book. Spiritual wholeness is the heart desire of all people and Stan Key has found the map. . . . Key sees important things scripturally and couples those incisive insights with real world application. These precepts have impressive potential to change the lives of those who study them. Wholeness ahead. Journey on!

> Matt Friedeman, PhD
> John M. Case Professor of Evangelical Studies
> Wesley Biblical Seminary

My love for roadmaps comes alive as the *Journey to Spiritual Wholeness* shows us how the map of the Exodus relates to our own spiritual journey. In a warm, engaging, readable, and enlightening manner this book converts theory into reality. The exodus of God's people gives us a simple yet doable guide for experiencing the beauty of a better land. It's hard to put this book down as it charts the course for God's best in our lives.

> Dave Engbrecht, PhD
> Senior Pastor
> Nappanee Missionary Church (Nappanee, IN)

Careful, methodical, and incisive, my friend Stan Key exhibits a rare gift in *Journey to Spiritual Wholeness*: He exegetes the deep truths of the Old Testament in such a clear, straightforward way that even we who have never been mistaken for scholars can easily grasp them. What true believer does not long for spiritual wholeness? Stan brings the entire quest into focus—and to within reach.

> Jerry B. Jenkins
> Bestselling Author
> *Left Behind* series

This little volume is a wonderful example of "biblical biography as spiritual journey." It not only provides practical teaching for every believer, but, in the process, it highlights the ongoing power of the living and active Word of God as it continues to speak and transform us today. I enthusiastically recommend this as an excellent resource for a small group or Sunday School class.

> Timothy C. Tennent, PhD
> President
> Asbury Theological Seminary

You'll never look at the Exodus story through the same lens again. [This book contains] stirring, convicting, and motivating messages for followers of Jesus. Teachers and preachers will be inspired to "preach the map."

> Ron Mackey
> Executive Director
> Deerfoot Lodge

In this book, with the sure touch of both a seasoned pastor and a gifted Bible student, Stan Key shows us how the apparently distant and obscure stories of the early books of the Bible relate directly to our lives today. In his words we find that it is ourselves who are captive in Egypt, wandering in the Wilderness, and hesitating at the Jordan. Nor is this a misappropriation of the biblical text for contemporary purposes. Rather, Stan helps us to see that understanding the truths of Scripture in these ways has an integrity and at the same time a realism that can and should involve all our biblical interpretation.

John N. Oswalt, PhD
Interim President
Wesley Biblical Seminary

In the spirit of Bunyan, Stan offers a comprehensive map to the spiritual journey of individual believers through a fresh reading of the old, familiar story of the Exodus. As such, Stan helps readers to see the story of the Exodus through a new lens that is informed by the complete gospel message in all its richness.

Matt Ayars, PhD
President
Emmaus University of Haiti

With his characteristic and signature charm and clarity, power and eminent practicality, preacher and teacher extraordinaire Stan Key (aptly enough) unlocks a vast swath of scripture by adroitly using the lens of the Exodus to shed light on how to enter the fullness of God's promise of spiritual victory— while avoiding notorious pitfalls along the way. At once as uplifting and enchanting as it is challenging and convicting, Key's long-awaited book on the geography of salvation is everything I hoped for and more. Rife with trenchant biblical insights, veritably singing with inimitable turns of phrase and dancing with lucid prose, it captures the imagination and invites readers to become fellow pilgrims with the ancient Israelites on a journey saturated with salvific significance today. The result is a treasure-laden pilgrimage readers should not, and with Key's help definitely will not, ever forget.

David Baggett, PhD
Professor of Philosophy
Liberty University

Drawing on his years of experience as a missionary, pastor, and teacher, Stan Key provides a penetrating challenge for Christians to take up the battle against aimless wandering. *Journey to Spiritual Wholeness* inspires a deeper longing to be led by the Spirit—to seek divine guidance and direction—that our lives would powerfully reflect the image of Christ.

Sandra C. Gray, PhD
President
Asbury University

I love what Stan Key has done in this book. He has taken an approach in reading the Old Testament that has an impeccable lineage, an approach grounded in how many of the New Testament writers interpreted it; how the early church fathers worked with it; and how many in our Holiness tradition preached it. Stan's work with the Exodus event and Promised Land conquest is theologically insightful, pastorally helpful, and spiritually practical. This book speaks with illustrative clarity about God's sanctifying work in the believer and how we can "possess" the life God makes possible to us through Christ in the power of the Holy Spirit. I can't wait to use it in my classroom.

> Christopher T. Bounds, PhD
> Professor of Theology/Wesley Scholar in Residence
> Asbury University

In this work, "Papa Stan" serves as a father to a new generation who never may have heard these life-giving, essential, inspirational lessons from the Exodus story. Written in a clear, engaging, personal style, this book makes the great lessons of the central story of the Old Testament accessible to all of us. It is a trustworthy source of wisdom, warning, instruction, and inspiration for a journey we are all on, like it or not. This is the Old Testament like I never read it before. The gospel was there all along! This book makes it clearer and takes it deeper! It has been strengthening and encouraging to me, personally, and I've already been using this material with my counseling clients. The response has been powerful!

> Brian Fast, PsyD
> Clinical Director
> CCAHope

I have often described Stan Key as my favorite preacher and one big reason for such a compliment are the ideas in this book. He makes you think thoughts you've never considered. The only thing better than reading this book is actually hearing Stan preach the Journey. Enjoy the ride!

> Judge Tim Philpot
> Retired Family Court Judge (Lexington, KY)
> Author, *Judge Z: Irretrievably Broken* (2016)

Pastor Key's teaching on the University of the Desert [has] great applicability for today. We often sneer at the inability of Israel to learn what they needed to learn—while repetitively and sometimes spectacularly failing the same courses ourselves. . . . Christ pointed out that the sick are the ones who need a doctor. Those struggling with the course are the ones who need a tutor. Let Pastor Key fulfill that role until we too are ready to fight the battle.

> Bruce Steffes, MD
> Former Chief Executive Officer/Chief Medical Officer
> Pan-African Academy of Christian Surgeons

There's no doubt in my mind that God has given Stan Key the rare and unique gift of keen insight into his Word. Coupled with a deep love for Christ and for his people, Stan's teaching continues to inspire me personally and open my eyes to see wonderful things in God's Word. God is using Stan, a pastor's pastor, to impact his people all over the nations. I truly thank God for this, Stan's latest release.

> Michael J. Thompson
> Founder and President
> OneWay Ministries

Stan Key has written a splendid new book on spiritual wholeness. His use of the Jewish Exodus to illustrate the spiritual life of each individual is brilliant. The metaphor of wandering in the desert strikes a chord which resonates in a way that more familiar descriptions of our fallen state as guilt or sin fail to reach many modern minds. Everyone can relate to times of being lost. God leads us to the "University of the Desert" as he did his own son, as part of our journey to [spiritual] wholeness. Stan uses the very details of the Exodus experience to illustrate the many lessons that we each must learn if we would arrive at the promised land—with humor, stories, poems, and a refreshing new view of the well-known. No one tells the story as Stan does. He writes deep truths with a light touch. I am eager to share this new book with family and friends.

> William C. Wood, MD
> Academic Dean
> Pan-African Academy of Christian Surgeons

Stan Key gifts us with an ancient, yet relevant, metaphor to shape our spiritual lives—the journey. The "mapplications" of the Israelite's journey from Egypt to Canaan will be a blessing to those who read this book. We will never experience the wholeness God has for us if we resist this call to adventure. So, pack your bags, find the map, and start moving toward the wholeness God has for you.

> Andy Miller III, Captain DMin
> Area Commander and Lead Pastor
> The Salvation Army (Tampa, FL)

As God leads Moses and the tribes toward their inheritance, he also teaches us many lessons for our own lives. As Stan compares their journey to our own spiritual walk, he puts the bow on the package with *Journey to Spiritual Wholeness*. . . . Stan is a gifted speaker and again brings his deep theological knowledge to the written page.

> Steve Luce
> President
> Indian Springs Holiness Campmeeting

In a world that increasingly devalues the Old Testament, my friend Stan Key reminds us again of its enormous value. Rooted in Paul's words to the Corinthians, Stan unpacks the powerful parallels between the Israelites' journey to Canaan and the believer's journey to "spiritual wholeness." Stan does something profoundly bold and liberating by showing that Canaan is not primarily reserved as a picture of heaven but is truly the land of "rest" for the believer today. On this pilgrimage with the people of God, you will discover more about your own spiritual journey. You will be encouraged that your journey is not unique, you will be challenged to be faithful every step of the way, and you will be thrilled to learn that your destiny is not the mediocre sands of the desert, but a place of spiritual blessing, rest, and victory. The parallel Stan draws between the life of the Christian and the children of Israel is beautiful, it is biblical, and it will be a blessing to all who read it.

Troy Keaton
Senior Pastor
EastLake Community Church (Moneta, VA)

Stan Key has presented, simultaneously, a work of scholarly reflection and one readily accessible to any serious student of the Scriptures. While focusing on the Book of Exodus, Key takes the whole [process of] crossing out of Egypt and through the wilderness as the guide for describing the Christian journey to the eternal Holy Land. . . . [O]ften drawing on the imagery of *Pilgrim's Progress*, he does gently correct Bunyan's reference to Sinai—liberation from spiritual bondage is not before but after the Law is received and purity becomes possible. Recognizing the canonical whole, Key uses Numbers, Leviticus, and Deuteronomy to explain that though this journey is not one without costs or unforeseen and unpleasant (even very painful) moments, it can be—by grace—one that offers holiness and wholeness.

James Thobaben, PhD
Dean of the School of Theology and Formation
Professor of Bioethics and Social Ethics
Asbury Theogical Seminary

Refreshing, challenging, inspiring, and humbling. In *Journey to Spiritual Wholeness*, Pastor Stan fleshes out the analogy of the Israelites' travels from Egypt to the Promised Land and our own present-day journey of spiritual freedom and growth. He skillfully points us to applications that will create in you a desire to deepen your understanding of Scripture while at the same time impacting your personal spiritual journey. Being struck by the truth that battles are a normal part of living in the Promised Land, my reality today ceased as a long journey through a desert but became characterized by the joy of experiencing the Promised Land. . . . [Y]et this road less traveled is not for the faint of heart, but for those who desire personal change and are willing to live in the battleground of the Promised Land.

Keir Thelander, MD
Chief Medical Officer
Pan-African Academy of Christian Surgeons

What an incredible biblical journey upon which I embarked as I read Stan Key's book, *Journey to Spiritual Wholeness*! The book took me from the Exodus . . . to my present situation. The children of Israel's voyage through the wilderness came alive because I saw my own wilderness in their wanderings. The best part is that I was shown the path to wholeness. What a great read! I recommend it to all traveling the highway of life who are searching for the way that leads to the fullness and abundance of life that Christ promised. You'll find it in this book!

Sammy Tippit, DMin
Author and International Evangelist
Sammy Tippit Ministries

Journey to Spiritual Wholeness

How the map of the Exodus illustrates our own spiritual journey

By Stan Key

OTHER TITLES BY STAN KEY

Journey to Spiritual Wholeness

How the map of the Exodus illustrates our own spiritual journey

By Stan Key

Francis Asbury Press

Wilmore, Kentucky

Francis Asbury Society

PO Box 7
Wilmore, KY 40390
859-858-4222
800-530-5673
fas@francisasburysociety.com
www.francisasburysociety.com

Unless otherwise noted, scripture quotations are from the Holy Bible, English Standard Version® (ESV®), copyright ©2001 by Crossway, a publishing ministry of Good News Publishers. Used by permission. All rights reserved.

Scriptures marked NASB are taken from the Holy Bible, New American Standard Bible® (NASB), Copyright © 1960, 1962, 1963, 1968, 1971, 1972, 1973, 1975, 1977, 1995 by The Lockman Foundation. Used by permission. www.Lockman.org

Scriptures marked NIV are taken from the Holy Bible, New International Version®, NIV® Copyright ©1973, 1978, 1984, 2011 by Biblica, Inc.® Used by permission. All rights reserved worldwide.

Scriptures marked NKJV are taken from the Holy Bible, New King James Version®. Copyright © 1982 by Thomas Nelson. Used by permission. All rights reserved.

Scriptures marked NLT are taken from the Holy Bible, New Living Translation, copyright ©1996, 2004, 2015 by Tyndale House Foundation. Used by permission of Tyndale House Publishers, Inc., Carol Stream, Illinois 60188. All rights reserved.

Scriptures marked KJV are taken from the King James Version (KJV): King James Version, public domain.

Scriptures marked MSG are taken from *THE MESSAGE*, copyright © 1993, 2002, 2018 by Eugene H. Peterson. Used by permission of NavPress. All rights reserved. Represented by Tyndale House Publishers, Inc.

ISBN 978-0-915143-31-3
Cover design by Hadley Slucher
Printed in the United States of America

Dedicated to John Bunyan (1628–1688)

Other than the Bible, his classic *Pilgrim's Progress* is the greatest journey to spiritual wholeness ever written.

"And he brought us out . . . that he might bring us in . . . ." (Deuteronomy 6:23)

To Be a Pilgrim

John Bunyan (1684)

A song from "The Pilgrim's Progress"

Who would true valor see,
Let him come hither;
One here will constant be,
Come wind, come weather.
There's no discouragement
Shall make him once relent
His first avowed intent,
To be a pilgrim.

Whoso beset him round
With dismal stories,
Do but themselves confound;
His strength the more is.
No lion can him fright,
He'll with a giant fight,
But he will have a right
To be a pilgrim.

Hobgoblin, nor foul fiend,
Can daunt his spirit:
He knows, he at the end
Shall life inherit.
Then fancies fly away,
He'll fear not what men say,
He'll labor night and day
To be a pilgrim.

Contents

Foreword xvii

Introduction 21

EGYPT

Chapter 1: Who Am I? 35

Chapter 2: Redeemed 49

FROM THE RED SEA TO SINAI

Chapter 3: The Bitter Place 63

Chapter 4: Wonder Bread 75

Chapter 5: Spiritual Warfare 85

Chapter 6: The Stress Test 99

AT SINAI

Chapter 7: Dearly Beloved, We Are Gathered Here 109

Chapter 8: Oh, How I Love Your Law! 123

Chapter 9: A House for God 139

Chapter 10: A Lot of Bull 155

Chapter 11: Living with the Holy One 167

FROM SINAI TO MOAB

Chapter 12: The "Grumpies" 181

Chapter 13: The Moment of Truth 193

Chapter 14: The Land of In-Between 209

Chapter 15: The Heart of the Matter 223

CANAAN

Chapter 16: Crossing Jordan 239

Chapter 17: Soldiers of Christ, Arise! 255

Questions for Discussion 267

Foreword

*By faith Abraham obeyed, when he was called
to go out to a place that he was to receive as
an inheritance. And he went out, not knowing
where he was going. (Hebrews 11:8)*

The story of Abraham teaches us that salvation is a journey.
Though he did not know where he was going, he was confident
that the one who called him knew the way. Abraham "went out" into
the unknown with nothing but the promise of God to guide him. He
walked with God—by faith. My father loved the story of Abraham and
made it a point to teach me, when I was very young, that it didn't really
matter *where* the journey took Abraham (or me!), as long as God was
leading the way! He would smile as he told me, "It's not complicated;
all you have to do is follow him."

This journey of faith in obedience to the Word of God, motivated
by love, flows through all Scripture and is the very essence of living in
spiritual triumph. Stan Key brings this journey masterfully into focus
as he recounts how the Israelites leave Egypt and travel through the
wilderness to the Land of Promise.

The journey begins when God answers the cries of the oppressed
Israelites pleading for deliverance. God raises up a leader, Moses, who,
working signs and wonders, finally persuades Pharaoh to let them go.
In an awesome display of power, God holds back the waters of the Red
Sea so that the children of Israel can cross through on dry land. But
rather than taking the short, easy road, God leads them south, into the
desert of the Sinai Peninsula.

At Mount Sinai, God enters into a sacred covenant of love with his redeemed people. Though the people promise to obey God and submit to his plan for their lives, they soon begin to grumble and complain about their circumstances. In their discontent, they build a golden calf and begin to worship it. Though God judges them severely for their faithlessness and willful disobedience, he nevertheless allows them to resume their journey to Canaan.

After leaving Sinai, they soon reach the border of the Promised Land at a place called Kadesh-barnea. Amazingly, the people turn back in fear and refuse to move forward to possess their God-ordained inheritance! In anger, God condemns them to wander in the desert for the next forty years, until the whole generation (everyone over twenty years of age) has perished.

Finally, a new generation arises who is ready to trust once again in the promises of God and walk with him by faith on the journey of salvation. Once again, God performs a miracle at the Jordan River, making possible their passage to the other side. Make no mistake! Canaan is not paradise. They still have battles to fight, crops to plant, and cities to build. Here in Canaan, the journey continues as God's people go from victory to victory, living fruitful and productive lives in the kingdom of God.

This book tells the story of the journey of the Hebrews from Egypt, through the desert, to Canaan. In these pages, Stan Key masterfully expounds what this story meant for the people of Israel so long ago who first made that journey. But, just as importantly, he explains how *their* journey illuminates *ours* today. Though he is a gifted writer and a diligent student of Scripture, Stan is also, at heart, a pastor. As the journey unfolds step by step, he asks probing questions and makes penetrating, practical applications (he calls them "mapplications"). He helps us see that the journey taken by the Hebrew children so long ago is far more than history: it is, in fact, our own story. Yes, following the highway of holiness often leads through trials and difficulties, but God uses even our disappointments to help bring us home. Even

Jesus "learned obedience through what he suffered" (Heb 5:8). All his followers have similar lessons to learn.

As my father would explain it, it all boils down to one simple command: "Follow me," Jesus said, "I am the Way." Even a child can do that. It takes faith and obedience, and often the way is painful and hard, but if God is the one who is guiding our steps, then we can be certain that we are on our way home. Like Abraham, we are going to a city whose builder and maker is God. Oh, the joy that is set before us as we "go out" with God!

—Robert E Coleman, PhD
Author, *The Master Plan of Evangelism*

Introduction

"And Jesus said to them, 'Follow me . . . .'" (Mark 1:17)

The Bible uses multiple metaphors to help us better understand the richness of salvation offered us in Jesus Christ (see "Table 0.1: Metaphors of Salvation"). For example, in Romans and Galatians, Paul describes salvation in terms of a *courtroom*. God is the Judge and we stand condemned, having broken his law. Jesus comes not only as our Advocate to plead our case; he actually takes our place and receives the punishment we deserve. Through his actions, our sins are pardoned and we are made right with God. Another biblical metaphor is one that describes salvation in *family* terms. We enter the Father's family when we are born of the Spirit and become a child of God. Other Scriptures picture salvation in terms of *marriage*. Jesus is the bridegroom who seeks to capture our hearts and live in intimacy in a covenant of love forever. While other metaphors could be cited,[1] the emphasis of this book is to see salvation as a *journey*, a walk with God.

The theme of *walking with God* is prominent throughout the biblical narrative, from Genesis to Revelation. It is one of the primary word-pictures the Bible uses to describe what our relationship with God is like. It is significant that many non-Christian writers also have seen life in terms of a journey, finding that this metaphor provides a powerful vocabulary for grappling with the meaning of human existence. Homer, in his epic tale *The Odyssey*, wrote of Odysseus' ten-year journey home after the Trojan War. Full of adventure, warfare, monsters, temptations, and romance, this classic remains a standard

---

1   The vine and the branches, the shepherd and sheep, the potter and the clay, etc.

Table 0.1: Metaphors of Salvation

	Courtroom	Father & Children	Marriage	Journey
Who is God?	Judge	Father	Bridegroom Husband	Lord King
Who is Jesus?	Advocate, lawyer	Brother	Bridegroom Husband	Guide Fellow traveler "The Way"
Who am I?	Guilty sinner Condemned	Newborn child Adopted child	Fiancée Wife	Pilgrim
What is the problem?	Sin, guilt I've broken God's law	I am dead, unborn, a child of the devil	Other lovers Adultery	I'm lost I'm headed in the wrong direction
What is the solution?	Forgiveness Pardon Justification	New birth Adoption	Marriage Covenant	Repent (turn around) "Follow Me"
How do I become a Christian?	Confess Repent Believe	Be born again	Enter a covenant Turn from other lovers	Decide to follow Jesus
How do I know I'm a Christian?	"There is now no condemnation . . ." (Rom 8:1)	"The Spirit of adoption . . . 'Abba!'" (Rom 8:15)	"My beloved is mine and I am his . . ." (Sg 2:16)	"All who are led by the Spirit of God are sons . . ." (Rom 8:14)
How should I then live?	"If anyone does sin, we have an advocate . . ." (1 Jn 2:1–2)	"As obedient children . . . be holy" (1 Pt 1:14–15)	Keep yourself pure (2 Cor 11:2)	Walk worthy of your calling (Eph 4:1)

text of Western literature. J. R. R. Tolkien (*The Lord of the Rings*), Mark Twain (*The Adventures of Huckleberry Finn*), Jonathan Swift (*Gulliver's Travels*), and Frank Baum (*The Wizard of Oz*), to name only a few, also have used a journey as the framework for the stories they've told. Robert Frost (1874–1963) has captured the power of this metaphor in his moving poem *The Road Not Taken*:

> *Two roads diverged in a yellow wood,*
> *And sorry I could not travel both*
> *And be one traveler, long I stood*
> *And looked down one as far as I could*
> *To where it bent in the undergrowth . . . .*

Two roads diverged in a wood, and I—
I took the one less traveled by,
And that has made all the difference.

Christian writers also have been quick to use the journey theme. A classic of Russian Orthodoxy is a simple devotional work entitled *The Way of the Pilgrim*. Dante's *The Divine Comedy* is a three-volume work that tells of a journey from the depths of hell to the heights of paradise. This masterpiece of literature begins with these words: "Midway along the journey of our life I woke to find myself in a dark wood, for I had wandered off the straight path . . . ." By far the most famous and influential Christian book about spiritual wholeness as a journey is *Pilgrim's Progress*. John Bunyan's classic is still read with great profit because of the insights it gives to understanding the journey to spiritual wholeness. Chronicling the journey from the City of Destruction by way of the Wicket Gate, the Hill of Difficulty, Vanity Fair, By-Path Meadow, Doubting Castle, and finally the crossing at the River of Death to reach the Celestial City, Bunyan's saga introduces us to what the Christian walk is like.

The Bible itself provides us with our most poignant depictions of life described as a journey. It is no accident that one of the earliest names used to describe the Christian faith was "The Way" (see Acts 9:2; 19:9, 23; 24:22; etc.). When Jesus called his first disciples by saying "Follow me," those original Christians understood that they were being invited on a journey. The importance of walking with God is emphasized in many other places in the Bible:

- "Enoch *walked* with God . . ." (Gn 5:22).
- "Noah was a righteous man, blameless in his generation. Noah *walked* with God" (Gn 6:9).
- "When Abram was ninety-nine years old the LORD appeared to Abram and said to him, 'I am God Almighty; *walk* before me, and be blameless'" (Gn 17:1).
- "Blessed is the man who *walks* not in the counsel of the wicked, nor stands in the way of sinners, nor sits in the seat of scoffers" (Ps 1:1).

- "And your ears shall hear a word behind you, saying, 'This is the way, *walk* in it . . .'" (Is 30:21).
- "What does the LORD require of you but to do justice, and to love kindness, and to *walk* humbly with your God?" (Mi 6:8).
- "*Walk* by the Spirit, and you will not gratify the desires of the flesh" (Gal 5:16).
- "*Walk* in a manner worthy of the calling to which you have been called" (Eph 4:1).
- "*Walk* in love, as Christ loved us and gave himself up for us . . ." (Eph 5:2).
- "Look carefully then how you *walk*, not as unwise but as wise" (Eph 5:15).
- "If we *walk* in the light, as he is the light, we have fellowship with one another, and the blood of Jesus his Son cleanses us from all sin" (1 Jn 1:7).
- "Yet you have still a few names in Sardis, people who have not soiled their garments, and they will *walk* with me in white, for they are worthy" (Rv 3:4).

> **66 Spiritual wholeness defines a level of Christian living that is unknown to many today.**

However, nowhere in the Bible is the journey of salvation more graphically displayed than in the Exodus. When the Hebrews traveled from Egypt, through the Red Sea, across the desert, to Sinai, to Kadesh-barnea, to the Plains of Moab, and finally crossed the Jordan River into Canaan to possess their inheritance we have an unforgettable description of a journey unmatched in all human history. Full of adventure, battle, romance, temptation, rebellion, and surprise, this journey from bondage to glorious freedom is one of the greatest stories ever told. By following the locations on the map where God led his redeemed people, we discover the journey to spiritual wholeness.

Spiritual wholeness defines a level of Christian living that is unknown to many today. It is neither a certain level of religious performance nor a certain kind of experience. I use the term to define a spiritual reality that is characterized by:

- Victory over sin.
- Being fruitful (the fruit of Christian character and ministry).
- Finding strength to cope with hardship and suffering.

THE MEANING OF THE MAP

For many years, when I read the Old Testament story of the Exodus, I sensed that this journey was more than interesting history. As I learned about the victories and trials of the Jewish people in their journey from Egypt to Canaan, I often had the impression I was reading my own life story. It almost seemed that *their* journey was *my* journey. However, I'd been taught the dangers of interpreting the Scriptures allegorically and didn't want to be guilty of misusing the text. I was fearful of reading into the Bible a message that wasn't there.

Then I discovered 1 Corinthians 10:1–13. To my shock, the apostle Paul used the Exodus as a gospel lesson for Gentile believers in Greece! He drew spiritual lessons from an Old Testament story, and he claimed that these lessons had relevance for people—who weren't even Jews—living centuries later. Certainly, Paul knew how to interpret the Bible. Yet here he was, under the inspiration of the Holy Spirit, using the map of the Exodus as his text for a gospel sermon. He was making "mapplications." He used the story of what happened to the Hebrews on their journey from Egypt to Canaan as an illustration to help contemporary Christians learn from the mistakes made so long ago.

> For I do not want you to be unaware, brothers, that our fathers were all under the cloud, and all passed through the sea, and all were baptized into Moses in the cloud and in the sea, and all ate the same spiritual food, and all drank the same spiritual drink. For they drank from the spiritual Rock that followed them, and the Rock was Christ. Nevertheless,

with most of them God was not pleased, for they were
overthrown in the wilderness.

Now these things took place as examples for us, that we
might not desire evil as they did. Do not be idolaters as
some of them were; as it is written, "The people sat down to
eat and drink and rose up to play." We must not indulge in
sexual immorality as some of them did, and twenty-three
thousand fell in a single day. We must not put Christ to the
test, as some of them did and were destroyed by serpents,
nor grumble, as some of them did and were destroyed by
the Destroyer. Now these things happened to them as an
example, but they were written down for our instruction,
on whom the end of the ages has come. Therefore let
anyone who thinks that he stands take heed lest he fall.
No temptation has overtaken you that is not common to
man. God is faithful, and he will not let you be tempted
beyond your ability, but with the temptation he will also
provide the way of escape, that you may be able to endure it.
(1 Corinthians 10:1–13)

Apparently, the apostle Paul believed that the map of the Exodus
could serve as a guide not only for Jews in the Old Testament but also
for Christians in the New Testament. The places on the map were not
just random locations of historical interest. For Paul, each stage of the
journey was pregnant with spiritual significance. These places on the
map were illustrative of the experiences all Christians should expect in
their own journey from bondage in sin to freedom in Christ.

Of all the churches in the New Testament, none had more moral
problems, doctrinal aberrations, divisions, and carnality than the
church in Corinth. Though they prided themselves on the signs,
wonders, and spiritual manifestations that were often in evidence
when they gathered for worship, this church was perhaps the most
dysfunctional group of believers in the New Testament. As Greeks,
they likely were familiar with the philosophy of Plato and Aristotle
and probably prided themselves on their superior knowledge. Yet the
church in Corinth was a tragic example of spiritual immaturity and
doctrinal confusion.

One of the primary ways Paul chose to address these complex and
deep-rooted problems in the church at Corinth was by preaching the

map. He wanted these Gentile believers to understand that the journey described in the Exodus of God's people from Egypt was applicable directly to them. It was not just history. Twice, Paul asserts that these Old Testament stories are "examples" given so that New Testament believers can profit from them (1 Cor 10:6, 11). The word Paul used is *tupos*, from which we get our English word "type." The term originally described the impression of a seal or stamp. Sometimes it referred to a mold or form that could be used to make duplicates. Paul was warning the Corinthians not to imitate the foolish and sinful behaviors of their spiritual ancestors on their journey to spiritual wholeness. He wanted the Corinthian believers to learn from the mistakes of the past. Paul would have agreed with British philosopher and statesman Edmund Burke when he famously said: "Those who don't know history are destined to repeat it."

We can draw at least four conclusions, or "mapplications," from what Paul said about the journey to these first-century Christians: be informed, be wise, be alert, and be encouraged.

First, be informed: *spiritual wholeness is a journey, not just a destination.* In addressing the problems at Corinth, Paul chose to use the metaphor of a journey; he preached the map. These Christians didn't need a sermon on forgiveness or the new birth. They needed an exhortation on the dangers of the journey: Watch your step, lest you fall! By preaching the map, Paul reminded his hearers that salvation is not just a ticket to heaven when you die. It is a *walk* toward spiritual wholeness. It is a daily response to Jesus' call, "Follow me." How can we call ourselves Christ-followers if we are not following Christ? "All who are led by the Spirit of God are sons of God" (Rom 8:14).

Second, be wise: *not all who start the journey reach the finish line.* No one could doubt the many spiritual blessings that characterized the Hebrew people when they began their journey. They had all experienced divine guidance through the pillar of fire (1 Cor 10:1), they all had been "baptized" in the Red Sea (1 Cor 10:2), they all had eaten the miracle bread that fell freely from heaven each day (1 Cor 10:3), and they all had drunk the miracle water provided for them in the desert

(1 Cor 10:4). "Nevertheless, with most of them God was not pleased for they were overthrown in the wilderness" (1 Cor 10:5). Paul wanted the spiritual zealots of the church in Corinth to understand that spiritual blessings do not guarantee spiritual maturity. A good start does not guarantee a good finish. By preaching the map, Paul gently but firmly reminded the believers in Corinth that a race is always determined at the finish line, not in the starting blocks. Jesus stated the issue quite forcefully: "Not everyone who says to me, 'Lord, Lord,' will enter the kingdom of heaven, but the one who does the will of my Father who is in heaven" (Mt 7:21).

Third, be alert: *there are certain dangers that nearly all pilgrims face at some point in their spiritual journey.* Paul did not mention every temptation and trial that the Hebrews faced during the Exodus, but he focused on four particular instances, because he knew that believers in Corinth struggled with the very same things.

> **Thinking one is immune from moral failure is perhaps the surest way to allow it to happen.**

1. *Idolatry* (1 Cor 10:7). When God's people worshiped the golden calf (Ex 32), they gave an unforgettable example of the tendency in every human heart to try to make God in our own image and to give our worship to what our own hands have made.
2. *Sexual immorality* (1 Cor 10:8). Moral failure with the Moabite women (Nm 25) was a graphic illustration of the way sexual temptation has been a stumbling stone for believers since the very beginning.
3. *Putting the Lord to the test* (1 Cor 10:9). To test the Lord means to try his patience, to presume upon his grace, to complain about his provision and care. God sent poisonous snakes to punish the Hebrews for their ungrateful and bitter attitudes (Nm 21:4–9).
4. *Grumbling* (1 Cor 10:10). Repeatedly during the Exodus journey, God's people murmured and whined about their circumstances. Such a bitter spirit can keep one doing laps in the wilderness forever.

In preaching the map, Paul gave a strong warning to the believers in Corinth: beware, lest these same sins bring about your downfall, too. Don't be naive. Thinking one is immune from moral failure is perhaps the surest way to allow it to happen. "Therefore, let anyone who thinks that he stands take heed lest he fall" (1 Cor 10:12).

It is interesting to note that Paul himself had a healthy concern for his own ultimate salvation. Earlier in this letter to the Corinthians, he had written candidly about this:

> Do you not know that in a race all the runners run, but only one receives the prize? So run that you may obtain it. Every athlete exercises self-control in all things. They do it to receive a perishable wreath, but we an imperishable. So I do not run aimlessly; I do not box as one beating the air. But I discipline my body and keep it under control, lest after preaching to others I myself should be disqualified. (1 Corinthians 9:24–27)

Paul knew that the fear of the Lord was the beginning of wisdom (Prv 9:10). He was keenly aware of the potential that lay in his heart to sin against grace and to wander from the God he loved. Thus, he advised the Christians in Corinth to be alert lest they fall.

Fourth, be encouraged: *God is faithful.* Preaching the map was not just a way to warn misguided believers about the dangers of the journey. The main reason Paul preached the map was to *encourage* the saints to keep pressing on. God was with them to help them each step of the way. "No temptation has overtaken you that is not common to man. God is faithful, and he will not let you be tempted beyond your ability, but with the temptation he will also provide the way of escape, that you may be able to endure it" (1 Cor 10:13). For those who may feel fearful and tired in their journey, this is good news indeed! Paul finished his "map sermon" by reminding the believers in Corinth of three glorious truths:

1. *You are normal.* Regardless of the challenges you may be facing in your journey, you can be sure of this: "no temptation has overtaken you that is not common to man." You are not alone in

this battle. Countless saints before you have faced similar battles, and some, far worse. Your temptations and trials are not evidence of being abandoned and alone but rather of being precisely on the path where you are supposed to be.

2. *God is faithful.* In the final analysis, it is not our hold on God that matters, but his hold on us. "God will not let you be tempted beyond your ability." This is no mere pious hope. It is a promise from God himself, addressed personally to you. He will never leave you nor forsake you.

3. *Victory is promised.* "With the temptation he will also provide the way of escape, that you may be able to endure it." As Peter put it so succinctly, "The LORD knows how to deliver the godly out of temptation" (2 Pt 2:9). The God who brought us out of Egypt will surely bring us into the Land of Promise (Dt 6:23).

WELCOME TO THE JOURNEY

The purpose of this book is not only to study the journey of the Hebrews from Egypt to Canaan but also to invite *you*, the reader, to pack your bags and embark on the greatest adventure you will ever take. Jesus himself is calling and urging you to come: "Follow me." The geographical progression of the original Exodus is illustrative of what tends to happen in the life of everyone who answers Jesus' call. Thus, working through the following chapters hopefully will serve as a sort of road map for you in your spiritual journey.

The biblical story of the Hebrew people is told primarily in the books of Exodus, Leviticus, Numbers, Deuteronomy, and Joshua. The book of Genesis serves as an indispensable prequel to this material.

- *Exodus* tells of the journey from Egypt to Mount Sinai.
- *Numbers* tells of the journey from Mount Sinai to the border of Canaan at Kadesh-barnea where the people rebelled, resulting in thirty-eight years of wandering, doing laps, in the desert.
- *Leviticus* is a collection of instructions concerning sacrifices, worship, the priesthood, and discerning the difference between

clean and unclean. All these regulations were given to Moses while the people camped at Mount Sinai.

- *Deuteronomy* is a series of sermons given by Moses in the Plains of Moab, just across the Jordan River from the Hebrews' inheritance in Canaan.

- *Joshua* tells how the people crossed the Jordan River and entered Canaan. It recounts the battles fought and how the land was divided among the tribes.

To understand the significance of the journey and the importance of the map, one first needs to make sure the big picture is clearly understood (see "Figure 1: The Map of the Exodus" on page 34). The meaning of various locations on the map makes sense only as one remembers the overall geography: first Egypt, then the desert, and finally Canaan. The unfolding significance of this geography and how we can find personal mapplications for our own journeys to spiritual wholeness will be explained as we follow the Hebrews' journey from place to place.

The first two chapters deal with Egypt (Ex 1:1–15:21). Every journey has a beginning, and this one starts with a group of Hebrew slaves living far from their ancestral home. What will cause them to leave the place where they have lived for 400 years? And how will they break free from the bonds of slavery? These chapters explore issues related to identity, bondage, homesickness, desire, and calling. We will discover that no one can begin the journey to spiritual wholeness without God supernaturally making a way.

Chapters 3–6 describe the three-month journey from the Red Sea to Mount Sinai (Ex 15:22–18:27). God's redeemed people discover that, though they are out of Egypt, they are still a long way from Canaan. Rather than finding themselves in a land of milk and honey, they learn that God has led them into a barren wasteland. In studying the lessons God teaches his redeemed people in this University of the Desert, we will learn how to prepare for our own spiritual battles.

Chapters 7–11 tell the story of all that transpired during the 12–18-month stay at Mount Sinai. These chapters explore the marriage covenant made between God and his people (Ex 19–40). For over a year, God revealed his plans for the Tabernacle and gave clear instructions concerning worship. Tragically, the people violated the covenant only a few weeks after it was made by committing spiritual adultery with the golden calf. Though they were out of Egypt, "Egypt" was not yet out of them! In these chapters, we will discover that there is more to spiritual wholeness than getting out of our bondage to sin. We also must find a way to purify our hearts. Chapter 11 explores the book of Leviticus and God's demand for holiness in the hearts and lives of his people.

Chapters 12–15 follow the journey of the Hebrews from Sinai to the Plains of Moab (Nm 11–32). The rebellion that takes place at Kadesh-barnea explains why a journey intended to take about two years turned into a forty-year nightmare of doing laps in the wilderness. The dramatic stories of Korah's rebellion, poisonous snakes, and the seductive Moabite women typify the kinds of experiences followers of Christ may expect to encounter as they walk their own journey to spiritual wholeness. Chapter 15 surveys the entire book of Deuteronomy by summarizing Moses' final message to the people he had pastored for forty years. What God really wants from his followers, his purpose in redemption, is whole-hearted love.

Chapters 16–17 bring a culmination to the journey to spiritual wholeness when the people finally enter Canaan by crossing the Jordan River and then fighting the battle of Jericho (Jos 1–6). They started their journey by crossing a body of water, which freed them from bondage. They had to cross a second body of water to enter the Land of Promise. These events reflect the crises of faith Christians experience on their own journeys. First, we must be brought out of our bondage to sin, and then we must be brought into a life of victory, fruitfulness, and rest.

As we journey with the Hebrews from Egypt to Canaan, we will discover how the Exodus journey is a powerful illustration for believers today. A rich supply of biblical events illuminates theological complexities and provides a reservoir of teaching profitable for pastoral care. In studying the points on the map of the Exodus, we obtain a creative biblical vocabulary for dealing with complex questions such as:

- Why do some who start the journey fail to finish?
- What is the role of the desert in the journey to spiritual wholeness?
- Where does the law belong in redemption?
- What is the meaning of the covenant?
- What is the difference between true worship and false worship?
- What is the victorious abundant life really like?
- How does crisis and process affect the Christian experience?
- How does one discover true rest?
- What is the heart of matter? What is it all about?

Pack your bags and get ready for an adventure! God himself invites you to follow him on a journey like no other. Come on, let's go!

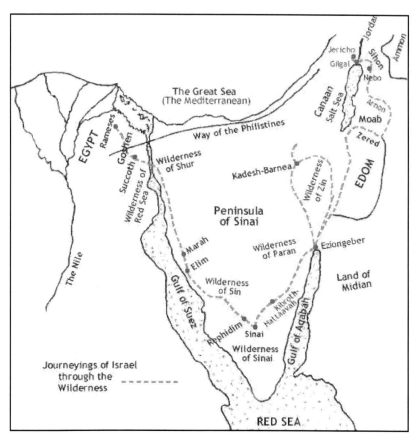

Figure 1: The Map of the Exodus

I
Who Am I?
(Exodus 1–4)

*"Once you were not a people, but now you
are God's people . . . ." (1 Peter 2:10)*

Tony Evans tells the delightful story about an eagle that was raised by turkeys.[1] Somehow an eagle's egg was knocked out of its nest and found itself on a turkey farm. When the little eaglet broke out of his shell, he looked around and saw a bunch of turkeys and drew what seemed to be a logical conclusion: "I must be a turkey." He began to eat like a turkey, walk like a turkey, gobble like a turkey, and even smell like a turkey. Occasionally, when he would gaze at his reflection in the water or stretch his wings, he would wonder about who he *really* was, but the daily grind of life on a turkey farm kept him locked in his turkey identity.

One day, a majestic eagle flew over the farm. Seeing the eaglet among the turkeys below, the eagle swooped down and said, "Hey, what are you doing in a place like this?"

"I'm hanging out with my family, the turkeys," the eaglet replied.

"Who told you that you were a turkey?" asked the eagle.

"Well," said the eaglet, "I was born with turkeys and raised by turkeys. I walk, eat, gobble, and smell like a turkey; so, I must be one of them."

---

1   Tony Evans, *The Promise: Experiencing God's Greatest Gift the Holy Spirit* (Chicago: Moody Press, 1996), 173.

"Someone has lied to you," said the eagle. "Stretch out those wings! Now flap!"

Obediently, the eaglet did as he was told. As he did so, he began to rise above the farm yard. Flapping harder, he rose higher and higher. "Now, follow me," shouted the eagle. As the eaglet began to rise into the sky, one of the turkeys looked up and said, "Where do you think you're going?" The eaglet looked back over his shoulder and said, "I'm going to be what I was created to be, you turkey!"

This story reminds us that no one embarks on the journey to spiritual wholeness until he comes to grips with the question of his true identity. Am I a turkey or am I an eagle? Am I trapped in a predetermined destiny or am I free to soar into a new and glorious identity? Who am I?

Before anyone starts a journey, there must first be a *reason* to begin. If we are content on the turkey farm, why leave? Why risk the journey when we are happy with the way things are? Why break the status quo if we like life as it is? Unless the reasons for leaving are greater than the reasons for staying, we will

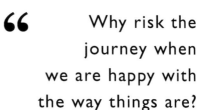

Why risk the journey when we are happy with the way things are?

never begin the journey that God has set before us. Though we may live among turkeys and even act like them, God wants us to know that we have a different identity and, therefore, we have a different destiny.

ALIENS IN A STRANGE LAND

As the book of Exodus opens, the Hebrew people have been living in the land of Egypt for almost 400 years. For much of this time, they have lived in relative freedom and comfort in the pleasant region of Goshen. Egypt was prosperous, stable, and culturally advanced. It would make sense for the Hebrews to think of Egypt as home and to take on Egyptian ways and customs. Just as the eaglet concluded that he must be a turkey, so the Hebrews, after 400 years, must have been tempted to conclude that Egypt defined both their home and their identity.

This is precisely the problem God faced when the time came for him to call his people to set out on their journey. His people were living, as it were, on a "turkey farm." As long as they were being treated well, why on earth would they want to leave? Though they may have occasional questions about their history and their true identity, as long as they were comfortable, they were content to stay.

In spiritual terms, Egypt is a picture of this world (see Rv 11:7–8). The Bible strongly states that no one can be a friend of this world and a friend of God at the same time (Jas 4:4; 1 Jn 2:15–17). God's people are not "turkeys," and their home is not "the farmyard." People who are happy with the status quo will never begin the journey to spiritual wholeness. We simply cannot soar with the eagles if we are content to waddle with the turkeys. As the puritan pastor Thomas Brooks (1608–1680) said so succinctly, "The world and you must part or Christ and you will never meet."

Though God's people live *in* the world, they are not *of* the world. This distinction explains why the Hebrews never assimilated into Egypt, even though they lived there for 400 years. Though raised on the "turkey farm," they knew deep in their hearts that they were not "turkeys." They were the children of Abraham. The beginning of their amazing story is told in Genesis 12:1–4.

WHY LEAVE?

God had a problem: how to motivate people to leave a place they didn't want to leave. Even God has difficulty getting the attention of people who are content with the status quo. What can be done for people who seem to *like* living the life of a "turkey"? The early chapters of Exodus describe how God responded to this challenge. He sovereignly orchestrated events so that the Hebrew people became so disenchanted with Egypt that they actually *wanted* to leave the place they had called home for four centuries! Specifically, God used four things to motivate his people to pack their bags and begin to walk with him on the journey to spiritual wholeness: pain, an identity crisis, hunger, and a call with a promise.

Pain

The book of Genesis ends with a picture of the Hebrews living comfortably in the pleasant land of Goshen. They had been welcomed there by a friendly and grateful Pharaoh. The Hebrew Joseph was a national hero for all he did to save Egypt from famine. We can assume that for many years, life was good and the Hebrews were happy living as welcomed guests in their new home. However, all this has changed by the time the book of Exodus continues the story. Exodus opens with a graphic depiction of slavery, suffering, and oppression (see Ex 1:6–22). A "new king" has come to the throne who does not remember how Joseph had saved the nation (Ex 1:8). Fearful that such a large minority might one day join Egypt's enemies and fight against them, he enslaved and oppressed the Jews. Cruel taskmasters were placed over them, forcing them to build the cities of Pithom and Raamses.

> 66 **Few things have a greater capacity to get our attention and cause us to desire change than pain.**

When it seemed the situation couldn't get worse, the king made a decree to kill all the male babies born into Jewish families.

Life became extremely painful for the Hebrews living in Egypt. What had once been a happy existence in a pleasant location now resembled life in a Nazi concentration camp. They groaned because of their slavery and cried out to God for deliverance. At first, it seemed that God wasn't listening, that he didn't care. As the plot unfolds, however, we discover that God is not deaf. Indeed, he is filled with compassion for those who suffer. Rather than rushing to bring pain relief, however, he first *used* their suffering to motivate them to leave the place they had called home for 400 years and begin a journey. The mapplication is clear: we will not begin the journey to spiritual wholeness until the pain of staying where we are becomes greater than the pain of moving to where God wants us to be.

One of the primary problems with the so-called "prosperity gospel" is that it has no theology of suffering and pain. It pretends that God's sole purpose is to bless his people so that they can be healthy, wealthy, and happy. It fails to realize that the Bible often speaks of how God permits bitter experiences to enter our lives to wake us from the deadly status quo and to motivate us to set out on a journey to the Land of Promise. Few things have a greater capacity to get our attention and cause us to desire change than pain. C. S. Lewis said it well: "God whispers to us in our pleasures; speaks in our conscience; but shouts in our pain. It is God's megaphone to rouse a deaf world."[2] God wants to use the pain in our lives to motivate us to press forward toward the goal he has set before us.

Americans, however, see little value in pain. We spend over 17.8 billion dollars every year on prescription pain relief medications alone.[3] Pain is an enemy that must be eliminated. Nothing good comes from pain, right?

Dr. Paul Brand wrote an insightful book about pain that has changed my thinking forever. Working as a medical missionary among leprosy patients in India, he learned that one of the side-effects of leprosy is that it destroys the body's ability to feel pain. Imagine that! What could be more wonderful than a pain-free existence? Dr. Brand shatters such naive notions by showing how valuable pain is to a person's overall health. Tragically, many lepers die an early death because they have no mechanism to warn them when something bad is happening. For example, while sleeping in his hut, a leper may inadvertently place his hand in the fire and not even realize that his flesh is burning. He may break a leg and yet continue to walk on it,

---

2   C. S. Lewis, *The Problem of Pain* (Glasgow: William Collins Sons and Co, 1940), 74.
3   Rafia S. Rasu, Kiengkham Vouthy, Ashley N. Crowl, Anne E. Stegeman, Bithia Fikru, Walter Agbor Bawa, and Maureen E. Knell. "Cost of Pain Medication to Treat Adult Patients with Nonmalignant Chronic Pain in the United States," *Journal of Managed Care & Specialty Pharmacy*, vol. 20, no. 9 (September 2014).

not realizing what has happened. He may go blind because he doesn't pause to wash a grain of sand from his eye. There is no pain to warn him that something is wrong. Writing about his research on pain, Dr. Brand states:

> I now regard pain as one of the most remarkable design features of the human body, and if I could choose one gift for my leprosy patients it would be the gift of pain . . . . Silencing pain without considering its message is like disconnecting a ringing fire alarm to avoid receiving bad news. [4]

What is true for the body is equally true for the soul. Where there is no ability to benefit from the pain and suffering that come into our lives, there is no spiritual health. In this sense, pain is one of God's choicest gifts. Rather than ignoring pain or trying to alleviate it, we should first seek to understand the message from God that it conveys. Imagine if the Israelites in Egypt had ignored their pain or perhaps tried to lessen its intensity. Imagine if they had numbed their senses through alcohol, shopping binges, or watching hours of mindless entertainment. I think they would still be in Egypt today!

> **" Pain is one of God's choicest gifts.**

Every parent knows how challenging it can be to motivate children to do what is in their own best interests. Whether it is eating vegetables, doing homework, or getting a job and moving out of the house, it is not easy to find ways to get children moving in the direction they need to go. God, our heavenly Parent (Father), has a similar problem with us. Sometimes, it seems that the pain of disciplinary action is the best strategy to prompt us to do what we ought.

> "My son, do not regard lightly the discipline of the LORD, nor be weary when reproved by him. For the LORD disciplines the one he loves, and chastises every son whom he receives." It is for discipline that you have to endure. God is treating

---

4   Paul Brand, *Pain: The Gift Nobody Wants* (New York: Harper Collins, 1993), 12, 188.

you as sons. For what son is there whom his father does not discipline? If you are left without discipline, in which all have participated, then you are illegitimate children and not sons. Besides this, we have had earthly fathers who disciplined us and we respected them. Shall we not much more be subject to the Father of spirits and live? For they disciplined us for a short time as it seemed best to them, but he disciplines us for our good, that we may share his holiness. For the moment all discipline seems painful rather than pleasant, but later it yields the peaceful fruit of righteousness to those who have been trained by it. (Hebrews 12:5–11)

It may sound startling to put it in these terms, but God is not so much interested in our happiness as he is in our holiness. He goes to great lengths to deliver us from bondage and sin, but delivering us from pain is, frankly, not his top priority. Pain is a gift of God because it motivates us to leave where we are and to step forward into the future he is preparing for us.

Identity Crisis

A second way that God motivates us to begin the journey to spiritual wholeness is creating within us a deep desire to know who we really are. The Jews had lived in Egypt for 400 years, but they knew they were not Egyptians. They knew that Egypt was not their home. Few people will begin the journey to spiritual wholeness without being motivated by the burning question: Who am I?

No one better typifies this search for identity than Moses himself. The second chapter of Exodus is a classic description of someone with a conflicted sense of self-identity. His birth mother was Jewish. His adoptive mother was Egyptian. When among the Egyptians, he would have been keenly aware of his alien Jewish roots and ethnicity. When among the Jews, his Egyptian culture and upbringing would have made him feel like an outsider. Moses is the classic example of a third-culture kid.[5] To make a confusing situation even more complex, he

---

5   Third-culture kid is a term used to refer to children who are raised in a culture outside of their parents' culture for a significant part of their childhood.

married a Midianite! Moses' struggle with self-identity was so great, he named his son Gershom (meaning "the alien," "the sojourner").

When Moses finally met God at the burning bush, the first question he asked was: "Who am I?" (Ex 3:11). Few questions go deeper or have more profound implications than this. Scriptures record Moses' identity crisis so that those who read his story can benefit from the painful lessons he slowly learned.

Who Am I?—A Universal Question

Moses was not the only one to ask this question. On three separate occasions, David asked it (see 1 Sm 18:18; 2 Sm 7:18; Ps 8:4). The disciplines of both philosophy and psychology highlight the fundamental importance of this question. The arts have numerous examples of how this question has inspired poetry, literature, and music. Casting Crowns puts the question to music in their hit song, "Who Am I?":

> *I am a flower quickly fading*
> *Here today and gone tomorrow*
> *A wave tossed in the ocean*
> *A vapor in the wind*
> *Still you hear me when I'm calling*
> *Lord, you catch me when I'm falling*
> *And you've told me who I am*
> *I am yours. . . .*
>
> *Not because of who I am*
> *But because of what you've done*
> *Not because of what I've done*
> *But because of who you are*

Today, the world's standards for identity and worth are based on performance, possessions, comparison, education, profession, and being part of the right crowd. The search for identity is further complicated by broken families, multiculturalism, and gender confusion. Perhaps never in history has the question "Who am I?" been asked by more people than today.

Moses did not get to choose his birth family or his adoptive family. He had no say in his ethnicity, gender, or even his name. It seemed that his identity was imposed upon him, a matter of fate. As he grew to adulthood, however, he began to realize that he *did* have some choice in the matter. He had the ability, at least to a certain degree, to determine who he was. Unfortunately, this realization resulted in Moses making a tragic choice. When he saw an Egyptian beating a Hebrew, "one of his people," he rose up and murdered him and buried his body in the sand (Ex 2:11–15).

While many interpret this act of violence as evidence that Moses struggled with anger issues, the real explanation goes much deeper. The murder of the Egyptian was an outward manifestation of Moses' inward identity crisis. Perhaps he wanted to prove his Hebrew identity in a manner that would be clear for all to see. Perhaps he thought he could validate his existence and find self-worth through force and violence. Regardless, Moses' actions had two tragic results. First, his biological family disowned him as a pretentious, self-appointed savior. "Who made you a prince and judge over us?" they sneered (Ex 2:14). Second, his adoptive family concluded that he was their enemy: "When Pharaoh heard of it, he sought to kill Moses" (Ex 2:15). In the difficulty of trying to figure out for himself who he was, Moses ended up shunned by both groups.

This story teaches us that we cannot define ourselves. Those who try to create their own identity only discover the ultimate futility of all attempts at self-definition. Jesus said it best: "Whoever would save his life will lose it, but whoever loses his life for my sake will find it" (Mt 16:25). No one discovers their true identity by self-effort. Only God can provide one's full identity.

Who Am I?—A Question that Must Be Addressed to God

When Moses met God at the burning bush, the first question he asked reflected the depth of his identity crisis: "Who am I?" (Ex 3:11). For eighty years he had been struggling to answer this question! This time, however, Moses was not asking his birth parents, his adoptive parents, his wife, his culture, his education, or his possessions. He was not looking in a mirror, asking himself. Finally, he was asking the only one who knew the answer. His question was addressed to his Creator: "God, who am I?" I can almost hear God say, "I thought you'd never ask!"

The truth is, no one is self-defining. It takes a mother and a father to produce a person and then give him or her a name and an identity. It takes a people and a culture to help its citizens understand who they are and their purpose in life. It takes an education and a profession to further refine one's sense of identity. Still, all of these contributing factors only partially answer the question. Just as Moses was able to rebel against some of the external forces that were seeking to define his identity and to strike out on his own on a course of self-discovery, so many today continue a frantic and futile search for identity. Ultimately, only God can tell us who we truly are. Moses' search for self finally ended at the burning bush, when he addressed the question to God.

> **" We find ourselves only when we find God.**

Who Am I?—A Question that Has an Answer

When God answers a question, his response is often surprising. At the burning bush, God's answer to Moses' question is startling. Moses asked, "Who am I?" God answered, "I will be with you" (Ex 3:12). What kind of an answer is *that*? Rather than responding to Moses' identity crisis in terms of philosophy, theology, psychology, biology, or sociology, God answered Moses by giving him the promise of his presence. In other words, Moses would discover his identity only as he developed his relationship with God. It is only as he lost himself in the one who had created and redeemed him that Moses found his true self. Dwight L. Moody summarized the story of Moses like this: "Moses spent his first 40 years thinking he was a somebody. He spent his second 40 years learning he was a nobody. He spent his third 40 years discovering what God can do with a nobody."

Moses was not the only one experiencing an identity crisis in this story. His people, the Hebrews, also were struggling to understand who they were. After living 400 years in Egypt, they were desperate to know who they really were. Were they Hebrews or had they perhaps become Egyptians? Were they slaves? Was Egypt their home? As Moses discovered his true identity in God, he was able to lead his people to discover their true identity as well. When the Hebrew people finally left Egypt and came to Mount Sinai, they had an experience similar to what Moses had at the burning bush. For the first time, they began to discover their true identity. At the holy mountain, their Creator and Redeemer said to them:

> You yourselves have seen what I did to the Egyptians, and how I bore you on eagles' wings and brought you to myself. Now therefore, if you will indeed obey my voice and keep my covenant, you shall be my treasured possession among all peoples, for all the earth is mine; and you shall be to me a kingdom of priests and a holy nation. (Exodus 19:4–6)

Everyone who embarks on the journey to spiritual wholeness is wrestling with the question, "Who am I?" When the search for self leads to God, it is time for the journey to begin. We find ourselves only when we find God. Our identity is discovered only when he is with us.

Hunger

A third motivation to leave the "turkey farm" and begin the journey to spiritual wholeness is hunger (i.e., desire, longing). As oppressed slaves, the Hebrew people knew hunger at a visceral and physical level, but God wanted them to learn about hunger on a spiritual level. Having a great quantity of Egyptian food was not the solution to their problem, no matter how often they might have thought so. The leeks, onions, garlic, cucumbers, melons, and fish of Egypt (see Nm 11:4-6) might have been tasty and might have provided temporary relief from the pangs of hunger, but the people needed something much more substantial. God was teaching his people that *what* they eat is even more important than *that* they eat. Egyptian food simply was not sufficient to empower them on the journey to spiritual wholeness. Eating leeks and onions was a type of spiritual "junk food" that gave a temporary rush but did little to strengthen their souls for the journey ahead.

At the burning bush, God told Moses that the place he had prepared for his people was "a land flowing with milk and honey" (Ex 3:8). *That* was the nourishment God intended for his people. It would sustain the body and fortify the soul. The real question was this: Which appetite would be stronger? Would the desire for leeks and onions cancel out the desire for milk and honey? The Hebrews would not succeed in leaving Egypt and reaching the Land of Promise until their desire for God's food was stronger than their desire for the food of Egypt. The lesson for Christians today is clear: No one gets far on the journey to spiritual wholeness until his appetite for the things of God is stronger than his appetite for the things of this world. In Chapter 4, we will return to the theme of hunger and treat it in greater detail.

A Call with a Promise

At the burning bush, God commissioned Moses to be the liberator who would lead the Hebrews out of Egyptian bondage to a beautiful place that he had prepared for them:

> Go and gather the elders of Israel together and say to them,
> "The LORD, the God of your fathers, the God of Abraham,
> of Isaac, and of Jacob, has appeared to me, saying, 'I have
> observed you and what has been done to you in Egypt, and I
> promise that I will bring you up out of the affliction of Egypt
> to the land of the Canaanites, the Hittites, the Amorites, the
> Perizzites, the Hivites, and the Jebusites, a land flowing with
> milk and honey.'" (Exodus 3:16–17)

Even if one has met God and discovered one's true identity, it is impossible just to start the journey to spiritual wholeness whenever we choose. God's people were slaves. They had cruel masters who would not let them go. They were trapped and had no hope of ever changing their oppressive situation—unless God intervened. Until God promised to deliver them from the oppressors' hand and to guide them on their journey, any hope for a new life was only a pious dream. At the burning bush, God gave Moses a solemn promise: "I promise that I will bring you up out of the affliction of Egypt . . ." (Ex 3:17). God extended to Moses and the nation of Israel the most amazing invitation that can ever be given to any human: Follow me.

This call is what the burning bush was all about. God had heard the cry of his people and was responding. The call first came *to* Moses. Then, it came *through* Moses to all of the Hebrew people. God's invitation to leave Egypt and begin a journey to the Land of Promise has several distinct characteristics:

1. *It was initiated by God.* Israel did not choose God. God chose Israel and called her to freedom and a glorious future (see Jn 15:16).

2. *It was a call to a journey as much as it was to a destination.* God was inviting the people to follow him: to go where he goes, do what he does, say what he says, think what he thinks. It was that simple. It was that profound.

3. *It was a call to a relationship more than to a task.* First and foremost, God's people were called to *be* something, not to *do* something. They were to be with God, to be his people, to believe his promises, and to obey his commands.

4. *It was a call that would cost them everything.* Though their salvation was free, it was not cheap. It was impossible to gain Canaan and keep Egypt. "Any one of you who does not renounce all that he has cannot be my disciple" (Lk 14:33).

2
Redeemed
(Exodus 5–14)

"The Lord will fight for you, and you have only to be silent." (Exodus 14:14)

One day, as a man was walking along, he fell into a pit. It was a deep pit and, try as he might, he simply couldn't get out. So, he sat down and waited to see what would happen. It wasn't long before a realist walked by the pit. Looking down at the man at the bottom, he said, "That's some pit." And he kept on walking. A little later an optimist came by. "Cheer up," he said. "It could be worse; it could be raining." Then he too kept walking. A sociologist passed by and decided to conduct a survey to determine how many others had fallen into pits in the area. When a politician saw what had happened, he hurried back to the capital and formed a task force to determine what should be done. A philosopher was profoundly moved by the man in the pit and went back to his office and began work on a book: "Pits and the Human Condition." A doctor tossed in a bottle of pills and said, "Take two tablets and call me in the morning." A lawyer gave the man his card and offered to help him sue the owner of the pit. "He should have erected a fence to prevent this from happening," he said. A psychologist came by and sat down on the edge of the pit, stroked his chin, and said in a very empathetic tone, "Tell me, sir, how do you *feel* about being in a pit?" A Hindu walked by the pit and said simply, "Your pit is an illusion." A Buddhist needed more time to explain his perspective: "The problem here is your desire to get out of the pit. If you would extinguish desire you would cease to suffer and you could enter Nirvana, right there in your pit!" A Muslim shook his finger at the man in the pit and told him sternly to submit to the will of Allah. A Calvinist walking by paused long enough to give the man in the pit a theological explanation for what had happened: "You were predestined to be in that pit." A Wesleyan gave a different reason: "You are in that pit because of your own free will." A fundamentalist could only say, "It's your own fault that you fell in that pit." An evangelical threw in a tract and said, "God loves you and has a wonderful plan for your life." A charismatic told the man in the pit to praise the Lord anyway! Finally, Jesus came by. He saw the man in the pit and had compassion on him. Going down into the pit, he pulled him out!

Israel was in a deep pit. Try as she might, she simply couldn't get out of her oppressive bondage in Egypt. She needed more than sympathy or words of theological explanation. She needed deliverance!

> **Things were going to get worse before they got better—a lot worse.**

After his experience at the burning bush, Moses returned to Egypt and announced to the Hebrews that God was ready to save his people and lead them to the Land of Promise. The response was encouraging.

> Then Moses and Aaron went and gathered together all the elders of the people of Israel. Aaron spoke all the words that the LORD had spoken to Moses and did the signs in the sight of the people. And the people believed; and when they heard that the LORD had visited the people of Israel and that he had seen their affliction, they bowed their heads and worshiped. (Exodus 4:29–31)

Israel was thrilled! God was going to pull them out of their pit. If they *believed* and if they *worshiped*, then their problems would all be solved. Right? Though the Israelites were off to a good start, they had no clue what was coming. Things were going to get worse before they got better—a lot worse.

THE BATTLE OF THE GODS

In obedience to what God had told him at the burning bush, Moses marched into the presence of Pharaoh with a message: "Thus says the Lord [Hebrew, *Yahweh* [1]], the God of Israel, 'Let my people go, that they may hold a feast to me in the wilderness'" (Ex 5:1). Pharaoh knew of many gods and even claimed to be one himself, but he had never heard of this deity named Yahweh. His response was curt and to the point: "Who is [Yahweh], that I should obey his voice and let Israel go? I do not know [Yahweh], and moreover, I will not let Israel go" (Ex 5:2).

The stage was now set. Pharaoh, the chief priest over all the gods of Egypt and himself a divine being, did not know Yahweh. God intended to remedy this tragic ignorance! The next chapters explain how Yahweh himself responded to Pharaoh's question. It was as if God spoke personally to Pharaoh saying, "You don't know Yahweh? Well then, let me introduce myself."

First, Pharaoh retaliated against the impertinence of Moses' request to free the slaves by making their lives even more miserable than before. Demanding that the Hebrews gather their own straw to make bricks, he increased their work load, accusing them of laziness (see Ex 5:4–21). Moses was deeply troubled by the fact that redemption was not working out the way he had anticipated. In desperation, he cried out to the Lord:

> O Lord, why have you done evil to this people? Why did you ever send me? For since I came to Pharaoh to speak in your name, he has done evil to this people, and you have not delivered your people at all. (Exodus 5:22–23)

---

1   Yahweh is God's personal name revealed to Moses at the burning bush. When English translations put the word "Lord" in caps, it indicates God's personal name (Yahweh) is being used.

Moses and the people of Israel were discovering that the greatest battle we face on the journey to spiritual wholeness is to continue to believe the promises of God even when all hell is breaking loose around us. Can we continue to believe in Yahweh when it seems that the gods of this world are far stronger?

Many readers of Exodus view the ten plagues (see chapters 7–12) as a divine temper tantrum. They see the violence and destruction associated with this series of catastrophes as evidence of an angry God who, like a bully, wants to hurt those who get in his way. Looking at the plagues this way misses the entire point! Pharaoh clearly stated that he didn't know Yahweh (Ex 5:2). The ten plagues were God's way of introducing himself to this pagan king. Repeatedly throughout the cosmic displays of Yahweh's majestic power, God emphasized the purpose of what was happening:

- Before turning the Nile to blood, God, through Moses, explained to Pharaoh the purpose of this plague: "By this *you shall know* that I am the LORD [Yahweh] . . ." (Ex 7:17).
- When the frog plague finally ended, Moses said: "so that *you may know* that there is no one like [Yahweh] our God" (Ex 8:10).
- When God spared the land of Goshen from the plague of flies, he explained the reason: ". . . that *you may know* that I am [Yahweh] in the midst of the earth" (Ex 8:22).
- Before the plague of hail, God once again explained clearly the reason: "so that *you may know* that there is none like me in all the earth" (Ex 9:14). And when the plague ended, Moses emphasized the point again: "so that *you may know* that the earth is [Yahweh's]" (Ex 9:29).
- Before the plague of locusts, God explained the reason to Pharaoh: "that *you may know* that I am [Yahweh]" (Ex 10:2).
- In explaining the reason for the final plague, the death of every firstborn in Egypt, Moses said to Pharaoh: "that *you may know* that [Yahweh] makes a distinction between Egypt and Israel" (Ex 11:7).

- In a final prophetic statement about what would happen if the Egyptians insisted on pursuing Israel into the Red Sea, God said: "and the Egyptians *shall know* that I am [Yahweh] . . ." (Ex 14:4).

Though it might not appear this way at first, the ten plagues were manifestations of God's love not only toward the Hebrews but also toward the Egyptians. God wanted Pharaoh to know who he was in the hopes that he could see the blasphemous foolishness of worshiping idols and give his trust and allegiance to Yahweh, the one who had revealed himself to Moses at the burning bush.

The ten plagues were not a random display of divine rage. They were a magnificent, carefully crafted, systematic dismantling of the entire Egyptian pantheon. This was God's chance to show Egypt (and the entire world) the vanity and impotence of idol worship. "On all the gods of Egypt I will execute judgments: I am [Yahweh]" (Ex 12:12). One might gain a truer understanding of the purpose of the plagues by calling this part of the story "The Battle of the Gods." God systematically exposed the impotency of virtually every major deity the Egyptians worshiped:

1. The first display of power (see Ex 7:14–25) was upon perhaps the most important deity in Egypt: the Nile River. When Moses extended his rod over the Nile, the life-giving waters were turned into death-dealing blood. It took no degree in theology for everyone in Egypt to immediately understand that this Yahweh was a great God indeed!

2. The Egyptians also worshiped a reptilian frog god. Yahweh seemed to be saying, "You like frogs? Well, let me give you what you worship!" What better way to learn the vanity of worshiping a god who cannot save than to have repugnant reptilian representatives jumping and croaking all over the house (see Ex 8:1–15).

3. When the magicians with their tricks and occult powers were unable to duplicate the invasion of gnats, they were forced to conclude that "this is the finger of God" (Ex 8:16–19).

4. The most remarkable aspect of the plague of flies was that they caused torment everywhere in Egypt *except* in the land of Goshen, where the Hebrews lived (see Ex 8:20–32).

5. Apis, the Egyptian bull god, was impotent in the face of the destruction that Yahweh sent upon all the livestock of Egypt (see Ex 9:1–7).

6. The plague of boils had a somewhat comical aspect when the magicians could not stand before Moses because of their discomfort (see Ex 9:8–12).

7. Before the plague of hail came, Moses urged the Egyptians to seek shelter from the coming disaster. God was clearly appealing to the Egyptians as well as to the Hebrews to put their trust in him (see Ex 9:13–35).

8. One of the greatest gods in Egypt was a vegetation deity named Osiris, who was of no help in protecting the Egyptians from an invasion of locusts that covered the face of the land, eating up everything that had not been destroyed already by hail (see Ex 10:1–20).

9. When three days of pitch darkness fell upon Egypt, everyone knew that Ra, the sun god, was nothing compared to Yahweh (see Ex 10:21–29).

10. The tenth and final plague was the death of the firstborn, including Pharaoh's own son, a divine being himself and the hope for Egypt's future (see Ex 11–12). With this display of divine omnipotence, Pharaoh realized that any further attempt to work against Yahweh was futile.

Once one understands the true purpose of the ten plagues, one can only bow in humble worship and proclaim: "Who is like you, O [Yahweh], among the gods? Who is like you, majestic in holiness, awesome in glorious deeds, doing wonders?" (Ex 15:11).

Redemption through Blood

With Egypt humbled into submission and broken by God's display of sovereign majesty, Pharaoh finally gave reluctant permission for the slaves to go free. The moment of redemption had come. As the people prepared to leave and begin their journey to Canaan, we are introduced to the real hero of the story (see Exodus 12–13). Surprisingly, the one that made it finally possible to begin the journey was not Moses or Pharaoh—but a lamb!

> Tell all the congregation of Israel that on the tenth day of this month every man shall take a lamb according to their fathers' houses, a lamb for a household . . . . Your lamb shall be without blemish, a male a year old. . . . and you shall keep it until the fourteenth day of this month, when the whole assembly of the congregation of Israel shall kill their lambs at twilight. "Then they shall take some of the blood and put it on the two doorposts and the lintel of the houses in which they eat it. They shall eat the flesh that night, roasted on the fire; with unleavened bread and bitter herbs they shall eat it. . . . In this manner you shall eat it: with your belt fastened, your sandals on your feet, and your staff in your hand. And you shall eat it in haste. It is the LORD's Passover. For I will pass through the land of Egypt that night, and I will strike all the firstborn in the land of Egypt, both man and beast; and on all the gods of Egypt I will execute judgments: I am the LORD. The blood shall be a sign for you, on the houses where you are. And when I see the blood, I will pass over you, and no plague will befall you to destroy you, when I strike the land of Egypt. . . .
>
> You shall observe this rite as a statute for you and for your sons forever. And when you come to the land that the LORD will give you, as he has promised, you shall keep this service. And when your children say to you, 'What do you mean by this service?' you shall say, 'It is the sacrifice of the LORD's Passover, for he passed over the houses of the people of Israel in Egypt, when he struck the Egyptians but spared our houses.'" And the people bowed their heads and worshiped. (Exodus 12:3–13, 24–27)

The Passover is a perpetual reminder to all those on the journey to spiritual wholeness that we will never arrive at our destination without the help of a lamb. The lamb shows us our need, dies in our place, and nourishes our souls.

Showing Our Need

The Hebrews, as well as the Egyptians, assumed they knew what their needs were. They needed provision, protection, and freedom. Little did they know that they had a greater need. Through the Passover lamb, they were made to realize that a death sentence lay on every household and divine judgment was about to fall on them all! Although Moses had warned of God's wrath and coming judgment for months, no one really paid any attention—until now! This little lamb, without even opening its mouth, made the message of salvation crystal clear: A covering of blood is required for salvation from the coming judgment.

Dying in My Place

The choice for every family in Egypt was simple: either a dead child or a dead lamb. On that first Passover, the people of God learned that God not only accepts a substitute but also provides one: "Behold, the Lamb of God who takes away the sin of the world" (Jn 1:29; see also Isa 53:4–6).

> **God not only accepts a substitute but also provides one.**

Nourishing My Soul

The lamb was sacrificed so there could be blood on the doorposts as well as food on the table. The Passover lamb was to be eaten to give God's people the strength they needed for the journey ahead. "In this manner you shall eat it: with your belt fastened, your sandals on your feet, and your staff in your hand. And you shall eat it in haste. . ." (Ex 12:11).

Redemption through Water

With a profound awareness of how the one true God had sovereignly chosen them, protected them, provided for them, and prepared a home for them, the people of God finally began their journey. With grateful hearts and full tummies, they set out. But which way? God had not provided them with a map, and most of the people had no understanding of geography. Being free from bondage was a wonderful thing, but knowing what to do with that freedom and which way to travel was another matter entirely! God had just the right answer:

> When Pharaoh let the people go, God did not lead them by way of the land of the Philistines, although that was near. For God said, "Lest the people change their minds when they see war and return to Egypt." But God led the people around by the way of the wilderness toward the Red Sea. And the people of Israel went up out of the land of Egypt equipped for battle. . . . And the LORD went before them by day in a pillar of cloud to lead them along the way, and by night in a pillar of fire to give them light, that they might travel by day and by night. (Exodus 13:17–21)

God provided his people with a divine GPS (global positioning system)! The pillar of cloud by day and the pillar of fire by night were a constant source of guidance so that the people of God did not lose their way. Far better than a map, God had given his people a guide.

Notice *where* the pillar of fire led the people. God did not "lead them along the main road that runs through Philistine territory, even though that was the shortest route to the Promised Land. . ." (Ex 13:17 NLT). God wasn't interested in speed or comfort for this journey. He had other purposes in mind. Instead, God led his people "by the desert road toward the Red Sea" (Ex 13:18 NIV).

But why would God lead hundreds of thousands of people into the desert? What will they eat? What will they drink? How will they survive? It is as we discover the answer to these questions that we learn the real purposes of God for his redeemed people.

The air must have been thick with joyful excitement and eager anticipation as the people of God set out on their journey. Perhaps they sang and danced as they followed the pillar of fire before them. Surprisingly, God led them to the edge of the Red Sea where steep mountains rose on both sides of them. They were boxed in. God had led them to a place where there was no way out—and the Egyptians were pursuing them!

> When the king of Egypt was told that the people had fled, the mind of Pharaoh and his servants was changed toward the people, and they said, "What is this we have done, that we have let Israel go from serving us?" So he made ready his chariot and took his army with him, and took six hundred chosen chariots and all the other chariots of Egypt with officers over all of them. And the LORD hardened the heart of Pharaoh king of Egypt, and he pursued the people of Israel while the people of Israel were going out defiantly. The Egyptians pursued them, all Pharaoh's horses and chariots and his horsemen and his army, and overtook them encamped at the sea, by Pi-hahiroth, in front of Baal-zephon. (Exodus 14:5–9)

It is difficult to imagine a more impossible situation. It seemed that God had led the Hebrews into a trap. The situation was such that most of the people threw up their hands in despair.

> They said to Moses, "Is it because there are no graves in Egypt that you have taken us away to die in the wilderness? What have you done to us in bringing us out of Egypt? Is not this what we said to you in Egypt: 'Leave us alone that we may serve the Egyptians'? For it would have been better for us to serve the Egyptians than to die in the wilderness." (Exodus 14:11–12)

What looks like a disaster, however, was going to be transformed into Israel's finest hour! At the Red Sea, God gave his people an unforgettable picture of redemption. In the biblical story, water is often closely associated with salvation. Just as the waters of the flood carried the ark to safety while at the same time destroying those who persisted in unbelief, so the water of the Red Sea provided redemption for the faithful but judgment on those who rebelled against God. As in baptism, water symbolizes a new beginning. The story of what happened at the Red Sea (Ex 14) illustrates with unforgettable clarity what it takes to accomplish our redemption.

Most importantly, it takes a promise from God. No one ever breaks the bonds of slavery and steps into the glorious freedom of the sons and daughters of God without a divine promise. True freedom is never the result of human effort or wishful thinking. Our sins are simply stronger than we alone can break. Without divine help, we remain in bondage forever. However, if the sovereign God makes us a promise of deliverance, then everything changes.

For the Hebrews, God's promise first came at the burning bush when he made an oath: "*I promise* that I will bring you up out of the affliction of Egypt to the land of the Canaanites . . . a land flowing with milk and honey" (Ex 3:17, emphasis added). This was a solemn promise from God himself, and it is one of many to be found in Scripture. Herbert Lockyer estimates that there are over 7,000 promises in the Bible.[2] If you feel trapped in an impossible situation, caught between a rock and a hard place, held in the clutches of forces that threaten to destroy you, find a promise from God and cling to it like a drowning man clings to a life preserver! Even a quick survey of Scripture reveals the rich treasure we have in these precious promises.

- "Call upon me in the day of trouble; I will deliver you . . ." (Ps 50:15).
- "Call to me and I will answer you, and will tell you great and hidden things that you have not known" (Jer 33:3).
- "Ask, and it will be given to you; seek, and you will find; knock, and it will be opened to you" (Mt 7:7).
- "All things are possible for one who believes" (Mk 9:23).
- "If you abide in me, and my words abide in you, ask whatever you wish, and it will be done for you" (Jn 15:7).

---

2   See Hebert Lockyer, *All the Promises of the Bible* (Grand Rapids: Zondervan, 1962).

- "God is faithful, and he will not let you be tempted beyond your ability, but with the temptation he will also provide the way of escape, that you may be able to endure it" (1 Cor 10:13).
- "If we confess our sins, he is faithful and just to forgive us our sins and to cleanse us from all unrighteousness" (1 Jn 1:9).

But a promise, to be effective, must be *believed*. No one experiences redemption who does not put into practice the obedience of faith. The promise of God is meaningless without faith. At the Red Sea, when faced with an impossible situation, the people of God discovered that faith meant more than an intellectual acknowledgment of the truth about God. Giving verbal assent to doctrinal truth is not what the Bible means by faith. Even demons have this kind of "faith" (see Jas 2:19). True faith is demonstrated when we step forward, as we trust in the promises of God. It is when we find ourselves trapped between the devil and the deep blue sea that we discover the real meaning of faith. The evidence for the presence or absence of faith was seen in how the people responded to the three commands that came to them at the Red Sea (see Ex 14:13–15): fear not, stand firm, and go forward.

> 66 **God often chooses to deliver us through our difficulties rather than from them.**

These three commands also reveal the presence or absence of faith in our own journey to spiritual wholeness. What mapplication do you need to make as you wrestle with some Red Sea moment in your own life?

Fear Not

Does God really expect us to be calm, cool, and collected when all hell is breaking loose around us? When the Bible tells us not to fear, it doesn't mean we are not to have *feelings* of fear. It doesn't mean we will never tremble. Rather, it means we are not to be controlled by our fears. None of us can control our emotions completely, but we can control whether or not we are paralyzed by our circumstances. My wife Katy has a phobia of flying, but not once has she ever said "no" to a ministry assignment because of her fear of boarding an airplane. Though her feelings of fear remain, her obedience to the will of God reveals the reality of her deep faith.

Stand Firm

Moses told the people to "stand firm, and see the salvation of the LORD, which he will work for you today. . . . The LORD will fight for you, and you have only to be silent" (Ex 14:13–14). It is easy to imagine the many things that the Hebrews would be tempted to do: run, hide, attack, negotiate, surrender, swim, etc. However, such responses would thwart the deliverance that God was about to perform. In this situation, the command was straightforward and clear: Be still and let God do the rest. It was *his* battle. We are all familiar with the adage, "Don't just stand there; do something!" For the Hebrews, their duty was just the opposite: "Don't do anything; just stand there!"

Go Forward

God had just told them to be still and do nothing. Then, he told them to march forward. This is a marvelous biblical paradox. Though the commands seem to be mutually exclusive, when we pause and think about it, they are really two ways of saying the same thing. We trust God and yet we do our part. The key here is timing. There is a time for passive trust; and, there is a time for active obedience. When we remember that God is ordering the people to go forward *into* the waters of the Red Sea, we see what the obedience of faith looks like in a real-life situation. It is only as we move forward in faithful obedience that the miracle of deliverance occurs. The sea opens and a highway appears *through* the waters. God makes a way where there is no way. The miracle of redemption at the Red Sea teaches us that God often chooses to deliver us *through* our difficulties rather than *from* them. The way out is the way through.

3
The Bitter Place
(Exodus 15:22–27)

"Behold, I am doing a new thing; now it springs forth, do you not perceive it? I will make a way in the wilderness and rivers in the desert." (Isaiah 43:19)

As the people realized the magnitude of what God had done in defeating the army of Egypt and setting them free, they spontaneously sang a song they had never sung before, the song of redemption:

> I will sing to the LORD, for he has triumphed gloriously;
> the horse and his rider he has thrown into the sea.
> The LORD is my strength and my song,
> and he has become my salvation;
> this is my God, and I will praise him,
> my father's God, and I will exalt him. (Exodus 15:1–2)

On the eastern shore of the Red Sea, the redeemed conducted one of the greatest worship services in human history as two million ransomed souls sang praises to God for delivering them from bondage and death. Miriam led the worship as all the women joined her with tambourines and dancing (see Ex 15:20). What a day of rejoicing it must have been!

What is often called "The Song of Moses" (Ex 15:1–18) summarizes in a powerful manner the amazing deliverance the people experienced.

Merely talking about what God had done was not enough. This experience required a *song*, which can be divided into three stanzas:

1. Praise to Yahweh for what he has done in the *past* (Ex 15:1–12). Perhaps it was pieces of broken chariot washing up on the shore that caused the people to remember all that God had done to make their deliverance possible: the ten plagues, the Passover lamb, the parting of the waters at the Red Sea, etc. "I will sing to the LORD, for he has triumphed gloriously . . ." (Ex 15:1).

2. Praise to Yahweh for what he is doing in the *present* (Ex 15:13–16). On the eastern shore of the Red Sea, with the pillar of fire before them, God was leading his people by his steadfast love and strength. The nations around them witness God's glory displayed in his people, and "they tremble" (Ex 15:14).

3. Praise to Yahweh for what he will do in the *future* (Ex 15:17–18). It is not our past that determines our identity but our future. The people sang of what God had prepared for their future: "You will bring them in and plant them on your own mountain, the place, O [Yahweh], which you have made for your abode . . ." (Ex 15:17). Praise the LORD for he "will reign forever and ever" (Ex 15:18).

> 66 No one enters the abundant life . . . without first passing through the desert.

As the worship service ended and the music faded, the people began to take stock of their surroundings. They knew they were no longer in Egypt, but where were they? Was it Canaan? Was it the land of milk and honey? Had they reached their inheritance?

THE UNIVERSITY OF THE DESERT

Although their redemption was complete, the Hebrews were only now beginning to grasp the reality that they were not home yet. Canaan was not contiguous with Egypt. God had brought them out of bondage, but he had not yet brought them in to the Land of Promise. The people were waking to the reality that their journey was only just beginning. It would take many months to reach their final destination. God was not leading his people to Canaan by the road that was quick and easy. He was intentionally leading them "by the way of the wilderness" (Ex 13:18). Their journey was about to take them into one of the most desolate pieces of real estate on Planet Earth: the Sinai Peninsula. The landscape around them looked more like Death Valley than a place of milk and honey.

Think for a moment about the characteristics of the Sinai Peninsula: no food, no water, no shelter from the extremes of temperature, barren soil where nothing grows, silence, scorpions, snakes, and Amalekites. Why would a good and loving God lead his redeemed people to a place like this? That's a good question!

Until we have a biblically informed theology of the desert, we cannot make sense of the journey to spiritual wholeness. Those who believe that redemption means an immediate relocation into the land of milk of honey are in for a rude awakening. The map is clear: A desert lies between Egypt and Canaan. God has built an object lesson into the journey.

No one enters the abundant life of his or her spiritual inheritance without first passing through the desert. In fact, nearly all the giants of faith mentioned in the Bible have a "desert experience" that helps to define their identities and ministries. Moses spent forty years in the desert of Midian before he met God at the burning bush (see Ex 2). David spent roughly ten years hiding in caves and desert places before he was elevated to the throne (see 1 Sm 22–30). Elijah learned perhaps his greatest lessons in the desert (see 1 Kgs 17:1–7; 19:1–18). John the Baptist spent his entire ministry in the wilderness (see Mt 3:1–6). After his conversion, Paul went "away into Arabia" for three years (see Gal 1:15–17). Even Jesus had his own desert experience when he was "led by the Spirit in the wilderness for forty days, being tempted by the devil" (see Lk 4:1–2). It seems that the desert is not a geographical anomaly. It is a spiritual necessity!

God sent his redeemed people into the desert because they needed an education. There were certain lessons that could not be learned in either Egypt or Canaan. They only could be learned at the University of the Desert. It is only when we experience life in the land of in-between that we can learn how to walk with God and accomplish his purposes. It is when we learn to live in the gap between a promise from God and its fulfillment that we discover the purposes of God in salvation. Moses stated the purpose of the desert eloquently:

> And you shall remember the whole way that the LORD your God has led you these forty years in the wilderness, that he might humble you, testing you to know what was in your heart, whether you would keep his commandments or not. And he humbled you and let you hunger and fed you with manna . . . that he might make you know that man does not live by bread alone, but man lives by every word that comes from the mouth of the LORD. Your clothing did not wear out on you and your foot did not swell these forty years. Know then in your heart that, as a man disciplines his son, the LORD your God disciplines you. (Deuteronomy 8:2–5)

The desert is a place of learning. Here, God humbles us, disciplines us, and tests us to know what is really in our hearts. We will never be prepared to face the giants that are camping on our inheritance in the Land of Promise until we learn the lessons God has prepared for us at the University of the Desert. Though these desert experiences may be frightening and even painful, we are in a good place. God is equipping us and growing us to maturity so that we can be ready to fight the battles that await us when we reach the Land of Promise. When we find ourselves in a "desert place," we should not immediately assume that we took the wrong road or that God is punishing us. In his great love and faithfulness, God has brought us to the University of the Desert, and he wants to give us the greatest education that grace can provide. He wants us to learn that salvation is about more than getting us out of "Egypt." It is also about getting "Egypt" out of us!

It took about three months for the people of Israel to travel from the Red Sea to Mount Sinai. During this important period (see Ex

15:22–18:27), God prepared a series of five different "tests"[1] that constitute the core curriculum of the University of the Desert (see the table below). Each test is custom designed by God himself to teach a lesson that is of vital importance for every traveler on the journey to spiritual wholeness.

Table 3.1: The Five Tests at University of the Desert

Reference	The Place	The Problem	The Solution	The Lesson
Ex 15:22–27 (see below)	Marah	Bitter water	A tree	"I am [Yahweh], your healer" (Ex 15:26).
Ex 16:1–36 (see Ch. 4)	Desert	Hunger	Manna	"Give us this day our daily bread" (Mt 6:11).
Ex 17:1–7 (see Ch. 5)	Rephidim	Thirst	A rock	Do not test the LORD.
Ex 17:8–16 (see Ch. 6)	Rephidim	Enemy attack	Intercessory prayer	Learn to fight God's way.
Ex 18:1–27 (see Ch. 7)	Near Mt. Sinai	Administrative overload	Delegation	Choose qualified persons, train them, organize them, empower them, and release them.

THE BITTER WATER TEST

> Then Moses made Israel set out from the Red Sea, and they went into the wilderness of Shur. They went three days in the wilderness and found no water. When they came to Marah, they could not drink the water of Marah because it was bitter; therefore it was named Marah. And the people grumbled against Moses, saying, "What shall we drink?" And he cried to the LORD, and the LORD showed him a log, and he threw it into the water, and the water became sweet. There the LORD made for them a statute and a rule, and there he tested them, saying, "If you will diligently listen to the voice of the LORD your God, and do that which is right in his eyes, and give ear to his commandments and keep all

---

1   For the importance of the word "test" during the desert journey, see Exodus 15:25; 16:4; 20:20 and Deuteronomy 8:2, 16; 13:3.

his statutes, I will put none of the diseases on you that I put on the Egyptians, for I am the LORD, your healer." Then they came to Elim, where there were twelve springs of water and seventy palm trees, and they encamped there by the water. (Exodus 15:22–27)

The people followed the pillar of fire for three days as it led them away from the Red Sea and into the desert. Each day, their thirst grew. Where was God leading them? Did he know what he was doing? How did he expect two million people to find water in a desert wasteland like this? At last, they came to an oasis, but when they put the water to their parched lips they discovered it was undrinkable!

Rather than trusting in God, the people grumbled and complained. They simply could not fathom why a good God would deliberately lead them to such a bitter experience. It made no sense. They could not imagine how even God could remedy a situation as impossible as this. In desperation, Moses cried out to the Lord for help. Though the words of his prayer are not recorded, I can imagine that he said something like this:

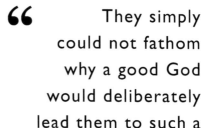

They simply could not fathom why a good God would deliberately lead them to such a bitter experience.

> Lord, I've seen you turn the Nile into blood, send an invasion of locusts, and make the sun go black. I've seen you create a way through the Red Sea and destroy our enemies. But can you handle this, Lord? I've got two million thirsty people in the middle of a barren desert, and they are expecting me to fix an impossible situation. Help, Lord!

It is interesting to note the absence of Moses' rod in this story. Up till now, nearly all the miracles in Exodus have involved Moses' shepherd's staff (see Ex 4:2–3; 7:8–20; 8:5, 16–17; 9:23; 10:13; 14:16; etc.). For this miracle at Marah, God used something different. The Scripture's description of how the Lord answered Moses' prayer is succinct and powerful. "And the LORD showed him a tree[2], and he threw it into the water, and the water became sweet . . ." (Ex 15:25). The text gives no indication of what kind of tree it was or how it sweetened the water, but many scholars have noted the fact that the New Testament often calls the cross of Jesus a "tree" (see Acts 5:20; Gal 3:13; 1 Pt 2:24). The similarity between the tree at Marah and the tree on which Jesus died cannot be coincidental. God was teaching these Old Testament travelers about a tree that can turn the bitterest experiences in life into something sweet. For God's followers today, regardless of how painful the ordeal or how impossible the circumstances, the cross of Christ has the ability, if we let it, to transform the most bitter reality into something miraculously sweet.

The story ends when the pillar of cloud moved again. This time, God had a wonderful surprise in store for his people. He led them to Palm Springs! Well, it actually was called Elim, but it was a touch of paradise with its twelve springs of water and seventy palm trees. Here they set up camp and stayed awhile, enjoying the beauty and refreshment of this desert oasis.

THE CREED OF MARAH

What a remarkable educational experience God prepared for his people at Marah! So many lessons were to be learned here, and *only* here, that one easily understands why "the bitter place" was the very first stop on the journey to spiritual wholeness. The lessons God wanted to teach his people here at Marah will be of tremendous benefit for the rest of the journey. They *must* learn how to deal with the bitter experiences of life.

One way to capture the lessons learned at Marah is to write them into a creed. By no means should the Creed of Marah ever replace the historic creeds of the Church, but this simple affirmation of faith

---

2   The Hebrew word can also mean "log."

can be of great benefit for any pilgrim in a bitter place. The creed is composed of four short affirmations:

> I believe *God* led me here. This is only a test.
> I believe God will provide for me *here*.
> I believe that in his perfect timing, God will lead me away from here.
> I believe God will one day use this experience to be a blessing and encouragement to others.

I Believe God Led Me Here

Many disciples of Christ testify to the perplexing reality that as they step out to follow the will of God it seems that all hell breaks loose around them. It seems that God often intends for the first stop on the journey to spiritual wholeness to be a difficult, painful, inexplicable situation that tastes very bitter. The first and most important affirmation we can make when we are following Christ and yet find ourselves in such circumstances is simply:

> I believe *God* led me here. It is only a test. I'm not in
> this mess because I took a wrong turn or because God is
> punishing me. I'm not here because of some decision my
> boss has made or because the government is not doing
> its job. This is not the fault of my spouse or the economy.
> Though I may not understand why God would lead me to a
> place like this, I believe he has something for me *here* that
> he wants to teach me. This is a test. Yes, I believe God led me
> *here* and I believe that his ultimate purposes for me are good.

When we confess our faith in God and put our confidence in his ability to lead us wisely, then the bitter experiences of life begin to lose their sting. We learn that "for those who love God all things work together for good, for those who are called according to his purpose" (Rom 8:28).

I Believe God Will Provide

God did not lead his people to Marah to destroy them. His purpose was not their misery but their blessing. He brought them to the bitter place so he could teach them what grace can do. He wanted them to learn once and for all the power of "the tree" to transform any bitter situation in life into something sweet. This lesson could not be learned in bondage in Egypt, and it could not be learned among the palm trees at Elim. It could only be learned at Marah, the bitter place. I believe God will provide for me *here*.

There is something, however, that can hinder God's good purposes for us at Marah: grumbling. If the bitterness of the water outside becomes the bitterness of our spirits inside, then we have a major problem. For this reason, the writer of Hebrews urges us to "see to it that no one fails to obtain the grace of God; that no root of bitterness springs up and causes trouble, and by it many become defiled" (Heb 12:15).

I Believe God Will Lead Me Away

Some people, unfortunately, begin to think that the bitter place is their home. They've been there so long they begin to think it is the end of the journey. So, they unpack their bags and set up camp. How tragic! Marah is not our home, and it should not be allowed to define our existence!

We may wonder how long we have to remain at the bitter place. The best answer is the most obvious one: until God moves. In the Bible, to "wait" on the Lord means to put our trust in him. Though our stay at the bitter place may seem like an eternity, we should not despair. We must put our faith and hope in God. He knows what he is doing. We must believe that God—one day, in his perfect timing—will lead us away.

> Write the vision; make it plain on tablets, so he may run who reads it. For still the vision awaits its appointed time; it hastens to the end—it will not lie. If it seems slow, wait for it; it will surely come; it will not delay. . . . but the righteous shall live by his faith. (Habakkuk 2:2–4)

I Believe God Will Use this Experience

Those who have been to Marah and have seen firsthand how the cross of Jesus can transform the experience into something sweet have a story to tell. Many are embarrassed by their experience at the bitter place and are tempted to keep silent about what happened: the divorce, the bankruptcy, the cancer, the failure. Perhaps it is just too bitter even to remember. It is difficult to tell others about our bitter experiences in life, but how important it is to share the stories of how God saved us, not only from bondage but also from bitterness! Many around us who find themselves in an impossible situation simply don't have the faith to believe that God can transform their bitter experiences into something sweet. So, tell them your story, of how God turned your experience at Marah into something sweet. Encourage them to find the hope and the faith to believe that God can do it for them as well.

For ten years, my wife Katy and I served as missionaries in France. We followed God where we believed he was leading us and we found ourselves in an impossible situation. After a decade of ministry, the missionary team had dwindled and fractured through conflict, the one little church we had helped to plant had split and finally our visas were denied. The mission decided that the field should be closed. I had the task of turning out the lights and locking the doors. In the history of our mission organization, we were "the field that failed." As Katy and I unpacked our bags here at home, we asked ourselves, "What was *that* all about?" Never had we experienced anything so bitter. Though God chose not to "explain" our experience, he did enable us to survive the ordeal and continue in ministry. He gave us grace to go even deeper and further in our journey with God than we ever dreamed possible.

For years, we kept silent about what had happened. We didn't want to talk about it. We didn't know what to say. It was just too painful, too humiliating, and too bitter. Over time, we discovered a revolutionary truth: God *wanted* us to tell others about our failure. More than that, we learned that others *needed* to hear about what had happened to us because many of them had had bitter experiences in ministry as well. We learned that there were many faithful followers of Christ who were currently in very bitter places. They needed hope. They needed someone to share a story about how God could deliver his people from places of bitterness and frustration. They needed to know that God could work his good and gracious purposes even when the situation seemed impossible.

Today, whenever I have a chance to speak to missionaries or pastors, I *always* mention our failure in France. I tell the story of how God led us to a bitter place and how he taught us lessons there that we never could have learned anywhere else. I talk about how something very, very bitter has been sweetened so that the final result is good. Nothing I share has impacted more people in more ways than that story of what God did for us in a very bitter place.

4
Wonder Bread
(Exodus 16:1–36)

"[The Lord] opened the doors of the heavens . . . .
Human beings ate the bread of angels; he sent them
all the food they could eat." (Psalm 78:23–25 NIV)

The Bible is a food-driven book. Adam and Eve first got into trouble when they allowed their appetites to be focused on the wrong thing: forbidden fruit. It wasn't murder, theft, or adultery that caused the fall, but eating the wrong kind of food:

> So when the woman saw that the tree was good for food, and that it was a delight to the eyes, and that the tree was to be desired to make one wise, she took of its fruit and ate, and she also gave some to her husband who was with her, and he ate. Then the eyes of both were opened, and they knew that they were naked. (Genesis 3:6–7)

Amazingly, salvation also comes into the world through food. Jesus said, "I am the living bread that came down from heaven. If anyone eats of this bread, he will live forever. . ." (Jn 6:51). The gospel teaches us that Jesus came to re-educate our taste buds. As the Holy Spirit works deep in our hearts, our appetites and desires are transformed. No longer do we hunger for the spiritual junk food that this world has to offer. Instead, our appetites are fixed on the "true bread from heaven" (Jn 6:32) that gives eternal life.

Our salvation hinges on the answer to one simple question: Is my hunger for Jesus greater than my hunger for this world? To rephrase the question in terms of the Exodus, we could ask: Is my appetite for the milk and honey of Canaan stronger than my appetite for the leaks and onions of Egypt? Jesus reminds us that *only* those who hunger and thirst for righteousness will be satisfied (see Mt 5:6).

THE HUNGER TEST: YOU ARE WHAT YOU EAT

The sixteenth chapter of Exodus introduces us to the reality that though the Hebrews had gotten out of Egypt, they still had Egyptian appetites:

> They set out from Elim and . . . came to the wilderness
> of Sin . . . on the fifteenth day of the second month after
> they had departed from the land of Egypt. And the whole
> congregation of the people of Israel grumbled against Moses
> and Aaron in the wilderness, and . . . said to them, "Would
> that we had died by the hand of the LORD in the land of
> Egypt, when we sat by the meat pots and ate bread to the full,
> for you have brought us out into this wilderness to kill this
> whole assembly with hunger." (Exodus 16:1–3)[1]

The problem here was much deeper than the lack of food. The real issue was hunger for the wrong thing. The redeemed people of God longed for the food they had eaten as slaves back in Egypt. Until a stronger appetite pulled them in the opposite direction, their risk of backsliding into bondage was very real. However, educating one's taste buds is harder than one might think.

Few travelers on the journey to spiritual wholeness simply wake up one day and prefer milk and honey to leaks and onions. Our hungers are shaped deep within us by fo es and influences that are beyond our ability to understand fully. No one can simply decide to have different desires. It doesn't work that way. Our hungers must be trained and nurtured. Our taste buds must be educated. This training is precisely why God brought his people to the University of

---

1   Elsewhere in Scripture we learn that the Hebrews' appetite for Egyptian food involved more than "the meat pots" and plenteous bread given to them as slaves. They also continued to have a "strong craving" for "the cucumbers, the melons, the leeks, the onions, and the garlic" that was part of their diet in Egypt (Nm 11:4–5).

the Desert. His program to provide bread from heaven for his people was not simply a plan to sustain their health and nourish their bodies with wholesome food. More importantly, this was God's method for cleansing their palates. The bread he gave them was designed to purge away the appetite for the garlic and onions of Egypt (or the hunger for this world) and to replace it with a ravenous appetite for the milk and honey of Canaan (or the hunger for things of God).

> Then the LORD said to Moses, "Behold, I am about to rain bread from heaven for you, and the people shall go out and gather a day's portion every day, that I may test them, whether they will walk in my law or not. On the sixth day, when they prepare what they bring in, it will be twice as much as they gather daily." So Moses and Aaron said to all the people of Israel, "At evening you shall know that it was the LORD who brought you out of the land of Egypt, and in the morning you shall see the glory of the LORD, because he has heard your grumbling against the LORD. For what are we, that you grumble against us?"

> In the evening quail came up and covered the camp, and in the morning dew lay around the camp. And when the dew had gone up, there was on the face of the wilderness a fine, flake-like thing, fine as frost on the ground. When the people of Israel saw it, they said to one another, "What is it?" For they did not know what it was. And Moses said to them, "It is the bread that the LORD has given you to eat. This is what the LORD has commanded: 'Gather of it, each one of you, as much as he can eat. You shall each take an omer, according to the number of the persons that each of you has in his tent.'" And the people of Israel did so. They gathered, some more, some less. But when they measured it with an omer, whoever gathered much had nothing left over, and whoever gathered little had no lack. Each of them gathered as much as he could eat. (Exodus 16:4–7, 13–18)

The Hebrew term *manna* means "what is it?" If English-speakers had been present, perhaps they would have called it *whatzit*. "It was like coriander seed, white, and the taste of it was like wafers made with honey" (Ex 16:31). They had never seen anything like this before. Each day their food just fell from heaven: wonder bread. Though the taste was somewhat bland and the daily sameness boring, the manna was nourishing, abundant, and free. They would grind it in hand mills, beat it in mortars, boil it in pots, and make cakes of it (see Nm 11:7–9). This was their traveling food, designed by God himself. It was uniquely suited to give daily strength for their journey through the wilderness.

J. R. R. Tolkien tells of a special kind of traveling food in his epic trilogy *The Lord of the Rings*. When Frodo and Sam visit the elves, they are given a food called *lembas*. It was a kind of bland wafer that could easily be carried in their back packs. To consume only a few crumbs would give immediate strength and courage. It wasn't designed for culinary pleasure but for traveling. *Lembas* had "a potency that increased as travelers relied on it alone and did not mingle it with other foods. It fed the will, and it gave strength to endure."[2]

Nutrition 101

Part of the core curriculum at the University of the Desert was a course that we might call "Nutrition 101." No one on the journey to spiritual wholeness will be permitted to opt out of this class. This is *not* an elective! This course includes a final exam (see Ex 16:4). Like many educational experiences, this exam will cause a measure of pain, but the end result will be good, very good. God causes us to feel hunger and then fills us with the bread of heaven to both cleanse our palates and nourish our souls for the journey. He gives us manna so that we might know "that man does not live by bread alone, but man lives by every word that comes from the mouth of the LORD" (Dt 8:3). This is only a test. The real battles await us up ahead in the Land of Promise. At the University of the Desert, however, God intends to teach us how to eat wisely. There are six questions on the test.

Do You Suffer from the Grumpies?

When I'm in a foul mood, my wife Katy, who knows me better than anyone else, typically discerns exactly what the problem is. "Oh, go get something to eat," she tells me. In a similar manner, the

---

2   J. R. R. Tolkien, *The Lord of the Rings: The Return of the King (Part III)* (Boston: Houghton Mifflin, 1955), 915.

Hebrews began to grumble and complain because they were hungry. Exodus 16 reminds us that when we begin to grumble and complain, the problem is often that we aren't eating properly. Our diet is not what it ought to be.

The word "grumble" occurs eight times in this story (see Ex 16:2, 7–11), but this is not the only place where a foul mood characterizes the redeemed people of God. Murmuring is one of the primary themes during the entire Exodus journey.[3] Though I've never seen grumbling included on anyone's list of the seven deadly sins, the Bible makes it clear that this spiritual malady is potentially fatal. A grumbling spirit poisons health, destroys relationships, quenches the Spirit, extinguishes faith, and keeps one doing laps in the wilderness forever!

It only takes a little reflection to understand how deadly the sin of grumbling truly is. To complain about how God is leading our lives is to arrogantly assume that we somehow are being mistreated. It is to shake our fist at God, telling him that he is failing us, leading us down the wrong path, and not providing for our needs. How quickly we forget the miracles of grace that redeemed us from our bondage and sin. How prone we are to focus on the problems of today, forgetting the salvation of yesterday.

One of the worst consequences of the grumpies is its contagious nature, which helps to explain why God treats the malady with such seriousness. One grumbler soon becomes two. Then three families are grumbling, and soon it's a whole community. Moses was surrounded by an entire nation of cry-babies, whining about their circumstances. The Israelites believed their complaint was against Moses. After all, *he* was the one who led them out of Egypt and promised them milk and honey. *He* was the "senior pastor," so holding him accountable and blaming him for their misery made sense.

When we find ourselves in a hard place, the temptation to find a scapegoat is always strong. It's so convenient to take the role of victim and blame others for what is happening. Yet it wasn't Moses

---

3   Beyond the references in Exodus 16, see also Ex 15:24; 17:3; Nm 11:1; 14:2, 27, 29, 36; 16:11, 41; 17:5, 10; and Dt 1:27.

who led the Hebrews into the wilderness. It wasn't Moses' fault that there was nothing to eat. God was fully responsible for this situation. Moses reminded them of the truth when he said, "Your grumbling is not against us but against the LORD" (Ex 16:8).

Grumbling is both sinful and foolish, because it is based on the false assumption that our inner happiness is determined by our outward circumstances. The Exodus journey shows us that God's people were happy neither in Egypt nor in the desert. Many of them will not be happy in the Land of Promise either! Happiness has little to do with outward circumstances and everything to do with the state of our hearts. One of the reasons God brought his people to the University of the Desert was to teach them the source of true contentment and joy. Just as the test at Marah was intended to teach them how to deal with bitterness by showing them a tree, so the hunger test aimed to train them how to deal with the grumpies by learning to eat well.

> **66 Happiness has little to do with outward circumstances and everything to do with the state of our hearts.**

This test was designed to teach them that the root cause of nearly all bad attitudes and foul moods is related to diet. It's not so much our environment that is causing us to gripe and complain but our eating habits. No one gets out of the desert until he is cured of the grumpies, and no one is cured of the grumpies until he learns to eat wisely. We will return to this theme in Chapter 12, where God's people learn even more important lessons during another episode of grumbling.

What Are You Hungry for?

The hunger test aimed to help the Hebrews realize that the real problem in the desert was not hunger itself, but hunger for the wrong things. They indeed were out of Egypt, but they were still controlled by Egyptian appetites. This was a serious problem and revealed the very reason God had brought them to the University of the Desert.

The problem with spiritual junk food is not its sugar content and poor nutritional value but that it ruins our appetite for healthy food. This is why, when we were children, our mothers refused to let us eat a cookie before dinner. The problem wasn't the cookie but the fact that eating it would make us unable to eat our vegetables. John Piper says it well: "The greatest enemy of hunger for God is not poison, but apple pie."[4]

The reason many of us are not more desirous for the things of God is because we've been eating too much junk food. When we feed our souls on worldly fare (e.g., movies, Facebook, video games, talk radio, TV, sports, etc.), is it any wonder we have so little spiritual hunger? It's not that these things are morally bad. It's just that they ruin our appetite for God.

> Come, everyone who thirsts, come to the waters; and he who has no money, come, buy and eat! Come, buy wine and milk without money and without price. Why do you spend your money for that which is not bread, and your labor for that which does not satisfy? Listen diligently to me, and eat what is good, and delight yourselves in rich food. (Isaiah 55:1–2)

At the University of the Desert, we realize that our destiny is determined by our appetites. Will we go back to Egypt to feed on leeks, onions, and garlic? Or will we press forward to the Land of Promise and eat the milk and honey that awaits us there? Eating manna every day allows us to cleanse our palates and educate our taste buds.

Have You Learned to Feed Yourself?

In the desert, God provided the bread. It was abundant, accessible, and free, but the people must go out and gather it for themselves. What a beautiful picture of divine grace and human responsibility! God gives the gift, but we must respond in obedient faith. In obedience, God's people are fed. He provides; we receive and consume. God brings us to

---

4   John Piper, *A Hunger for God* (Wheaton: Crossway, 1997), 14.

the University of the Desert so that we can grow in spiritual maturity by learning to feed ourselves.

> For though by this time you ought to be teachers, you need someone to teach you again the basic principles of the oracles of God. You need milk, not solid food, for everyone who lives on milk is unskilled in the word of righteousness, since he is a child. But solid food is for the mature, for those who have their powers of discernment trained by constant practice to distinguish good from evil. (Hebrews 5:12–14)

When Do You Eat?

Good nutrition is not just *what* we eat but *when*. God's course in Nutrition 101 teaches us the importance of *daily* bread. Each morning, the people were to gather what they needed for that day. If someone tried to store manna for future days, it would breed worms and stink (see Ex 16:20). God gave only what was necessary for today. This principle was enshrined in the prayer Jesus taught his disciples: "give us this day our daily bread" (Mt 6:11). On the sixth day, the **We should read our Bibles and pray every day for the same reason we eat breakfast every morning.** people of God were to gather twice as much. The reason is so that they could properly observe the Sabbath (see Ex 16:23–26).

We should read our Bibles and pray every day for the same reason we eat breakfast every morning. It's good for us. It's nutritious. It makes us grow big and strong. To view Bible study as a "discipline" is to miss the point. We read God's Word because we are hungry and our souls need nourishment for the journey. Without the strength it gives, we simply cannot make it through the day. If one is having trouble establishing a daily pattern of reading God's Word, perhaps the real problem is not a lack of discipline, but a lack of hunger!

Do You Have any Eating Disorders?

Our world today is inundated with a plethora of disorders and illnesses related to poor eating habits. Obesity (overeating), anorexia (not eating at all), and bulimia (binging and purging) are just a few of the dysfunctions we witness around us. These disorders can be detected before they reach a crisis level by the presence of tell-tale behaviors, such as:

- skipping meals,
- nausea,
- obsessing about one's image,
- excessive exercise,
- diet by day, binge by night,
- obsession over labels and the nutritional value of foods, or
- eating compulsively with little or no exercise.

It takes only a moment to see parallels in our spiritual lives to these dysfunctional patterns. Nutrition 101 is designed to help Christians on the journey to spiritual wholeness think rightly about spiritual food and learn to establish healthy patterns that will sustain them as they walk through the wilderness of this world.

In Whom Is Your Trust?

God's primary purpose in bringing his redeemed people to the University of the Desert and giving them manna was to teach them how to trust in him and live by faith. Daily bread from heaven was the perfect object lesson to teach God's people about his covenant faithfulness to provide for their needs each day. Every morning before opening the flap of their tent, God's people would choose to believe that there would be enough manna lying around to get them through the day. Then tomorrow, they would do it all over again. "The just shall live by faith" (Gal 3:11 KJV). That is what the journey to spiritual wholeness is all about.

True Bread

God gave manna in the desert to remind his people that they needed more than manna in the desert. The real lesson being taught in Nutrition 101 was the need for the "true bread" that can sustain the body and the soul! Man does not live by bread alone but by "every word that comes from the mouth of the LORD" (Dt 8:3). Jesus knew Exodus 16 very well. He obviously had spent much time meditating on its true meaning when he preached his "Bread Sermon" in John 6. After miraculously feeding 5,000 people with five loaves and two fish, Jesus explained the real meaning of what he had just done:

> Truly, truly, I say to you, it was not Moses who gave you the bread from heaven, but my Father gives you the true bread from heaven. For the bread of God is he who comes down from heaven and gives life to the world. . . . I am the bread of life. Your fathers ate the manna in the wilderness, and they died. This is the bread that comes down from heaven, so that one may eat of it and not die. I am the living bread that came down from heaven. If anyone eats of this bread, he will live forever. And the bread that I will give for the life of the world is my flesh. . . . For my flesh is true food, and my blood is true drink. (John 6:32–33, 48–51, 55)

Don't settle for junk food when God is offering you Wonder Bread! As William Williams wrote (1745):

> *Guide me, O Thou great Jehovah,*
> *Pilgrim through this barren land.*
> *I am weak, but Thou art mighty;*
> *Hold me with Thy powerful hand.*
> *Bread of Heaven, Bread of Heaven,*
> *Feed me till I want no more;*
> *Feed me till I want no more.*

5
Spiritual Warfare
(Exodus 17:1–16)

"For we do not know what to pray for as we ought, but the Spirit himself intercedes for us with groanings too deep for words." (Romans 8:26)

The next stop on the Hebrews' journey was a place called Rephidim. Though scholars debate the exact location, our text seems to indicate that it was near Mount Sinai. In this desert encampment, two important events took place, both of which were clearly tests and part of the core curriculum that God had prepared for his people at the University of the Desert. This chapter focuses primarily on the second test, the battle with the Amalekites, because the first test, lack of water, was really a type of re-test.

THE LACK OF WATER TEST

The people had done so poorly on the bitter water test at Marah that God gave them another chance at Rephidim. Though these tests have important differences, they both were designed to teach the Hebrews to trust God to meet their basic needs when in a desert wasteland. God considered this lesson to be of such importance that he gave the test twice!

> All the congregation of the people of Israel moved on from the wilderness of Sin by stages, according to the commandment of the LORD, and camped at Rephidim, but there was no water for the people to drink. Therefore the

people quarreled with Moses and said, "Give us water to drink." And Moses said to them, "Why do you quarrel with me? Why do you test the LORD?" But the people thirsted there for water, and the people grumbled against Moses and said, "Why did you bring us up out of Egypt, to kill us and our children and our livestock with thirst?" So Moses cried to the LORD, "What shall I do with this people? They are almost ready to stone me." And the LORD said to Moses, "Pass on before the people, taking with you some of the elders of Israel, and take in your hand the staff with which you struck the Nile, and go. Behold, I will stand before you there on the rock at Horeb, and you shall strike the rock, and water shall come out of it, and the people will drink." And Moses did so, in the sight of the elders of Israel. And he called the name of the place Massah and Meribah, because of the quarreling of the people of Israel, and because they tested the LORD by saying, "Is the LORD among us or not?" (Exodus 17:1–7)

The people should have been prepared for this test. They had seen God move in a miraculous manner at Marah when they were thirsty, so surely, they could trust him at Rephidim. Unfortunately, they manifested the very same dysfunctional patterns of grumbling and unbelief they had shown before. In this situation at Rephidim, however, a new element was introduced. Until now, the word "test" has been used to describe God's actions toward his people: he tested *them*, wanting *them* to learn an important lesson. This time, the situation was reversed: the people were testing *God*! Moses was incredulous: "Why do you test the LORD?" he asked (Ex 17:2).

We can easily understand the nature of a test when God is the teacher and his people are the students, but what does it look like when the people test God? The specific nature of the peoples' sin at Rephidim is seen in the audacious question they asked: "Is the LORD among us or not?" (Ex 17:7). These people have seen the Nile turned to blood, hailstones the size of baseballs, a plague of frogs, three days of darkness, the Red Sea divided, and bitter water miraculously turned sweet. That very day, they had gathered free food that fell from heaven to provide sustenance for them and their families. Yet they asked: "Is the LORD among us or not?" It would not be surprising if such an attitude tried God's patience and pushed him to the limit!

Amazingly, God responded to the situation with grace and mercy once again. He told Moses to take his staff and go to the rock at Horeb and strike it. When Moses did as God directed, water flowed out in abundance so that everyone's thirst was quenched.[1] To make sure the people never forgot this lesson, the place was named Massah, a Hebrew term meaning "testing" (see Ex 17:7).

FOUL FIEND: THE SPIRITUAL WARFARE TEST

The second test that happened at Rephidim was Israel's first battle. Minding their own business as they followed the pillar of fire, the people of God discovered that an enemy army was blocking their path. This was something new. They had never had to fight before. God was introducing his people to yet another test that is part of the core curriculum at the University of the Desert: the spiritual warfare test.

In his spiritual classic, *Pilgrim's Progress*, John Bunyan describes how a traveler named Christian makes his way toward the Celestial City. After visiting House Beautiful, Christian is given armor to prepare for what lies ahead. Entering the Valley of Humiliation, he encounters a hideous, fire-breathing dragon, a "foul fiend," standing in the middle of the road. The name of this monster is Apollyon, a Greek term meaning "destroyer" (see Rv 9:11). He has scales like a fish, wings like a dragon, feet like a bear, and a mouth like a lion. Christian is terrified and wants to turn and run back in the direction from which he came. Remembering that he has been given no armor to cover his back, he realizes he would be more vulnerable if he turned and ran than if he stood and fought. Struggling for courage, he pulls out his sword and steps toward the monster.

> Despite all that Christian could do to avoid it, Apollyon wounded him with arrows in his head, his hand, and his foot. This caused Christian to fall back a little. Apollyon, therefore,

---

1 Be sure not to confuse this incident with what happened many years later in the desert near Kadesh-barnea when, once again, water was supplied to thirsty people from a rock (see Nm 20:1–13). In this later situation, Moses lost his temper and disobeyed God's command. As a result, he was not allowed to enter the Land of Promise.

followed with another sudden and forceful attack. Christian took courage again and resisted as bravely as he could. This severe combat lasted for over half a day, even until Christian was almost worn out. . . . While Apollyon was preparing for his last blow, which he would use to bring an end to this good man, Christian skillfully reached out his hand for his sword and grasped it, saying, "Do not gloat over me, my enemy! Though I have fallen, I will rise." Then Christian gave him a deadly thrust, which made Apollyon back away as if he had received a mortal wound . . . . With that, Apollyon spread out his dragon's wings and quickly sped away, so that Christian saw him no more.[2]

Bunyan's vivid description of Christian's battle with Apollyon is wonderfully similar to the battle between the Amalekites and the Israelites at Rephidim. Amalek was a terrifying enemy blocking the Hebrew's path. Armed and dangerous, the Amalekites were intent on either turning the Israelites back to Egypt or killing them in battle. What could a rag-tag, undisciplined group of former slaves do in the face of a battle-hardened enemy? Previously, God had done all the fighting for Israel. Now, the time had come for the people of God to learn the art of warfare. God knew many battles were coming for the Hebrews, especially after they entered Canaan. So he made sure that Spiritual Warfare 101 was one of the core courses his people had to take at the University of the Desert. On their journey to spiritual wholeness, they had to learn to fight—God's way.

> **" Now, the time had come for the people of God to learn the art of warfare.**

Then Amalek came and fought with Israel at Rephidim. So Moses said to Joshua, "Choose for us men, and go out and fight with Amalek. Tomorrow I will stand on the top of the hill with the staff of God in my hand." So Joshua did as Moses told him, and fought with Amalek, while Moses, Aaron, and Hur went up to the top of the hill. Whenever Moses held up his hand, Israel prevailed, and whenever

---

2   John Bunyan, *The Pilgrim's Progress in Modern English* (Alachua, FL: Bridge-Logos, 1998), 81–82.

he lowered his hand, Amalek prevailed. But Moses' hands grew weary, so they took a stone and put it under him, and he sat on it, while Aaron and Hur held up his hands, one on one side, and the other on the other side. So his hands were steady until the going down of the sun. And Joshua overwhelmed Amalek and his people with the sword. Then the LORD said to Moses, "Write this as a memorial in a book and recite it in the ears of Joshua, that I will utterly blot out the memory of Amalek from under heaven." And Moses built an altar and called the name of it, The LORD Is My Banner, saying, "A hand upon the throne of the LORD! The LORD will have war with Amalek from generation to generation." (Exodus 17:8–16)

As descendants of Esau, the Amalekites were distant cousins of the Jews, which might explain some of their hatred and hostility. Sometimes the fiercest opposition to obeying the will of God comes not from outsiders but from the members of one's own family. The Amalekite attack was fierce and cruel. They practiced an early form of terrorism. Years later, writing about this incident, Moses remembered their unscrupulous methods:

Remember what Amalek did to you on the way as you came out of Egypt, how he attacked you on the way when you were faint and weary, and cut off your tail, those who were lagging behind you, and he did not fear God. (Deuteronomy 25:17–18)

Rather than fighting in conventional ways, the Amalekites snuck up from behind and picked off the stragglers one by one. Such terror tactics must have spread fear and panic among the Hebrews.

Amalek had the dubious distinction of being the first nation in history to fight against the redeemed people of God. Many other nations, of course, came later, but Amalek was the first. This is why the battle at Rephidim is so important. Not only was God teaching an important lesson to the Jews but also he was making a statement to the watching world. God wanted all nations everywhere to understand clearly what happens to those who attack his people. The consequences for Amalek's hostility were severe: "I will utterly blot out the memory of Amalek from under heaven" (Ex 17:14).

Until we learn to think like a soldier, live like a soldier, and fight like a soldier, we will never reach our destination. Paul pressed this point home with his disciple-in-training, Timothy: "Fight the good fight of the faith" (1 Tm 6:12); "Share in suffering as a good soldier of Christ Jesus" (2 Tm 2:3). All the spiritual giants of history have understood this principle. In his great hymn, *A Mighty Fortress*, Martin Luther writes of the spiritual combat that awaits us as followers of Christ:

> *And though this world with devils filled,*
> *Should threaten to undo us,*
> *We will not fear, for God hath willed*
> *His truth to triumph through us.*
> *The Prince of Darkness grim,*
> *We tremble not for him;*
> *His rage we can endure,*
> *For lo! his doom is sure,*
> *One little word shall fell him.*

Anyone who sets out on the journey to spiritual wholeness soon discovers that he has enemies. Jesus did not want us to be surprised by this fact.

> If the world hates you, know that it has hated me before it hated you. If you were of the world, the world would love you as its own; but because you are not of the world, but I chose you out of the world, therefore the world hates you. (John 15:18–19)

Until followers of Christ learn that the world hates them and wants to thwart their progress, the journey to spiritual wholeness will be one enormously frustrating experience. Indeed, those unprepared for conflict may become so discouraged that they give up and quit. God brings his redeemed children to the University of the Desert because he wants to introduce them to the reality of spiritual warfare and to give them the basic equipment they need to be victorious.

In the Gap

Soldiers of God must realize that, when it comes to spiritual warfare, the issue is not just *that* we fight but *how*. There is no spiritual merit in fighting as such. The real lesson to be learned in the test at Rephidim is not the willingness to fight or even the readiness to lay down our lives. What we most need to learn is *how* God's battles are to be fought. Paul states the issue succinctly:

> For though we walk in the flesh, we are not waging war
> according to the flesh. For the weapons of our warfare are
> not of the flesh but have divine power to destroy strongholds.
> (2 Corinthians 10:3–4)

The most striking thing about the battle at Rephidim is *how* it was fought. While Joshua was down in the valley fighting, Moses was up on the mountain praying. The staff of Moses was more important than the sword of Joshua. There could be no victory in the valley without prayer on the mountain. At Rephidim, God taught his people how to use their ultimate weapon, their nuclear option: intercessory prayer.

Most Christian pilgrims find it comparatively easy to identify with Joshua and his soldiers as they slug it out in the valley with the Amalekites. Using a sword comes somewhat naturally to most of us. Joining Moses, Aaron, and Hur on the mountain feels strange. The pressing need, it seems to most of us, is down in the valley. There on the field of battle is where the future is decided. What is needed is soldiers to fight, not saints to pray! Yet that is not what God taught the Hebrews at Rephidim.

Intercessory Prayer was another course in the core curriculum at the University of the Desert. God taught his people that prayer is not something that prepares us for the battle. Prayer *is* the battle! The prayer meeting on the mountain at Rephidim is perhaps the classic Old Testament illustration of the power of intercession. We make a mistake, however, if we think of intercessory prayer only in terms of a prayer meeting, when a few saints gather, circle their chairs, bow their heads, close their eyes, and then ask the Lord to intervene in a certain situation. It is true that intercession often involves such activities. It certainly did at Rephidim for the three men on the mountain. However, authentic intercession is more than a prayer meeting. It is a lifestyle, a consistent practice of positioning oneself in the gap, between the needs on earth and the resources in heaven. There on the mountain, Moses and his friends were positioned so that they could talk to God about men and talk to men about God. Intercessory prayer was standing in the gap. At Rephidim, we are introduced to four great principles of a life of intercession: identification, unity, agony, and authority.

Identification

As they were praying on the mountain, Moses, Aaron, and Hur were not detached spectators praying from a distance as if the battle did not impact them personally. Nothing could be further from the truth! These prayer warriors knew that their own destiny was intertwined with the destiny of those for whom they prayed. One of the great lessons God was teaching his people at Rephidim is that no one can pray effectively for others who is not ready to identify with the needs and concerns of those for whom he prays.

> **Authentic intercession is more than a prayer meeting. It is a lifestyle.**

To be honest, most prayer meetings I have attended seem oblivious to this first principle of intercession. We pray for Sue's surgery, Bill's need for a job, the persecuted church in Iran, and AIDS orphans in Africa. However, we pray from a distance. We refuse to allow our emotions to be touched by the desperate realities in these situations. The outcome of what happens in these tragic cases doesn't impact us. Is it any wonder that our prayers are so weak and ineffective?

When Moses interceded, he identified fully with those for whom he prayed. His emotions, his hopes, his fears were all wrapped up in the reality that was the focus of his prayer. Perhaps the most dramatic illustration of his life as an intercessor is seen in the way he prayed for the Hebrew people after they sinned with the golden calf:

> The next day Moses said to the people, "You have sinned a great sin. And now I will go up to the LORD; perhaps I can make atonement for your sin." So Moses returned to the LORD and said, "Alas, this people has sinned a great sin. They have made for themselves gods of gold. But now, if you will forgive their sin—but if not, please blot me out of your book that you have written." (Exodus 32:30–32)

I've participated in many prayer meetings in my life, but I can honestly say that I have *never* heard anyone intercede for others like that! Moses so closely identified with the Hebrews that he asked to receive God's judgment upon himself if God chose not to forgive them.

The ultimate intercessor is, of course, Jesus Christ. His life is the perfect illustration of what it means to stand in the gap and intercede for others. Salvation could not be accomplished from the throne room of heaven by a distant decree. For men and women to be redeemed, God had to come and live among us, fully identifying with those he came to save. He became poor for our sakes (see 2 Cor 8:9). He was tempted in all points like we are tempted (see Heb 4:15). He learned obedience through the things that he suffered (see Heb 5:8). He wept at the death of a friend (see Jn 11:33–35). He bore our griefs and carried our sorrows (see Is 53:4). He tasted death for everyone (see Heb 2:9). He became sin—for our sake (see 2 Cor 5:21).

To intercede for others is to fully identify with them and their situation. Intercessory prayer is to enter into the reality of what others are experiencing. This is how redemption comes to the world. This is what God wants to teach us about prayer. François Fénelon said it well: "Intercessory prayer is only another name for love."

Unity

Moses was not alone when he interceded. Aaron and Hur were at his side: praying, encouraging, helping, holding up his arms. The three were in agreement as they prayed. When there is unity on the mountain, there is victory in the valley. It is possible that Jesus was thinking about this incident at Rephidim when he said:

> Truly, I say to you, whatever you bind on earth shall be bound in heaven, and whatever you loose on earth shall be loosed in heaven. Again I say to you, if two of you agree on earth about anything they ask, it will be done for them by my Father in heaven. For where two or three are gathered in my name, there am I among them. (Matthew 18:18–20)

The Greek word "agree" is *sumphoneo*, the origin of our English word "symphony." To produce a symphony, the players in an orchestra must work together in unity. They are playing different parts and using different instruments, but they all follow the same score. The point is not that everyone plays the same note. That would be unison. The beauty of the music is heard in the harmonies, as the differences are unified in one glorious symphony. So it is in intercession. The point is not that everyone prays in an identical manner. Rather, to agree together in a deep unity of purpose makes corporate prayer a beautiful symphonic expression of our cries to God.

Agony

At eighty years of age, it is little wonder that Moses needed help to hold up his arms. Prayer hurts. At Rephidim, God taught his people about the agony of intercession that is necessary to successfully complete the journey to spiritual wholeness. While there is no redemptive value in any pain that *we* may feel in prayer, there is tremendous redemptive value in entering in to the pain that *God* feels for the world.

> Likewise the Spirit helps us in our weakness. For we do not know what to pray for as we ought, but the Spirit himself intercedes for us with groanings too deep for words. And he who searches hearts knows what is the mind of the Spirit, because the Spirit intercedes for the saints according to the will of God. (Romans 8:26–27)

True intercession happens when the one who is praying gets so close to the heart of God that he feels what God feels as he prays. The Spirit of God is looking for a heart with whom he can groan for the sins and sufferings of the world. When the intercessor allows the Spirit to pray through him, he becomes a sort of channel through which God talks to himself! God the Spirit is praying through us back to God the Father using groans more than words to plead for help. When we intercede for others, we give the Holy Spirit permission to groan in us. True intercession, then, is a participation in the life of the Trinity. Such prayer always will be "according to the will of God" (Rom 8:29), because God is talking to himself through us. As such, our prayers have nuclear power, because such prayers always will be answered.

The cross was the place where the ultimate intercessor stood in the gap to plead with the Father on behalf of sinners. There, suspended between earth and heaven, Jesus absorbed the pain and sin of the world like a sponge. In the body of Jesus writhing in agony on the cross, God's grace and human need met in a glorious collision of redemptive power. His pain made possible the salvation of the world.

The drama intensifies when we discover that God invites us to join him in this ministry of intercession. He wants us to do what his Son came to do: to stand in the gap, to become intercessors. "As the Father has sent me, even so I am sending you," Jesus tells his disciples (Jn 20:21). Authentic intercessors understand their calling to ministry includes an invitation to complete "what is lacking in Christ's afflictions" (Col 1:24). The agony *we* may feel in this work is important only to the extent that our suffering is an expression of his suffering. The power of suffering comes from the fact that it is not *our* suffering, but *his*! He is simply groaning out his agony in and through us. It is as we enter into the pain that God constantly feels for this sin-broken world that his redemptive potential is released to those around us!

> But we have this treasure in jars of clay, to show that the surpassing power belongs to God and not to us. We are afflicted in every way, but not crushed; perplexed, but not driven to despair; persecuted, but not forsaken; struck down,

but not destroyed; always carrying in the body the death
of Jesus, so that the life of Jesus may also be manifested in
our bodies. For we who live are always being given over to
death for Jesus' sake, so that the life of Jesus also may be
manifested in our mortal flesh. So death is at work in us, but
life in you. (2 Corinthians 4:7–12)

Authority

Unfortunately, the story of what happened on the mount of
intercession at Rephidim does not include the content of Moses'
prayer. We can be certain, however, that his words were *not* the
following:

> O Sovereign Lord, help us to submit to these Amalekites
> that stand in our path and to receive their opposition as part
> of your divine purpose for us. Give us grace to accept these
> harsh circumstances of Amalekite domination in our lives.
> And if our journey ends here at Rephidim, then, Lord, we
> will accept that too as part of your will for our lives. Amen.

Though Moses knew how to submit to a Sovereign Lord, we can be
sure that his prayer at Rephidim was not one of passive acquiescence.
Moses understood both God's character and his ways well enough
to know that this moment of Amalekite opposition was not a call to
passivity and submission but rather a call to authority and resistance.
Though there is certainly a time to submissively pray "not my will but
your will be done," true intercessors understand that this comes *at
the end* of prayer, not the beginning. We might imagine that Moses'
prayer at Rephidim went something like this:

> O Lord, these uncircumcised pagans are brazenly seeking
> to thwart your purposes and blaspheme your Name. If they
> succeed in stopping your people on their path to the Land of
> Promise, the nations will laugh at you and conclude that you
> are nothing more than the tribal deity of the Jews, weak and
> ineffective. It is *your* reputation that is at stake here, Lord.
> And don't forget those promises you made to Abraham about
> the land you were going to give to his descendants. O Lord,
> this is your chance to let the world see your power to save
> those who trust in you. Glorify your Name, O Lord. Amen.

True intercessors always pray with authority. They know God, and they know his promises. They pray boldly because the battle is not about them but about God.

The victory at Rephidim was won not because God found someone to fight but because he found someone to intercede. All it takes is two or three, agreeing in prayer, and the battle is won. God is still looking for intercessors, because prayer is the ultimate weapon for the people of God. It is our nuclear option.

Faith Is the Victory

John Yates (1837–1900)

Encamped along the hills of light,
Ye Christian soldiers, rise,
And press the battle ere the night
Shall veil the glowing skies.
Against the foe in vales below
Let all our strength be hurled;
Faith is the victory, we know,
That overcomes the world.

Refrain:
Faith is the victory!
Faith is the victory!
Oh, glorious victory,
That overcomes the world.

His banner over us is love,
Our sword the Word of God;
We tread the road the saints above
With shouts of triumph trod.
By faith, they like a whirlwind's breath,
Swept on o'er every field;
The faith by which they conquered death
Is still our shining shield.

On every hand the foe we find
Drawn up in dread array;
Let tents of ease be left behind,
And onward to the fray.
Salvation's helmet on each head,
With truth all girt about,
The earth shall tremble 'neath our tread,
And echo with our shout.

To him that overcomes the foe,
White raiment shall be giv'n;
Before the angels he shall know
His name confessed in heav'n.
Then onward from the hills of light,
Our hearts with love aflame,
We'll vanquish all the hosts of night,
In Jesus' conqu'ring name.

6
The Stress Test
(Exodus 18:1–27)

Pick out from among you seven men of good repute,
full of the Spirit and of wisdom, whom we will appoint
to this duty. But we will devote ourselves to prayer
and to the ministry of the word. (Acts 6:3–4)

The fifth and final test at the University of the Desert was of a different nature than the previous four. Here, God intended to teach his people, and especially their leader, the indispensable importance of working together. No one gets across the desert alone. We need one another and the different gifts each one brings if we are going to reach our destination on the journey to spiritual wholeness.

A humorous story illustrates this point. A bricklayer was trying to move 500 pounds of bricks from the top of a four-story building to the sidewalk below. The problem was that he was trying to accomplish this feat alone. He wrote a letter to his insurance company describing what happened:

> It would have taken too long to carry the bricks down by hand, so I decided to put them in a barrel and lower them by a pulley which I had fastened to the top of the building. After tying the rope securely at the ground level, I then went up to the top of the building. I fastened the rope around the barrel, loaded it with the bricks, and swung it out over the sidewalk for the descent. Then I went down to the sidewalk and untied the rope, holding it securely to guide the barrel down slowly. But, since I weigh only 140 pounds, the 500-pound load

jerked me from the ground so fast that I didn't have time to think of letting go of the rope. And as I passed between the second and third floors, I met the barrel coming down. This accounts for the bruises and lacerations on my upper body. I held tightly to the rope until I reached the top, where my hand became jammed in the pulley. This accounts for my broken thumb. At the same time, however, the barrel hit the sidewalk with a bang and the bottom fell out. With the weight of the bricks gone, the barrel weighed only about 40 pounds. Thus, my 140-pound body began a swift descent, and I met the empty barrel coming up. This accounts for my broken ankle. Slowed only slightly, I continued the descent and landed on the pile of bricks. This accounts for my sprained back and broken collar bone. At this point, I lost my presence of mind completely and let go of the rope. And the empty barrel came crashing down on me. This accounts for my head injuries.

As for the last question on the form, "What would you do if the same situation arose again?" please be advised that I am finished trying to do the job alone.[1]

THE DANGERS OF WORKING ALONE

In Exodus 18, we discover Moses working alone. This situation was threatening to bring Moses to the point of burnout and was creating great frustration for the hundreds of thousands of people who were living under his leadership. The crisis became so great that it threatened the success of their journey. While the previous tests at the University of the Desert focused on the need to learn basic spiritual lessons such as trust, prayer, providence, and contentment, this test was different. The problem here was administrative. The core curriculum at the University of the Desert included a course that taught the people of God the importance of organizing tasks, managing resources, and delegating responsibilities. Though this lesson might not appear to have been as spiritual as the previous ones,

---

1   John C. Maxwell, *Developing the Leader Within You* (Nashville: Thomas Nelson, 1993), 113–14.

we soon discover that failing this test has the potential to thwart the very purposes of God.

> The next day Moses sat to judge the people, and the people stood around Moses from morning till evening. When Moses' father-in-law saw all that he was doing for the people, he said, "What is this that you are doing for the people? Why do you sit alone, and all the people stand around you from morning till evening?" And Moses said to his father-in-law, "Because the people come to me to inquire of God; when they have a dispute, they come to me and I decide between one person and another, and I make them know the statutes of God and his laws." Moses' father-in-law said to him, "What you are doing is not good. You and the people with you will certainly wear yourselves out, for the thing is too heavy for you. You are not able to do it alone. Now obey my voice; I will give you advice, and God be with you! You shall represent the people before God and bring their cases to God, and you shall warn them about the statutes and the laws, and make them know the way in which they must walk and what they must do. Moreover, look for able men from all the people, men who fear God, who are trustworthy and hate a bribe, and place such men over the people as chiefs of thousands, of hundreds, of fifties, and of tens. And let them judge the people at all times. Every great matter they shall bring to you, but any small matter they shall decide themselves. So it will be easier for you, and they will bear the burden with you. If you do this, God will direct you, you will be able to endure, and all this people also will go to their place in peace." (Exodus 18:13–23)

Jethro, Moses' father-in-law, was very impressed with the amazing things God had done in redeeming the Hebrews from bondage in Egypt. After Moses told him the story of the plagues, the Red Sea, and the miracles in the desert, Jethro exclaimed, "Now I know that the LORD is greater than all gods" (Ex 18:11). Yet as he watched Moses carrying out his administrative duties, Jethro realized there was something that was "not good": Moses was carrying the weight of administration alone (see Ex 18:17–18). Unless this problem were remedied, the mission of God would fail.

From the outside, the life of a leader often appears enviable. The salary, the office space, the constant attention, and the perks make the position seem like a dream job. However, from the inside, leadership is a heavy burden. Not everyone can handle it. For those who try to go it alone, a crash is inevitable. This is especially true for leaders in ministry. The Bible gives a surprising amount of detail about the inner world of Moses, one of the greatest leaders in human history. Those he led grumbled constantly about his leadership and blamed him for their hardships. It is little wonder that Moses was often discouraged, depressed, frustrated, and angry.[2] In fact, his level of frustration eventually led him to sin in such a way that he was denied entrance into the Land of Promise (see Nm 20:1–13). His example serves as a warning to all ministry leaders: Those who fail to learn how to handle the stress of leadership jeopardize their witness and risk finishing the race poorly.

NAMING THE PROBLEM

To get an idea of the situation, imagine a courtroom, a counseling office, and a seminary classroom all rolled into one. Moses was being called on to act as a judge, a counselor, and a theological professor. Whether the issue was a property dispute, marital conflict, or a doctrinal question, the people—approximately two million of them!— had only one place to go: Moses. Israel hadn't yet received the Law or the Tabernacle. There were no priests, lawyers, or counselors. Anyone who needed to "inquire of God" about a matter had to make an appointment with Moses (see Ex 18:15).

It takes little imagination to picture the results of such a system. For the people, the lack of staff and the simplistic organizational structure created a bureaucratic nightmare. They stood around "from morning till evening" (Ex 18:13–14) waiting their turn to share their situation with Moses. By the time they saw him, they were worn out. Their frustration increased as their basic needs remained unmet.

---

2   For a picture of Moses' emotional struggles related to leadership, see Exodus 32:19 and Numbers 11:13–15; 14:5; 16:4.

For Moses, the consequences were catastrophic. The weight of such a load was crushing. Moses was heroically trying to do a task that was logistically impossible. Jethro stated the issue succinctly: "For the thing is too heavy for you. You are not able to do it alone" (Ex 18:18). In other words, Moses was on the point of burnout. He was on the verge of failing the stress test. If Moses were to go under, what would happen to the flock he was leading?

The problem was administrative overload. The consequences were two-fold: mounting frustration for the people and crippling fatigue for Moses. Eugene Peterson captures the reality well in his translation: "You'll burn out, and the people right along with you" (Ex 18:18 MSG).

"Burnout" is a secular term, dating from the 1970s, used to describe a state of emotional, mental, and physical exhaustion caused by excessive and prolonged stress and overwork. It occurs when someone feels overwhelmed and unable to meet life's demands. The classic symptoms include:

- anger, irritability, a quick temper.
- feelings of loneliness and of being unappreciated.
- depression, apathy, mood swings.
- fatigue, exhaustion, lack of motivation, little enthusiasm.
- difficulty in making decisions, inability to concentrate.
- headaches, high blood pressure, insomnia.
- wasting time in mindless pursuits (e.g., video games, playing solitaire, etc.).
- feeling overwhelmed and that nothing one does makes a difference.
- thinking every day is a bad day.

It is not clear that Moses and the people had reached such a condition, but it is *very* clear that they were headed that direction. Left unaddressed, Moses certainly would have cracked under the strain, and the people might have risen in revolt as their basic needs remained unmet. Burnout is serious business. It has the capacity to derail the very purposes of God.

Secular approaches to dealing with burnout tend to rely on secular solutions: exercise, diet, sleep, laughter, time management, vacation, etc. While such responses certainly have value, they fail to deal with the deeper issues involved. God has a method for dealing with burnout that gets at the root causes, not just the surface symptoms. God sent Jethro just in time to avert disaster by giving wise counsel that brought godly solutions.

Embracing the Solution

How blessed Moses was to have such a good and wise father-in-law! Jethro's advice remedied the situation and made possible the continuation of the Israelites' journey to spiritual wholeness. Fortunately, Moses was humble enough to listen and learn. The counsel Jethro gave to Moses is not only of historical interest, however. His advice continues to help men and women in ministry even today. His counsel can be summarized in five short commands: choose qualified persons, train them, organize them, empower them, and release them.

> **" God has a method for dealing with burnout that gets at the root causes, not just the surface symptoms.**

Choose Qualified Persons

Moses needed help. The burden was too great to carry alone. However, in the rush to find workers, he had to be careful not to choose the wrong kind of workers, lest he make a bad situation even worse. The selection process had to be discerning. The point was not to draft those who were available, but rather to enlist those who were qualified. Jethro wisely told his son-in-law that three qualifications were non-negotiable (see Ex 18:21). They must be men who:

- *Feared God.* These assistants had to be persons who had a personal relationship with the living Lord. This was foundational. To bring on staff someone who did not know God, regardless of how talented such a person might have been, would have resulted in deeper difficulties than they already had.
- *Were trustworthy.* Moses was looking for men whose commitment to truth was greater than their commitment to anything else. Such persons would be of tremendous assistance in the work of God, because they had an inner moral compass that knew how to discern right from wrong, truth from error.
- *Hated a bribe.* Jethro encouraged Moses to look for leaders who were not motivated by selfish ambition or personal advantage. It was only those whose first commitment was to the will and purposes of God who were fit to lead on the journey to spiritual wholeness.

Train Them

The men chosen were to receive on-the-job training for the work they were called to do. Some would be chiefs over thousands, others over hundreds, others over fifties, and others over tens. This system was thus in some ways like our own judicial system with its varying levels of courts of appeal. A matter that could not be resolved by a lower court was passed on to a higher court. Only the most difficult cases came to Moses (see Ex 18:21–22). Such a system ensured that leaders at each level were held accountable for their actions and, at the same time, were trained as they watched how the system worked.

Organize Them

Jethro's suggestion to divide the camp into groups of thousands, hundreds, fifties, and tens was ingenious (see Ex 18:21). Though many think of "small group ministry" as a contemporary innovation, the truth is that this strategy is over 3,000 years old. Jethro's plan was profoundly simple and simply profound. It ensured that every member of the Israelite congregation had a place to be heard and to receive help. Whether the congregation had 100 members or 100,000, the plan worked beautifully.

Empower Them

Once the structure was established and the leaders trained, Moses was to delegate authority to the new leaders. At each level, those in charge were thus able to act in the name of those who had commissioned them. This meant even the man who led a group of ten people could speak and act with the authority of Moses! Later in the journey through the desert, we will see this principle of delegation and empowerment spelled out with even more clarity:

> Then the LORD said to Moses, "Gather for me seventy men of the elders of Israel, whom you know to be the elders of the people and officers over them, and bring them to the tent of meeting, and let them take their stand there with you. And I will come down and talk with you there. And I will take some of the Spirit that is on you and put it on them, and they shall bear the burden of the people with you, so that you may not bear it yourself alone." (Numbers 11:16–17)

Release Them

Finally, Moses deployed the men who had been chosen, trained, organized, and empowered. He sent them forth to do the work, to care for the people. As they faithfully executed their duties, the mission of God was accomplished and the people marched forward to possess their inheritance.

It is tempting to imagine that Jesus may well have been thinking of Jethro's advice when he called his disciples. Though he was the Second Person of the Trinity, he knew he needed help in accomplishing his mission. Calling the twelve, he established a method of operating that is unequaled in human history. Each disciple would be nurtured and cared for, *and* the evangelization of the world would become possible as small groups of disciples multiplied over the face of the earth. Robert Coleman, in his classic work, *The Master Plan of Evangelism*, outlines the method Jesus used to train his men. The similarity of Jesus' plan to Jethro's is remarkable.

1. Selection—People were his method, not programs.
2. Association—He spent time with them, lived with them, hung out with them.
3. Consecration—He expected obedience. When he said, "Follow me," he meant it.
4. Impartation—Jesus gave himself to the disciples because he loved them.
5. Demonstration—Jesus told his disciples what to do, and he showed them how.
6. Delegation—He gave them work to do.
7. Supervision—Jesus held them accountable for their assignments.
8. Reproduction—As Jesus poured into the twelve, so he expected that they would, in turn, pour their lives into others. Paul summarized the process well when he said to Timothy: "And what you have heard from me . . . entrust to faithful men, who will be able to teach others also" (2 Tm 2:2).

SHALOM!

When Moses implemented Jethro's advice and formed small groups with qualified leaders, the results were both immediate and far reaching. Jethro had promised Moses that if he followed his advice, "you will be able to endure, and all this people also will go to their place in peace" (Ex 18:23). In Hebrew, the word "peace" is *shalom*, which denotes much more than the absence of conflict. It speaks of one's total well-being, experiencing satisfaction and contentment in the deepest depths of one's soul.

We can imagine what such *shalom* looked like when Jethro's advice was followed:

- For *Moses*, life was finally in balance once again. The stress was off, the burden was lighter because it was shared, and rest was finally possible. He was free to devote his time and energy to those areas where he was most gifted and called.
- For *the people*, there was deep contentment and satisfaction. They had someone to hear their concerns and respond to their needs.
- For *the group leaders*, there was the joy of having a job to do and a mission to accomplish. Whether leading a group of ten or one thousand, they found great meaning in being co-laborers together with God in the greatest liberation movement in the history of the world.

The fifth test at the University of the Desert teaches us the importance of organizing our lives in such a way that stress, fatigue, and frustration don't hinder the work of God. God wants us to learn that burnout can be just as deadly on the journey to spiritual wholeness as lack of food, lack of water, or enemy attacks. While the previous four tests were resolved by a divine miracle, this test demanded a more human solution. Though we don't often think of good administration and governance as a gift of God, Exodus 18 helps us to see that no one completes the journey to spiritual wholeness without help in organizing and structuring their lives.

7

Dearly Beloved, We Are Gathered Here . . .

(Exodus 19–24)

"I remember the devotion of your youth,
your love as a bride, how you followed me
into the wilderness . . . ." (Jeremiah 2:2)

Years ago, a country preacher went into a bar to try to talk some sense into old Leroy. Though he had warned him of the danger of sin on numerous occasions in the past, nothing seemed to work. Today, however, the preacher had a new strategy to try. Finding Leroy at his usual place, the preacher sat down on a stool next to him at the bar. Reaching into his pocket, he pulled out a live worm and dropped it into Leroy's glass of liquor! It took only a few moments for the worm to shrivel up and die. Leroy stared in dumbfounded amazement. Seizing the moment, the preacher looked intently into his bloodshot eyes and asked, "Now, Leroy, what do you think the Lord might be trying to say to you through this illustration?" Scratching his head and thinking hard, Leroy finally said, "Well, I guess God wants me to know that if I drink more hard liquor I won't get worms."

Two people can look at the same situation and draw very different conclusions. Few events in the Bible illustrate this reality better than what happened at Mount Sinai. Different people, examining the same event, see two very different realities. Many regard Sinai as a terrifying place where an angry God thunders down his rules and obligations.

For these people, the smoke-covered mountain conjures up images of legalism, pharisaism, and works righteousness. As Christians, we don't need that stuff anymore. We're under grace now, not law, right?

A classic illustration of this negative view comes from John Bunyan's *Pilgrim's Progress*. As Christian travels from the City of Destruction toward the wicket gate that leads to life, he encounters Mr. Worldly-Wiseman, who encourages him to go first to "yonder high hill," where he will meet Mr. Legality, who will tell him how to find relief from the burden he carries on his back. The hill is none other than Mount Sinai.

> So, turning out of the way he was going, Christian went toward Mr. Legality's house for help. But when he reached the hill, it seemed so high, and the side of the hill that was next to the pathway had such a great overhang, that Christian was afraid to venture farther lest the hill should fall on his head. So, he stood still there not knowing what to do. Furthermore, his burden now seemed heavier to him than while he was in his original course of travel. Flashes of fire came out of the hill, making Christian afraid he would be burned. Here, therefore, he sweat and shook with fear . . . .[1]

“ We are expected to obey the law not to be saved but because we already are.

With all due respect, John Bunyan is confused about both the place and the purpose of Mount Sinai. He places the mountain *before* redemption, as if it were in Egypt. The message of this mountain, for Bunyan, seems to be a legalistic form of works righteousness. The map of the Exodus illustrates a radically different reality. Mount Sinai is not in Egypt at all! The people arrived at Sinai three full months *after* crossing the Red Sea. In other words, the law was never intended to be the *cause* of salvation but the *result*! We are expected to obey the law not to be saved but because we already are.

---

1   John Bunyan, *The Pilgrim's Progress in Modern English* (Alachua, FL: Bridge-Logos, 1998), 19.

Far from being a terrible place to be avoided, Sinai was a beautiful place where God gathered his redeemed people to himself and began to reveal his deeper purposes in accomplishing their redemption. At Sinai, God invited Israel into a covenant of love that would define their relationship forever. The laws given at Sinai were neither onerous obligations nor efforts to earn salvation. Rather, they served as wedding vows, where both bride and groom pledged their covenant faithfulness each to the other. The Exodus journey teaches us that, seen in proper perspective, what happened at Mount Sinai was, in reality, the greatest of all weddings.

Few discoveries in my own spiritual journey have done more to transform my thinking and shape my theology than discovering that Mount Sinai is a wedding ceremony. God and Israel got married! It is my purpose in this chapter to show Mount Sinai in these terms as well. I hope I'll have more success in my endeavor than the preacher did with old Leroy.

My Treasured Possession

Historians and theologians agree that what happened at Mount Sinai was one of the defining moments in human history. Traditionally identified as the 7,500-foot peak near the southern tip of the Sinai Peninsula, the mountain was the destination toward which Israel had been traveling since their deliverance at the Red Sea. Here, God gave his people instructions about how to live and how to worship. Obedience to the law was the fruit of redemption, not the root. As they camped at the mountain for 12–18 months, three major events occurred:

1. The covenant was established (see Ex 19–24). Israel was married to God.
2. The tabernacle was built (see Ex 25–31, 35–40). Israel learned how to worship. (See Chapter 9, "A House for God")
3. The golden calf was set up and then destroyed (see Ex 32–34). Israel learned how *not* to worship. (See Chapter 10, "A Lot of Bull")

This chapter deals with the establishment of the covenant. Though redeemed and set free, the people did not yet have a clear understanding of their relationship with their Redeemer. At Sinai, God revealed that the purpose of salvation was not just getting them out of Egypt. More importantly, it was about bringing them to himself. Sinai was about a new relationship more than it was about a new religion.

> On the third new moon after the people of Israel had gone out of the land of Egypt, on that day they came into the wilderness of Sinai. . . . There Israel encamped before the mountain, while Moses went up to God. The LORD called to him out of the mountain, saying, "Thus you shall say to the house of Jacob, and tell the people of Israel: 'You yourselves have seen what I did to the Egyptians, and how I bore you on eagles' wings and brought you to myself. Now therefore, if you will indeed obey my voice and keep my covenant, you shall be my treasured possession among all peoples, for all the earth is mine; and you shall be to me a kingdom of priests and a holy nation.' These are the words that you shall speak to the people of Israel." So Moses came and called the elders of the people and set before them all these words that the LORD had commanded him. All the people answered together and said, "All that the LORD has spoken we will do." And Moses reported the words of the people to the LORD. . . . On the morning of the third day there were thunders and lightnings and a thick cloud on the mountain and a very loud trumpet blast, so that all the people in the camp trembled. Then Moses brought the people out of the camp to meet God, and they took their stand at the foot of the mountain. (Exodus 19:1–8, 16–17)

The particulars of Israel's covenant responsibility are laid out in a series of laws, the essential core being what we typically call the Ten Commandments:

> And God spoke all these words, saying, "I am the LORD your God, who brought you out of the land of Egypt, out of the house of slavery.
> "You shall have no other gods before me.
> "You shall not make for yourself a carved image . . . .
> "You shall not take the name of the LORD your God in vain . . . .

"Remember the Sabbath day, to keep it holy. . . .
"Honor your father and your mother . . . .
"You shall not murder.
"You shall not commit adultery.
"You shall not steal.
"You shall not bear false witness against your neighbor.
"You shall not covet . . . ." (Exodus 20:1–17)

The covenant was finally ratified in a dramatic fashion in Exodus 24, when more vows were made, sacrifices offered, blood sprinkled, and a ceremonial meal shared with God.

> Moses came and told the people all the words of the LORD and all the rules. And all the people answered with one voice and said, "All the words that the LORD has spoken we will do." And Moses wrote down all the words of the LORD. He rose early in the morning and built an altar at the foot of the mountain, and twelve pillars, according to the twelve tribes of Israel . . . . Then he took the Book of the Covenant and read it in the hearing of the people. And they said, "All that the LORD has spoken we will do, and we will be obedient." And Moses took the blood and threw it on the people and said, "Behold the blood of the covenant that the LORD has made with you in accordance with all these words." Then Moses and Aaron, Nadab, and Abihu, and seventy of the elders of Israel went up, and they saw the God of Israel. There was under his feet as it were a pavement of sapphire stone, like the very heaven for clearness. And he did not lay his hand on the chief men of the people of Israel; they beheld God, and ate and drank. (Exodus 24:3–11)

There are at least four reasons why this covenant-making ceremony at Sinai is best understood as a wedding: the beloved was pursued, vows were spoken, there was a public ceremony, and there was fear and trembling.

The Beloved Was Pursued

In the book of Exodus, we discover the prototypical love story. Most of the other famous romance stories in history are but a vague echo of this original. God, the Mighty Prince, fell in love with a maiden in distress. Though she was poor and destitute, he loved her with an everlasting love. Taking the initiative, he left heaven to pursue the object of his affection. It was only at Sinai that he revealed the true intentions of his heart: "I bore you on eagles' wings and brought you to myself. . . . You shall be my treasured possession among all peoples . . ." (Ex 19:4–5).

God's love for Israel was not a detached philanthropic condescension. It was a pursuing, initiating, masculine kind of compassion that sought to woo and win Israel's love in return. It was a love that sought to know and to be known. In calling Israel his "treasured possession," God's aim was not to control and manipulate but to cherish, honor, and bless the one he loved.

Every other love story in history must take its cue from this one. Whether we are thinking of Cinderella, Sleeping Beauty, or Rapunzel, all other love stories are but faint echoes of the Great Story. The prince loved a damsel in distress, rescued her, and brought her to the palace where they married and lived happily ever after.

> **" Most of the other famous romance stories in history are but a vague echo of this original.**

Vows Were Spoken

Though many couples today choose to live together without vows, the Bible envisions marriage differently. God intended much more than co-habitation with Israel, and he wanted something more personal than a prenuptial contract. He was looking for covenant intimacy. Vows have the capacity to transform a romantic relationship into a marriage. The traditional marriage ceremony captures this reality by making the vows central to what is happening:

> Will you have this woman to be your wedded wife? Will you love her, comfort her, honor and keep her, in sickness and in health; and forsaking all others keep thee only to her so long as you both shall live?

After the bride makes the same vow, the couple turns to face each other and then speaks these words of covenant promise to one another:

> I [groom] take thee [bride], to be my wedded wife, to have and to hold, from this day forward, for better, for worse, for richer, for poorer, in sickness and in health, to love and to cherish, till death do us part.

Nothing is more beautiful than vows like these. When spoken in sincerity and truth, they lay a solid foundation for a future home and family that will be a source of great blessing for years to come.

Vows were at the heart of the covenant ceremony being ratified at Mount Sinai between God and Israel. Three times, Israel vowed to God: "All that the LORD has spoken, we will do" (Ex 19:8; 24:3, 7). Seen in the context of the Ten Commandments, Israel was making a solemn promise to turn away from all other gods and to be true to her heavenly Husband in good times and in bad until death. As with all love stories, making such promises was not seen as a legalistic duty but an incredible privilege.

It is important to recognize that Israel was not the only one making vows at Sinai. God himself made a solemn oath to be true to Israel and to forever keep his vows. He pledged covenant fidelity to the one he had chosen to be his wife from among all the nations of the earth. The specifics of God's promise to Israel are seen in Exodus 23:

> Behold, I send an angel before you to guard you on the way and to bring you to the place that I have prepared. . . . I will be an enemy to your enemies and an adversary to your adversaries. . . . [I] will bless your bread and your water, and I will take sickness away from your days. . . . I will make all your enemies turn their backs to you. And I will send hornets before you, which shall drive out the Hivites, the Canaanites, and the Hittites from before you. . . . And I will set your border from the Red Sea to the Sea of the Philistines, and from the wilderness to the Euphrates, for I will give the inhabitants of the land into your hand, and you shall drive them out before you. . . . (Exodus 23:20–31)

The Lord vowed to be the kind of husband to Israel that every bride dreams of having. He would protect her, lead her, provide for her, bless her, honor her, be faithful to her, and never leave her or forsake her. What love!

The vows Israel made to God, and the vows God made to Israel, were far more than a contract or a prenuptial agreement. They were a holy covenant, and, as such, these vows were exclusive, comprehensive, and irrevocable.

Exclusive

Wedding vows are intended not only to unite the bride and the groom in a covenant of love but also to exclude forever any other potential lovers from that sacred union. "Forsaking all others" is at the core of what it means to be married. When a man marries a woman, he is not only saying "Yes" to his bride. He is saying, at the same time, a decisive and definitive "No" to millions of other options. From that moment on, he becomes a one-woman man.

> To worship another god was to break Israel's wedding vows.

The same thing was happening at Mount Sinai. Although the whole earth belonged to God, he had chosen Israel to be his bride (see Ex 19:5). God loved all nations, but his relationship with Israel was unique. Israel's vows to God were equally exclusive. The first commandment made this clear: "You shall have no other gods before [or, besides] me" (Ex 20:3). Israel was saying "Yes" to God, but she also was saying "No" to all competing idols and deities. At Sinai, Israel became a one-God nation. Years later, when Israel gave her heart to other gods (Baal, Asherah, etc.), it is no surprise that the prophets accused her of spiritual adultery. To worship another god was to break Israel's wedding vows.

Comprehensive

Not only are wedding vows exclusive but also they are meant to cover every possible situation. Once those promises are made, there is no place or time when one of the spouses can say, "Here, in this situation, my vows don't apply." The wedding vows do not permit the husband or wife to compartmentalize their lives into areas where they are free to act as if they are not married. Israel was married to God not only during worship services at the Temple but also at home, at work, at the marketplace, and at play.

Irrevocable

Many today get married with an attitude that says, "as long as we both shall love," or "as long as things are going well." That is no vow! A vow is a promise "till death do us part." There is no escape clause hidden in the fine print of the marriage covenant.

Similarly, the covenant God and Israel made at Sinai was for keeps. God wanted his bride to know that he loved her with an everlasting love. When God makes a vow, he will be faithful to what he has promised! Israel might wander and go astray, but God never will. Though Israel's future pursuit of other lovers would raise the possibility of divorce (see Jer 3:8), we can be sure the unfaithfulness was always on Israel's side, never on God's. Paul stated the paradoxical nature of this truth powerfully:

> Here is a trustworthy saying: If we died with him, we will also live with him; if we endure, we will also reign with him. If we disown him, he will also disown us; if we are faithless, he remains faithful, for he cannot disown himself. (2 Timothy 2:1–13 NIV)

There Was a Public Ceremony

Almost intuitively, we understand that a wedding should be beautiful, solemn, and dignified. The magnitude of what is happening dictates that the ceremony should be carefully planned. It is not a casual event but a sacred assembly. Therefore, people should dress in their best clothing and display proper etiquette. The music should be of the highest quality, and all those involved should be on their best behavior. The ceremony should reflect the importance of the occasion.

When one pauses to think about it, it is easy to imagine that our contemporary wedding practices have their origin in the amazing covenant-making ceremony that took place at Mount Sinai. Israel washed and dressed in her best clothing (see Ex 19:10, 14). When the service concluded, they shared a special meal with God, a type of reception (see Ex 24:11). In this prototypical wedding ceremony, God ensured that the occasion was an awe-inspiring moment:

> On the morning of the third day there were thunders and
> lightnings and a thick cloud on the mountain and a very loud
> trumpet blast, so that all the people in the camp trembled.
> Then Moses brought the people out of the camp to meet
> God, and they took their stand at the foot of the mountain.
> Now Mount Sinai was wrapped in smoke because the LORD
> had descended on it in fire. The smoke of it went up like the
> smoke of a kiln, and the whole mountain trembled greatly.
> And as the sound of the trumpet grew louder and louder,
> Moses spoke, and God answered him in thunder. The LORD
> came down on Mount Sinai, to the top of the mountain.
> (Exodus 19:16–20)

In contrast to modern weddings, it was the arrival of the groom at Mount Sinai that was the focus of everyone's attention. God's arrival at the wedding was punctuated with thunder, lightning, a thick cloud, an earthquake, and an unforgettable trumpet solo. The only thing in biblical history comparable to this is that climactic moment in the book of Revelation when the Bridegroom returns once again to marry his bride, the Church:

> Then I heard what seemed to be the voice of a great
> multitude, like the roar of many waters and like the sound of
> mighty peals of thunder, crying out,
>
> "Hallelujah!
> For the LORD our God
> the Almighty reigns.
> Let us rejoice and exult

and give him the glory,
for the marriage of the Lamb has come,
and his Bride has made herself ready;
it was granted her to clothe herself
with fine linen, bright and pure" . . . .

And the angel said to me, "Write this: Blessed are those who are invited to the marriage supper of the Lamb." And he said to me, "These are the true words of God." . . .

Then I saw heaven opened, and behold, a white horse! The one sitting on it is called Faithful and True . . . . His eyes are like a flame of fire, and on his head are many diadems . . . . On his robe and on his thigh he has a name written, King of kings and Lord of lords. (Revelation 19:6–16)

There Was Fear and Trembling

No wedding is complete without the knees of someone knocking in terror at the magnitude of what is taking place. The traditional English ceremony doesn't hide this reality but highlights it by reminding the bride and groom that these vows are not to be entered into "unadvisedly, but reverently, discreetly, and *in the fear of God.*"

I remember well how my knees knocked as I recited my vows on my wedding day. To be sure, it was the happiest day of my life. At the same time, there was something terrifying about it. Though I had meditated on the meaning of these words before our wedding day, I knew that I didn't have a clue what I was getting myself into. As Katy came down the aisle in all her radiant beauty, I cast all prudence to the wind and sealed the deal. My fear of making the covenant was trumped by my fear of missing the opportunity of a lifetime!

Though it sounds almost irreverent to say, there might have been "fear and trembling" even in the heart of God that day at Sinai. I wonder if perhaps he felt a bit nervous about entering an unbreakable covenant with a bride like Israel. Did he really know what he was getting himself into? Did he realize what it would cost him to pledge covenant fidelity to someone as fickle as Israel? When the mountain "trembled greatly" (Ex 19:18), is it possible that God's knees were knocking?

The New Covenant

The covenant at Sinai is more than an isolated fact in Israel's history. For Christians, its importance lies in the fact that it points beyond itself to a reality much, much bigger. It is only when we understand the covenant at Sinai that we can fully comprehend the New Covenant that Jesus came to make available to all people everywhere.

> Behold, the days are coming, declares the LORD, when I will make a new covenant with the house of Israel and the house of Judah, not like the covenant that I made with their fathers on the day when I took them by the hand to bring them out of the land of Egypt, my covenant that they broke, though I was their husband, declares the LORD. For this is the covenant that I will make with the house of Israel after those days, declares the LORD: I will put my law within them, and I will write it on their hearts. And I will be their God, and they shall be my people. And no longer shall each one teach his neighbor and each his brother, saying, "Know the LORD," for they shall all know me, from the least of them to the greatest, declares the LORD. For I will forgive their iniquity, and I will remember their sin no more. (Jeremiah 31:31–34)

What's new about the New Covenant? Not the content. It is still a covenant of grace made by a God of infinite love with an unworthy people. It still takes the blood of a Lamb and the waters of baptism to get started. It still involves faith, not works. None of those elements have changed. They are as old as Mount Sinai. So, what's new about the New Covenant?

For one thing, there is a new *motivation*. The coming of Jesus means that God's law is no longer written on tablets of stone. Now it is written within us, on our hearts. No longer is obedience a matter of external obligation. Now, because of the ministry of the Holy Spirit, obedience is the desire of our hearts. "If you love me, you will keep my commandments," Jesus said (Jn 14:15).

Secondly, the New Covenant offers a new *relationship*. At Sinai, most of the people only knew *about* God. Only a few people, like Moses, had the privilege of knowing God personally, face to face (see Ex 33:11).

The New Covenant makes it possible for all people everywhere to "know the LORD." It was only when the veil in the Temple was torn in two (see Mt 27:51) that all worshipers could get up close and personal with God. The salvation offered us in Jesus Christ is not a religion but a relationship!

Finally, the New Covenant offers a new *power*. The death of Jesus on the cross and the coming of the Holy Spirit at Pentecost mean that worshipers can have the assurance of sins forgiven and the joyful security that comes from a right standing before God. Indeed, the finished work of Christ means that sinful actions can be forgiven and that sinful hearts can be purified! Redemption in the New Covenant is much more than behavior modification. It is the promise of a new creation!

8
Oh, How I Love Your Law!
(Exodus 20)

*"Now we know that the law is good, if one
uses it lawfully." (1 Timothy 1:8)*

The memory of the conversation is etched forever in my mind. I had been pastor of the congregation for perhaps two years when Sally[1] made an appointment to come and talk. Raised in a Christian home, Sally had attended our church since she was a child. She had been part of the youth group and later the program for Christian singles. She also had volunteered to serve in several different ministry areas of our fellowship. In many ways, Sally was the quintessential product of our church. Now in her late twenties, things were not working out well, and she found herself in a crisis of faith.

Sally explained that she no longer read the Bible or prayed. Her attendance at Sunday worship was sporadic at best, and she had dropped out of all fellowship and ministry activities. She acknowledged that she no longer believed the promises of God because they just hadn't "worked" for her. She was romantically involved with a non-Christian and making plans for marriage. As she shared more details of her immoral lifestyle, I could sense the cynicism and unbelief that had taken root in her heart. As she continued her story, my face apparently reflected anxiety and concern. Sensing my struggle, she paused; "Oh, Pastor Stan," she said reassuringly, "Don't be alarmed! I'm saved."

---

1   Not her real name.

It was one of those moments when I could almost hear the "click" go off in my brain as the light suddenly came on. This conversation with Sally became a game-changer for me. My thinking was never again the same. "Sally," I said, mustering all the pastoral courage I could find, "If you don't believe the promises, that makes you an unbeliever. Listen to your own words! How can you call yourself a follower of Christ if you are not following Christ?" Offended by my words, Sally shot back: "I know I'm saved! It all happened at summer youth camp when I was a teenager. On Friday night, during the campfire service, I prayed the sinner's prayer and threw a pine cone on the fire and asked Jesus into my heart. I got saved. And of course, once you're saved, you are always saved—even if you are living in sin."

I really don't remember where the conversation went after that. I only know that was the day I declared war on antinomianism.[2] Though the seven-syllable word may sound frightening, the term is really quite easy to understand. It refers to the unconsciously held belief that salvation by grace alone means that one's moral behavior has little or nothing to **That was the day I declared war on antinomianism.** do with one's spiritual state. The most troubling reality I confronted in dealing with Sally was that she was not an exception to the rule. She was, rather, an illustration of the kind of Christian our evangelical church was producing. To my horror, I realized that the church I pastored had produced many people exactly like Sally! Though they lived like the devil, they were quick to say that they were saved. In Sally's mind, she had not abandoned the faith. She was simply living out the implications of the gospel she had heard and believed.

As I reflected on my conversation with Sally, I realized that her belief system was not only bad theology but also sheer irrationality. If someone claims to be a jogger and yet never jogs, we raise our eyebrows in incredulity. If someone claims to be a Republican but always votes

---

2   Antinomianism (from Greek, literally meaning "anti-law" or "lawless") is an ancient heresy that uses God's grace as a license to sin.

for Democrats, we assume they are not thinking clearly. If someone claims to be a vegetarian but loves to eat at Dakota Steakhouse, we question their sincerity. Yet, in the church today, if someone claims to be a follower of Christ and yet consistently doesn't follow Christ, we tend to nod our heads in pious approval. We have made it possible to be a Christian without being Christ-like. Brothers and sisters, these things ought not to be so!

Dietrich Bonhoeffer speaks against the antinomianism that characterizes so many who call themselves Christian in his book, *The Cost of Discipleship*:

> Cheap grace is the deadly enemy of the church . . . . Cheap grace means the justification of sin without the justification of the sinner. Grace alone does everything, they say, and so everything can remain as it was before . . . . Cheap grace is the preaching of forgiveness without requiring repentance, baptism without church discipline, Communion without confession . . . . Cheap grace is grace without discipleship, grace without the cross, grace without Jesus Christ . . . . We Lutherans have gathered like eagles round the carcass of cheap grace, and there we have drunk of the poison which has killed the life of following Christ . . . . The word of cheap grace has been the ruin of more Christians than any commandment of works.[3]

Because "cheap grace" characterizes so much of the American evangelical church today, we should not be surprised to discover that the lives of many Christians are indistinguishable from those of non-Christians. In his book, *The Divine Conspiracy*, Dallas Willard gives a helpful illustration:

> Think of the bar codes now used on goods in most stores. The scanner responds only to the bar code. It makes no difference what is in the bottle or package that bears it, or whether the sticker is on the "right" one or not. The calculator responds through its electronic eye to the bar code and totally disregards everything else. If the ice cream sticker

---

3   Dietrich Bonhoeffer, *The Cost of Discipleship* (New York: Simon & Schuster, 195), 43–45, 53, 55.

is on the dog food, the dog food is ice cream, so far as the scanner knows or cares.[4]

Sally believed that she had the bar code of salvation on her soul and therefore it didn't really matter how she lived. She was "saved" and her sins were forgiven: past, present, and future. Obeying the moral law of God was therefore optional. The bar code made it official. Sally believed that keeping the law was unnecessary because she had been saved by grace through faith. She further believed that once she was saved she could never fall, regardless of how immoral her lifestyle became.

The Pharisees, on the other hand, believed that keeping the law was indispensable to salvation. They taught that one must obey the law to be saved. Sally had fallen into one ditch (antinomianism), but the Pharisees fell into another (legalism).

So, how do law and grace go together? Where does the moral law of God fit into the Christian life? An examination of the map of the Exodus helps us to answer these important questions.

> **They were to keep God's commandments not to be saved, but because they already were..**

Mount Sinai Is Not in Egypt

God gave the law at Mount Sinai. The first thing to notice about this momentous event is its location. A quick look at the map shows us that Mount Sinai is not in Egypt. This location is theologically significant. The moral law was given *after* redemption, not before. God did not give the law while the Hebrew people were still in Egypt. He did not say, "Here are my commandments. If you obey these laws, then I will deliver you." That would have meant that salvation was by works. God redeemed his people by grace alone through faith. Salvation was not

---

4   Dallas Willard, *The Divine Conspiracy: Rediscovering Our Hidden Life in God* (New York: HarperCollins, 1998), 36.

earned or deserved. It was not the reward for obedience. Rather, it was the free gift of God's amazing grace.

It was *after* they had been liberated from bondage that God led his people to Mount Sinai, where he introduced them to his moral demands. They were to keep God's commandments not to be saved, but because they already were. The law was never intended to be the *way to* God. It was given rather as expression of the *walk with* God. Obedience was the fruit of salvation, not the root.

Apparently, the Pharisees in Jesus' day never quite understood the map. They worked hard to obey the law, thinking it would somehow earn God's favor. Someone needed to tell them that Mount Sinai is not in Egypt. First comes salvation, then obedience.

The Law Reveals the Law-giver

At Sinai, the redeemed began to realize that God had much more in mind than merely getting them out of bondage. God brought them out so that he could enter into a marriage covenant with them. He wanted a relationship of intimacy and love. Yet how can redeemed sinners walk in daily fellowship with the Holy One? This is the question the law was intended to answer.

The law reveals the character of God. Thus far in the journey to spiritual wholeness, God has revealed his power. He defeated the gods of Egypt. He parted the waters of the Red Sea and provided bread from heaven every day. However, until this point, there have been only brief glimpses of his character. Who is this God that redeemed us? What are the qualities of his being that define his character? Who is this husband we have married? The giving of the law at Sinai is one of the primary ways God answers these questions.

In his commentary on the book of Exodus,[5] John Oswalt explains how God's self-revelation at Sinai had to counteract many false notions about God that were prominent in the world of that time. Because many of these pagan notions about God were present in the hearts and minds

---

5   John N. Oswalt, *Exodus: The Way Out* (Wilmore: Francis Asbury Press, 2013), 145–53).

of the redeemed, God came down at Mount Sinai to help his people understand who he truly was. Oswalt mentions six characteristics of the pagan understanding of God that had to be corrected so that his redeemed people could know him for who he truly is:

1. *God is not to be identified with the created order.* Paganism taught that the cosmos is all there is. There is nothing beyond the created order. Therefore, "God" (or "gods") must be identified with this world. Thus, the earth is god, the sky is god, the trees are god, you are god, I am god, good is god, evil is god, etc. The God of Sinai wanted his people to know he is the one who created the cosmos, and he must never be identified with it!

2. *God gives purpose to life.* The religions of the ancient world tended to teach that the world is the result of random actions of various gods vying for power and influence. There is no overarching purpose or goal for human existence. We are born, we live, we die; more people are born, they live, they die. Reality is a cyclical rhythm of survival. The God of Sinai

> 66 God is holy, and he expects his people to reflect his character.

revealed that history is linear, not cyclical, and because history is going somewhere, the lives of his people have significance!

3. *God is one.* Paganism looked at the diversity of the cosmos and concluded there must be diversity in the divine as well: a god of the moon, a god of the storm, a god of vegetation, a god of the river, etc. At Sinai, God spoke plainly about the unity of his being: "Hear, O Israel: The LORD our God, the LORD is one" (Dt 6:4). Because God is one, the world around us can be conceived of as a uni-verse, not a multi-verse.

4. *God is a moral being.* The multiple gods of paganism were competing for power and prestige constantly, using any trick at their disposal to obtain their selfish purposes. Pagans worshiped immoral gods so that they could manipulate them to grant their selfish requests. How different is the God of Sinai! He is righteous,

just, and true. The point of belonging to him is not to get our own way but rather to do the right thing. God is holy, and he expects his people to reflect his character.

5. *God cannot be manipulated or controlled.* All of the gods of the pagan nations were capable of being manipulated so that they performed in conformity to the worshiper's demands. By speaking certain words (incantations), performing certain actions (magic), or by offering certain sacrifices (bribes), these gods could be coerced into performing in certain ways. Not so the God of Sinai! He is majestic in holiness and does whatever he chooses. Sacrifice is never intended as a bribe but as an expression of thanksgiving or a request for mercy.

6. *God is not a sexualized being.* Pagan religion believed that sexuality was the primary force in life. The gods were sexually promiscuous as were those who worshiped them. By contrast, the God of Sinai is holy. While he celebrates the beauty of marital sexual fidelity between one man and one woman, he warns that perverting his created sexual order will bring judgment and social chaos.

The Exodus journey alerts us to the fact that God needed to educate his redeemed people to correctly understand who he is. They had been schooled in the theology of paganism. Though they had put their trust in the one true God and experienced his saving power, they did not yet fully understand his holy character. They continued to think about ultimate reality in patterns learned from their pagan neighbors. At Mount Sinai, God came to root out these false notions and replace them with a theology grounded in the truth. This was the purpose of the giving of the law.

Jesus Summarizes the Law

The law reveals who God is, but it also explains what he expects of his people. Redemption is free and undeserved, but Israel discovered that there are responsibilities that come with the covenant. The laws given at Sinai relate to virtually every area of life: property disputes, economic justice, protection of life, compassion for the defenseless, etc. The Ten Commandments, recorded in Exodus 20:1–21 (also found in Dt 5:1–21), serve as a sort of summary of the entire code.

The first four commandments[6] define our vertical relationship with God. The final six commandments[7] define our horizontal relationships with one another. God wanted his people to understand that the journey to spiritual wholeness is more than just getting right with him. It also involves how we treat and interact with one another.

Jesus was no doubt thinking of both the vertical and horizontal aspects of our faith when a lawyer came to him with a question: "Teacher, which is the great commandment in the Law?" (Mt 22:36). He was asking Jesus to summarize the entire law of God, the Torah, all 613 rules and regulations. He wanted Jesus to boil it all down to its most essential core. The response Jesus gave is one of the most sublime truths he ever spoke:

> And Jesus said to him, "You shall love the Lord your God with all your heart and with all your soul and with all your mind. This is the great and first commandment. And a second is like it: You shall love your neighbor as yourself. On these two commandments depend all the Law and the Prophets. (Matthew 22:37–40)

Love God. Love your neighbor. This is the essence of what the law demands. This is the heart of what God expects from his redeemed people, and it can be explained in two rules:

- Look up to God, the one who redeemed you, and love him with your entire being. If you love him as you should, you won't worship anyone or anything else. You will never try to shape him to fit your conception, but you will let him reveal himself to you as he truly is. If you love him, you'll never use his name tritely or as a swear

---

6   1) You shall have no other gods besides me; 2) You shall not make for yourself a carved image; 3) You shall not take the name of the Lord your God in vain; 4) Remember the Sabbath day to keep it holy.

7   5) Honor your father and mother; 6) You shall not murder; 7) You shall not commit adultery; 8) You shall not steal; 9) You shall not bear false witness against your neighbor; 10) You shall not covet.

word and you will certainly remember to worship him in the great congregation weekly.

- Look out to those around you and love them even as you love yourself. Show honor to your parents. Never violate the life or property of others. Keep sex within marriage. Never slander, lie, or be jealous of those who may have more than you.

Is it possible to imagine a greater summation of God's law than this? Yes. The apostle Paul took Jesus' two commands (love God, love neighbor) and found the element common to both: love. In one majestic sentence, Paul boldly proclaimed: "Love is the fulfilling of the law" (Rom 13:10). It doesn't get more basic than that!

JESUS INTERNALIZES THE LAW

How shocking it must have been to his listeners when Jesus said: "Unless your righteousness exceeds that of the scribes and Pharisees, you will never enter the kingdom of heaven" (Mt 5:20). No one in Jesus' day was more zealous for the law than the Pharisees. They devoted their entire lives to obeying the minutest details of the Mosaic requirements. What could Jesus possibly mean when he tells his followers that their righteousness must *exceed* that of the Pharisees?

Jesus knew the law better than the Pharisees. He also knew the Pharisees. He knew that they majored in outward conformity to behavioral standards. He knew that their righteousness was based in their spiritual disciplines and hard work, not in the grace of God. He also knew that many Pharisees were more interested in *appearing* righteous rather than actually *being* righteous. Jesus also knew that the law itself declared that outward conformity without inward purity was pointless. God was interested in something much deeper than behavior modification. God was interested in the heart.

> And now, Israel, what does the LORD your God require of you, but to fear the LORD your God, to walk in all his ways, to love him, to serve the LORD your God with all your heart and with all your soul, and to keep the commandments and statutes of the LORD, which I am commanding you

today for your good? . . . Circumcise therefore the foreskin of your heart, and be no longer stubborn. (Deuteronomy 10:12–13, 16)

When Jesus said that the righteousness of his followers must exceed that of the Scribes and Pharisees, he simply was reasserting what Moses had already said so long ago: The obedience that God requires is an obedience that comes from the heart. Few things rouse God to greater anger than when his people practice outward forms of piety while their hearts are callous and cold. Jesus was angered by the fact that many of the Pharisees were so meticulous in their observance of the law that they tithed mint, dill, and cumin; yet they neglected "the weightier matters of the law: justice and mercy and faithfulness" (Mt 23:23).

Jesus knew that the law must be internalized and obedience must come from the heart. This explains why, in the Sermon on the Mount, he emphasized that a mere refraining from murder fails to understand the law's true intent:

> **66 Jesus knew that the law must be internalized and obedience must come from the heart.**

> You have heard that it was said to those of old, "You shall not murder; and whoever murders will be liable to judgment." But I say to you that everyone who is angry with his brother will be liable to judgment; whoever insults his brother will be liable to the council; and whoever says, "You fool!" will be liable to the hell of fire. (Matthew 5:21–22)

Similarly, when it comes to keeping the commandment against adultery, Jesus knew that God is interested in far more than outward behavior:

> You have heard that it was said, "You shall not commit adultery." But I say to you, that everyone who looks at a

woman with lustful intent has already committed adultery
with her in his heart. (Matthew 5:27–28)

While Jesus never minimized the importance of our actions and
outward behaviors, he knew that true obedience, the kind desired by
God, comes from the heart.

Using the Law Lawfully

Many today continue to struggle with the place of the law in
their Christian experience. Some, like Sally, see the law as having no
relevance to their relationship with God (antinomianism). Others, like
the Pharisees, see the law as a whip to drive us to work harder and
perform better so that we can make ourselves righteous and acceptable
to God (legalism). We must be vigilant and avoid both errors at all
costs. Paul warned of this danger when he said, "Now we know that
the law is good, *if one uses it lawfully*" (1 Tm 1:8, emphasis added).
When the law is misused, it can do great damage.

One of the most common ways the law is misused is when
Christians fail to distinguish between the moral law and the ceremonial
law. Many of the laws given at Mount Sinai relate to ceremonies,
rituals, and customs that have been rendered obsolete by the coming
of Christ and the establishment of the New Covenant. The book of
Hebrews especially underscores this reality by showing how the high
priesthood of Jesus has nullified the Levitical priesthood of Aaron and
how the sacrifice of Jesus as the Lamb of God has rendered all other
animal sacrifices of the Jewish Temple null and void. For reasons such
as these, most of the classical theologians of history have insisted on
the importance of separating the moral law from the ceremonial law.
It is the former that we are meant to obey, *not* the latter! For example,
John Wesley commented on Jesus' statement that he had come not to
destroy the law but to fulfill it (see Mt 5:17):

> The ritual or ceremonial law, delivered by Moses to the
> children of Israel, containing all the injunctions and
> ordinances which related to the old sacrifices and service of
> the Temple, our Lord indeed did come to destroy, to dissolve,

and utterly abolish . . . . But the moral law, contained in the Ten Commandments, and enforced by the Prophets, he did not take away. It was not the design of his coming to revoke any part of this . . . . Every part of this law must remain in force upon all mankind, and in all ages; as not depending either on time or place, or any other circumstances liable to change, but on the nature of God, and the nature of man, and their unchangeable relation to each other.[8]

Even when we focus squarely on the moral law of God, questions remain: Is it even possible to keep these laws? What if I stumble and fall? What if I disobey? Should we perhaps regard the law as an ideal to aspire to rather than a rule to keep? We've seen the abuse that can happen when we use the law in an unlawful manner, but how are we to understand the right use of the law? What is the law's purpose? As Paul put it: "Why then the law?" (Gal 3:19). A survey of New Testament teachings helps us to clarify the right use of the law. These principles should become part of every Christian's spiritual journey.

> **Not only does the law reveal who God is, it reveals who we are.**

The Law Reveals the Nature of God

The law is a sort of verbal photograph of God. It tells us what he likes and what he hates. It reveals what he is passionate about and those things about which he is indifferent. It lets us know what makes him angry and what fills him with joy. If we really want to know what God is like, we need only to look in his law. As John Wesley put it so succinctly: the law is "the face of God unveiled. . . . [It is] the heart of God disclosed to man."[9]

The Law Convicts Us of Sin

Not only does the law reveal who God is, it reveals who we are. Like a mirror, when we read the law of God, we see the truth about

---

8   John Wesley, "Upon Our Lord's Sermon on the Mount" from *The Works of John Wesley*, 3rd ed. vol. V (Grand Rapids: Baker, 1978), 311f.
9   Ibid., "Sermon #34: The Original, Nature, Property, and Use of the Law," 438.

ourselves. We see ourselves for who we really are. The law shows us our guilt, and it reveals our God-given potential. It tells us the truth about who we are, but, at the same time, it shows us what we can become. "Through the law comes knowledge of sin" (Rom 3:20). Though this revelation often brings pain and discomfort, it is a great and blessed privilege to have a true and accurate self-understanding.

> If it had not been for the law, I would not have known sin. I would not have known what it is to covet if the law had not said, "You shall not covet." . . . Apart from the law, sin lies dead. I was once alive apart from the law, but when the commandment came, sin came alive and I died. The very commandment that promised life proved to be death to me. For sin, seizing opportunity through the commandment, deceived me and through it killed me. (Romans 7:7–11)

The reason many in the church today are so complacent about their sin and live in such delusion about their relationship with God is simply because the moral law of God is not being preached. Someone needs to hold up a mirror so that the people of God can see themselves for who they truly are. However, don't forget that, while the law reveals the problem, it also points to the solution.

The Law Leads Us to Christ

In writing to the Galatians, Paul explains that one of the great purposes of the law is to point us to Christ. "Therefore the Law has become our tutor *to lead us* to Christ, so that we may be justified by faith" (Gal 3:24 NASB, emphasis added). The term "tutor," in Greek, is *paidagogos*, from where we get the English word "pedagogue," or teacher. Other translations render it as "guardian" or "instructor." In the first century, the "pedagogue" was charged with the duty of supervising the life and moral instruction of young boys. These tutors accompanied their students everywhere they went. It was only when the boy became a man that the close supervision was removed.

Paul says that the moral law acts like a tutor or guardian while we are still babes in the faith. It defines boundaries so that we have a clear understanding of what is expected of us. Like a divine chaperone, it accompanies us everywhere we go, ensuring that we don't make foolish choices. As we grow in our faith and internalize the moral law of God, we discover a diminishing need for such close, well-defined supervision. The law leads us to Christ. Once we have him living and ruling in our hearts, sanctifying our thoughts and our motives, we naturally and automatically do what the law demands.

The Law Can Be Obeyed

Amazingly, Scripture assumes that the people of God can keep the law. Even Moses promised the people at Sinai, "This commandment that I command you today is not too hard for you, neither is it far off. . . . But the word is very near you. It is in your mouth and in your heart, so that *you can do it*" (Dt 30:11–14, emphasis added). However, it is with the promise of the New Covenant that the ability to obey God's moral law is most clearly articulated:

> **❝ If God commands me to be holy, it means he stands ready to make it possible.**

But this is the covenant that I will make with the house of Israel after those days, declares the LORD:
I will put my law within them, and I will write it on their hearts. And I will be their God, and they shall be my people. (Jeremiah 31:33)

No one stated this reality more succinctly than Jesus himself: "If you love me, you will keep my commandments" (Jn 14:15).

A loving father would never command his children to do something that was impossible to obey. In this sense, the commandments should be seen as veiled promises. God will enable us to do what he has commanded. The law of God becomes, then, not a long list of duties and obligations but rather a wonderful collection of promises! If God commands me to be holy, it means he stands ready to make it possible. If he commands me to love my neighbor, he will empower me to do it.

Jesus promised the gift of the Holy Spirit to all who follow him. This wonderful gift was first given on the Jewish feast day of Pentecost, when Israel celebrated the giving of the law on Mount Sinai. The choice of the day is significant. The Spirit of God was poured out on the people of God so that they could be empowered to walk in obedience to the will of God as expressed in the moral law given at Sinai.

> For God has done what the law, weakened by the flesh, could not do. By sending his own Son in the likeness of sinful flesh and for sin, he condemned sin in the flesh, in order that the righteous requirement of the law might be fulfilled in us, who walk not according to the flesh but according to the Spirit. (Romans 8:3–4)

We obey the law of God *not* in order to be saved but because we already are! Living in this tension between grace and works is one of the greatest challenges of the journey to spiritual wholeness. Few have articulated the mystery better than Augustine, who famously summarized the paradoxical relationship of faith and works in one simple statement: "The law was given that grace might be sought; and grace was given that the law might be fulfilled."[10] Hallelujah!

---

10   *De Spiritu et Littera*, 19, 34: CSEL 60, 187.

9
A House for God
(Exodus 25–31, 35–40)

"Heaven is my throne and the earth is my footstool; what is the house that you would build for me . . . ?" (Isaiah 66:1)

One of the best ways to get to know someone well is to visit his or her home. As a pastor, I seldom feel that I really understand who people are until I have seen where they live. Is the house a palatial mansion or a humble apartment? Is the yard well-kept and attractive or is it overgrown with weeds? Is the house neat and clean or a chaotic mess? What magazines are lying on the coffee table? Is the TV a focal point or is it a marginal accessory? Is music playing? What kind? Are children present? Pets? Yes, one can learn a great deal about people simply by visiting where they live.

This is especially true of those men and women who we might consider famous or influential in history. To visit their homes is to gain real insight into what they were really like. To understand George Washington, one must visit Mount Vernon. The true genius of Thomas Jefferson will never be appreciated fully until you've seen his home at Monticello. And one simply cannot fathom the megalomania of Louis XIV until one strolls the corridors and gardens of the palace he built at Versailles.

As shocking at it may sound, we can never understand fully who God is and what he is like until we visit his house. Once there, we can grasp immediately what he values and considers important. It is only when we visit God's house that we learn his true character and how he is to be approached.

At Mount Sinai, God gave Moses detailed instructions concerning the house where he intended to live. Now that God and Israel were married, he would dwell in the midst of his people. First, however, an appropriate dwelling must be prepared. The specifications Moses was to follow in building God's house were grand in scope and meticulous in detail. It is interesting to note that the Bible devotes just two chapters to the creation of the universe, whereas over thirty chapters are needed to describe the architecture, the materials, the furniture, and the function of God's house.[1] While God completed the work of creation in a mere six days, it required forty days just to give Moses the blueprints for the tabernacle.

After the covenant with Israel had been established and the law given, God showed Moses the plans for the house where he intended to live:

> **The tabernacle was the place where Israel would meet with God.**

The LORD said to Moses, "Speak to the people of Israel, that they take for me a contribution. From every man whose heart moves him you shall receive the contribution for me. . . . And let them make me a sanctuary, that I may dwell in their midst. Exactly as I show you concerning the pattern of the tabernacle, and of all its furniture, so you shall make it." (Exodus 25:1–2, 8–9)

God was insistent. The house had to be "exactly as I show you concerning the pattern." The divine blueprint was to be followed in minute detail. No deviation from the pattern would be tolerated. To

---

1   If one considers the Tabernacle in the wilderness (see Ex 25–40), the Temple built by Solomon (see 1 Kgs 5–8; 2 Chr 2–7), and Ezekiel's vision of the future Temple of God (see Ez 40–48), one discovers an enormous amount of Scripture devoted to describing God's house.

make sure Moses understood the importance of this, God repeated it over and over again:

- "And see that you make them *after the pattern* for them, which is being shown you on the mountain" (Ex 25:40).
- "Then you shall erect the tabernacle *according to the plan* for it that you were shown on the mountain" (Ex 26:30).
- "You shall make [the bronze altar] . . . . *As it has been shown you* on the mountain, so shall it be made" (Ex 27:8).

The message is clear: God's tabernacle had to be built according to God's specifications. If the dwelling place was not properly constructed, God would refuse to live there. Moses got the message and made certain that all the work was done "according to all that the LORD had commanded" (Ex 39:32, 43).

GOD WITH US

The plans for the tabernacle included detailed instructions for a wide variety of structures, furnishings, and functions needed for God's dwelling place:

- The tent and the courtyard
- The interior furnishings (the Ark of the Covenant, the table, the incense altar, the lampstand)
- The exterior furnishings (the altar of burnt offerings, the basin)
- Garments for the priests (the breast piece, the ephod, the robe, the tunic, the turban, etc.)
- Various accessories, such as the oil for the lampstand, the incense, the materials to be used, etc.

The tabernacle was the place where Israel would meet with God. The intent of all these architectural instructions was to enable the people of God to get close to the one who had redeemed and married them. The purpose was worship. Because God is holy, it was crucial for his people to learn to approach him in the right manner. No one gets far on the journey to spiritual wholeness without learning how to correctly worship the Holy One.

The reader of Exodus may be struck by the fact that the story of the Golden Calf (see Ex 32–34) is placed right in the middle of all this material about the tabernacle. Sandwiched between these amazing chapters on building a house for God is a story that describes one of the darkest moments in Israel's history. The next chapter examines this sad story in greater detail. The book of Exodus not only instructs us in *how* to worship the Holy One but also gives us a dramatic illustration of how *not* to. The structure of this section of the book of Exodus helps us to understand its message:

Table 9.1: Exodus 25–40

Ex 25–31 The Plan for the Tabernacle	Ex 32–34 The People Worship the Golden Calf	Ex 35–40 The Construction of the Tabernacle
How to Worship God	How *Not* to Worship God	How to Worship God
God Reveals His Purpose	God Reveals His Wrath	God's Glory Fills the Tabernacle

Once the problem of wrong worship with the golden calf had been dealt with, God placed his seal of approval on right worship by coming himself to live in the house that had been built:

> Then the cloud covered the tent of meeting, and the glory of the LORD filled the tabernacle. . . . For the cloud of the LORD was on the tabernacle by day, and fire was in it by night, in the sight of all the house of Israel throughout all their journeys. (Exodus 40:34, 38)

These final words of the book of Exodus provide the climax for the entire operation of redemption. This is the moment for which the entire book has been preparing us. With God's house properly built and the people committed to worshiping the Holy One in the proper way, God came in glory to take up residence among his people: Emmanuel, God with us. The journey out of Egypt was complete. The Hebrew people were married to God. They had the law, the tabernacle, and the very presence of the living God in their midst. They were ready to break camp and move northward toward the Land of Promise.

However, before we follow them on that journey, let's pause to study the tabernacle. The architecture and furnishings of this amazing structure teach us how to approach the Holy One who loves us and has redeemed us.

"Reading" the Cathedral

When we lived in France as missionaries, we loved to visit the many Gothic cathedrals that dot the countryside. None is more magnificent than Chartres. Many would claim it is perhaps the finest example of Gothic architecture in the world. With towering spires, flying buttresses, vaulted ceilings, and magnificent stained glass, it is truly a masterpiece. Walking into the massive nave causes one to look up in awe at the splendor and to speak in hushed, almost reverential tones.

When our girls were small, we drove one Saturday from our home near Paris to visit this architectural marvel. Joining a rather large group of tourists, we soon learned that our guide was a renowned authority on the cathedral. In fact, he had devoted his life to studying Chartres both inside and out. He spoke with passion and began our tour with words that went something like this:

> Ladies and gentlemen, welcome to Chartres Cathedral. In the middle ages, when this church was built, most people were illiterate. The designers thus wanted to build a structure that could be "read" by everyone. They wanted to make sure that the message of the gospel was clearly communicated through the shapes and spaces and stones and windows that are all around us. This afternoon, let's imagine ourselves stepping back in time. You are an illiterate farmer coming to visit the cathedral. My job as your host is to help you to simply "read" the building. Did you notice the shape of the cathedral as you walked up from the outside? It is cruciform. This church is an enormous cross! Nothing is more central to the Christian faith than Jesus' death on a cross. Keep walking . . .

> Look there; way up above us to your left is one of the many stained glass windows of Chartres. That particular window

depicts the tree of Jesse. The root is Jesse and from him grows a massive tree with many branches representing the many kings of Judah that came from his lineage. That branch there to the left is King David. Then moving up the tree you can see Solomon, Asa, Hezekiah, and Josiah. And look at the very top. The culmination of the entire tree is King Jesus. He is the King of kings and Lord and lords. It's all written there in the window. Keep walking . . .

For perhaps two hours our guide walked us through the building, "reading" the cathedral as we went. Sadly, I never detected any personal identification with the gospel message our guide so eloquently preached. His interest seemed to be fixated on the art, the architecture, and the history associated with the church. Yet for the tourists, the message of the building was clear. It was all about a King who died on a cross and shed his blood so that sinners like us could be forgiven and find a new start.

Similarly, the tabernacle that Moses built was a building that contained a message. God planned every detail, every ceremony, and every artistic expression so that even illiterate slaves would not fail to understand what this tent in the desert was all about. Let's take a tour. I'll be your guide. Let's "read" the message the Divine Architect communicates to us through this amazing structure (see "Figure 2: The Tabernacle").

ONE DOOR

Approaching God's house is a little like approaching a nuclear reactor. You had better know what you are doing! Holiness, like radioactive material, is a tremendous blessing when it is handled properly. But for those who don't know what they are doing, the results can be catastrophic. The structure of the tabernacle helps us to understand that God is holy—and we aren't! To approach the Holy One, therefore, demands that we follow the instructions very carefully.

Perhaps the first thing that we should notice is there is only one door. The fence that establishes the perimeter around the tabernacle

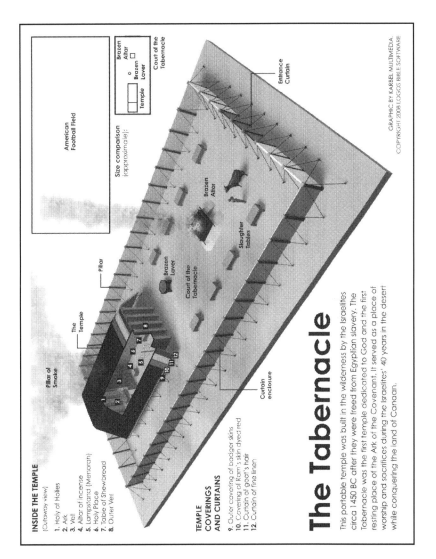

Figure 2: The Tabernacle

has a single opening. The message is clear: there is one and only one way to approach God.

In our world of political correctness, such a message is highly offensive. Many today want to pretend that there are many "doors" that lead to God. Probably no religion has stated this more eloquently than the Baha'i faith. And nowhere do the adherents of this faith communicate their belief more forcefully than in the architecture of their temple in Wilmette, Illinois. The beautiful building has not one door, but nine; nine entrances leading to a central point where all those who enter the temple converge. The message is simple and clear: many roads lead to the Divine Absolute. In fact, all nine religions of the world are legitimate options for finding God. Some may enter by the Muslim door, others by the entrance for Hindus. There are other doors for Jews, Buddhists, Christians, etc. The architecture says it all: there are many ways to God, so choose the door that suits you best.

Jesus may well have had the architecture of the tabernacle in mind when he said, "I am the door. If anyone enters by me, he will be saved . . ." (Jn 10:9); and, "I am the way, and the truth, and the life. No one comes to the Father except through me" (Jn 14:6). Perhaps nothing Jesus ever said was more scandalous and offensive than this. Jesus claimed to be the only path to God. All other doors lead astray.

While many in our postmodern world struggle with such a narrow concept of truth when it comes to finding our way to God, they have no difficulty at all accepting a narrow way when it comes to the truth about mathematics. Though we may understand the logic of someone who passionately claims that $2+2=22$, we are quick to assert that such an answer is false. There is one and only one correct answer to the equation: $2+2=4$. All other answers are wrong. We intuitively understand that, when it comes to mathematics, truth is very narrow. The very same rationale must be at work when it comes to the truth about God. The house where God lives has only one door. One enters through Jesus Christ or one does not enter at all.

> Enter by the narrow gate. For the gate is wide and the way is easy that leads to destruction, and those who enter by it are many. For the gate is narrow and the way is hard that leads to life, and those who find it are few. (Matthew 7:13–14)

The High Priest: Our Mediator

Once inside the gate of the tabernacle, the worshiper would find himself in a courtyard. Where to from here? The atmosphere didn't encourage one to wander around trying to figure things out for oneself.

Thankfully, the instructions God gave Moses for the tabernacle ensured that someone would be present to extend a warm welcome and then provide guidance for what comes next. A priest was present to guide the worshiper in his approach to God. He was more than a guide, however. He was a mediator—a sort of bridge, a connecting link—between sinful worshipers and a Holy God. No one experienced God in the tabernacle without his help!

Though the analogy is limited, imagine yourself seeking an audience with the President of the United States. No one casually wanders into the White House and meanders around until he finds his way to the Oval Office! An escort is required, someone to usher you past the guards and the locked doors until you are introduced to the president. In a similar manner, no one enters the presence of the Holy One without a mediator to show the way and make the introduction.

In Moses' day, priests were chosen from the tribe of Levi to help worshipers meet God. To be a priest required more than a willing heart and good intentions. It was not a role for volunteers. The instructions Moses received on the mountain concerning priests indicated that these men must be born into the right family, trained in the proper manner, and consecrated so that they were empowered to fulfill their role effectively.

The New Testament explains that Jesus Christ has replaced the Levitical priesthood and is now a new kind of High Priest who is infinitely better suited for the task. Though not of the tribe of Levi himself, Jesus was able to become the greatest of all High Priests because the order of his priesthood was both higher and earlier than that of the Levites. He was "designated by God a high priest after the order of Melchizedek" (Heb 5:10). Jesus became the ultimate High Priest and mediator "not on the basis of a legal requirement concerning bodily descent, but by the power of an indestructible life" (Heb 7:16). Because his priesthood is of a higher order, Jesus' ability to usher us into the very presence of God is infinitely better than what the Levitical priests could do.

> The former priests were many in number, because they were prevented by death from continuing in office, but he holds his priesthood permanently, because he continues forever. Consequently, he is able to save to the uttermost those who draw near to God through him, since he always lives to make intercession for them. (Hebrews 7:23–25)

THE ALTAR OF BURNT OFFERING

After meeting the priest, the worshiper was confronted with the large altar standing in the middle of the courtyard, blocking one's path to the tent of meeting, where God dwelt. This imposing structure was unavoidable and reminds us of what is perhaps the most important thing to know in approaching God: No one meets God without an appropriate sacrifice preparing the way. This already had been made perfectly clear in the law given to Moses when God said,

> **66** **Jesus is both our High Priest and our sacrifice. He plays simultaneously the role of mediator and offering.**

"None shall appear before me empty-handed" (Ex 23:15). It would be the height of arrogance to seek an audience with the Holy One without a gift, but what kind of offering is adequate for meeting God?

The Hebrew people already had learned that, for their redemption from Egyptian bondage, a Passover lamb had to be killed (see Ex 12–13). Not just any lamb would do, however. He had to be "without blemish, a male, a year old" (Ex 12:5). The lamb was to be killed and the blood smeared on the doorposts and lintels of their houses. Then, the lamb was to be eaten, giving strength for the journey ahead. The death of the lamb made redemption possible.

The book of Leviticus spells out other types of sacrifice and offerings that were to be made on this altar in the courtyard (see Leviticus 1–5).

The most important sacrifices were those that dealt with sin in the life of the worshiper. Meeting God is contingent on finding a solution for the sin problem that separates us from him.

The priest would meet the worshiper with the sacrificial lamb he had brought and lead them to the altar. The ceremony that took place next was simple, yet dramatic:

1. The priest or the worshiper would place his hands on the head of the lamb and confess aloud the sins the worshiper had committed and for which he sought forgiveness. This action was meant to symbolically portray the transference of sin from the worshiper to the lamb. The lamb thus became the sin-bearer.
2. Taking a knife, the priest would slit the throat of the lamb and burn the body as an offering. The lamb died in the place of the worshiper, as a substitute. The wages of sin is death, but because the lamb died in the place of the worshiper, forgiveness became a reality and access to God was possible.

When John the Baptist described Jesus as the Lamb of God who takes away the sin of the world (see Jn 1:29), he was portraying Jesus in a form that every first-century Jew would have understood. He was the ultimate sin-bearer, the one spoken about by Isaiah the prophet that would come one day to save his people:

> But he was pierced for our transgressions; he was crushed for our iniquities; upon him was the chastisement that brought us peace, and with his wounds we are healed. All we like sheep have gone astray; we have turned—every one—to his own way; and the LORD has laid on him the iniquity of us all. (Isaiah 53:5–6)

The book of Hebrews makes things even more clear. Jesus is both our High Priest and our sacrifice. He plays simultaneously the role of mediator *and* offering. Even under the Mosaic dispensation, people intuitively recognized that the blood of bulls and goats *really* could not take away sins (see Heb 10:4). People in Old Testament times understood that the rituals at the tabernacle pointed to something richer and fuller that was yet to come.

> And every priest stands daily at his service, offering repeatedly the same sacrifices, which can never take away sins. But when Christ had offered for all time a single sacrifice for sins, he sat down at the right hand of God, waiting from that time until his enemies should be made a footstool for his feet. For by a single offering he has perfected for all time those who are being sanctified. (Hebrews 10:11–14)

THE BASIN FOR WASHING

Having come through the gate and been guided by the priest concerning the sin offering on the altar, worshipers in the tabernacle came next to a large basin made of bronze. Before one could enter the tent where God dwelt, one had to first wash, seeking cleansing from all defilement—both external and internal. In the days of the Old Testament, only the priests were permitted to enter the tabernacle and so only the priests were required to bathe. In the New Testament, however, we learn that cleansing is part of the gift of salvation that is made available to every believer. No one can have true fellowship with God until the defilement of sin is dealt with.

While the altar offered forgiveness for external acts of sin, the basin offered cleansing for the internal sinful nature. It is interesting to note that the basin was made of the mirrors of the women (see Ex 38:8). Apparently, when one looked into the basin, one could see a true reflection of oneself. As he approached the Holy One, the structures and rituals of the tabernacle enabled the worshiper to see himself for who he truly was. God demands that we confront our sinful behaviors, but he also intends for us to confront our sinful nature. The redemption God offers deals with both external sins and internal sin.

The basin reminds us that the problem of sin is worse than we think. It also promises us that the redemption God offers is better than we ever dreamed. God makes it possible for our sinful actions to be forgiven, and he makes it possible for our sinful natures to be cleansed. A simple chart helps us to understand our need for a deeper work of grace:

Table 9.2: Understanding Our Need for a Work of Grace

The Altar of Burnt Offering	The Bronze Basin
• Forgiveness for outward sins	• Cleansing from inward sin
• Deals with the guilt of sin	• Deals with the power of sin
• What Christ can do for us	• What the Spirit can do in us
• Changes our status	• Changes our nature
• Makes possible clean hands	• Makes possible a pure heart
• Justification	• Sanctification

The altar for forgiveness coupled with the basin for cleansing helped worshipers in Old Testament times understand both the depth of the problem and the extent of the solution. If we are to have genuine fellowship with God, we need more than forgiveness for the bad things we've done. We need cleansing for the egotistical perversity that defines who we are. We need more than clean hands; we need a pure heart (see Ps 24:3–4).

The Tent: Two Rooms

The tent was quite small (150' x 75') and divided into two rooms. In Moses' day, only the priests could enter the tabernacle itself and only the High Priest was allowed to enter the Most Holy Place, and that only once a year. Though all worshipers could have a measure of access to God and experience a degree of intimacy in relationship, face-to-face fellowship with the Holy One was severely restricted.

The forward room was called the Holy Place. Here the Levites could come to perform ritual acts of worship. There were three pieces of furniture in this room:

- *The Table of Bread.* Twelve loaves, symbolizing the twelve tribes of Israel, were kept on this table. The bread reminded Israel of their need for spiritual nourishment that comes from God alone.
- *The Lamp Stand.* This golden stand, which held seven candle sticks, provided light for those who came to worship.

- *The Altar of Incense*. Here, specially prepared incense was burned, symbolizing the prayers of God's people.

At the far end of the Holy Place was a magnificent veil that separated the Holy Place from the Most Holy Place (or the Holy of Holies). This inmost room was designed as a cube (15' x 15' x 15') and contained the Ark of the Covenant, made of gold. The top of the ark was a type of platform called the Mercy Seat. On this platform, the High Priest would pour blood from the animal slain for the sins of the nation on Israel's most holy of all days, Yom Kippur (the Day of Atonement). Above the ark were two winged creatures called cherubim, one at each end of the chest with their wings stretched toward one another. It was in this space, above the Mercy Seat and between the wings of the cherubim, where God resided. It was the precise location of God's "home," and it was where Israel knew the Presence (Face) of God could be found: "There I will meet with you, and from above the mercy seat, from between the two cherubim that are on the ark of the testimony, I will speak with you . . ." (Ex 25:22).

> **If your concept of God is wrong, then the more religious you become, the more dangerous you become to yourself and to others.**

It is only as we understand the architecture and function of the tabernacle that we grasp the enormity of what was signified when the veil of the Temple was torn in two at the moment of Jesus' death. The Scripture simply states that as Jesus was dying on the cross, the curtain of the temple was torn in two, "from top to bottom" (Mt 27:51; Mk 15:38; Lk 23:45). This miracle was believed by the writers of Scripture to be a work of God himself. In this dramatic manner, God made it crystal clear that, for once and for all, he has opened the way into his most intimate presence for all people through the sacrifice of his only Son on the cross. Christ's blood makes it possible for anyone and everyone to have immediate and full access into the very throne room of God. "Let us then with confidence draw near to the throne of grace, that we may receive mercy and find grace to help in time of need" (Heb 4:14–16).

CONCLUSION

William Temple, one-time archbishop of Canterbury, made a profound observation when he said that if your concept of God is wrong, then the more religious you become, the more dangerous you become to yourself and to others. The tabernacle was God's own great visual aid to help his people to worship him *in the right way*. The architectural design and the liturgies used helped God's people to have a solid grasp of who he truly is and how he should be approached. The next chapter shows the catastrophic results that come when worshipers have the wrong concept of these most fundamental realities.

10

A Lot of Bull
(Exodus 32)

*"All who worship images are put to shame, those
who boast in idols . . . ." (Psalms 97:7 NIV)*

Imagine a new bride, just six weeks after the wedding, in an
adulterous relationship with another man. We recoil in disgust at
the cold-hearted wickedness of a woman who would behave with such
brazen audacity, yet this is precisely the reality that is depicted for
us in graphic detail when the people of God commit adultery—with
a bull! Only six weeks earlier, Israel and God had made solemn vows
of covenant fidelity to one another in a dramatic ceremony at Mount
Sinai (see Ex 19–24; see also Chapter 7, "Dearly Beloved, We Are
Gathered Here..."). Scarcely was the honeymoon over before Israel
was in bed with someone else! What happened?

The sad story is told in Exodus 32. Three times in this passage,
Israel's action in worshiping the golden calf is called a "great sin"
(Ex 32:21, 30, 31). This was no minor infraction. It was brazen
treachery, willful rebellion, and high treason. God's reaction to what
Israel had done was similar to what any faithful husband might do
were he confronted with the reality of his new bride's infidelity. He
was shocked, hurt, and angry. Initially, his response was rage. He
threatened to annul the covenant and punish his treasonous partner:

> And the LORD said to Moses, "Go down, for your people,
> whom you brought up out of the land of Egypt, have

corrupted themselves. They have turned aside quickly out of the way that I commanded them. They have made for themselves a golden calf and have worshiped it and sacrificed to it and said, 'These are your gods, O Israel, who brought you up out of the land of Egypt!'" And the LORD said to Moses, "I have seen this people, and behold, it is a stiff-necked people. Now therefore let me alone, that my wrath may burn hot against them and I may consume them, in order that I may make a great nation of you." (Exodus 32:7–10)

This heated exchange between God and Moses took place on Mount Sinai, a short distance from the orgy of sensuality going on in the valley below. When Moses came down the mountain and entered the camp, the wayward spouse suddenly realized the gravity of situation:

And as soon as he came near the camp and saw the calf and the dancing, Moses' anger burned hot, and he threw the tablets out of his hands and broke them at the foot of the mountain. He took the calf that they had made and burned it with fire and ground it to powder and scattered it on the water and made the people of Israel drink it. (Exodus 32:19–20)

When Moses threw the tablets of the covenant to the ground and broke them, he was not just having a temper tantrum, as some have imagined. Yes, he was angry, but his behavior was an acted parable. He was illustrating, in a manner that is impossible to misunderstand, that the covenant with God (represented by those tablets) was broken, or perhaps, potentially broken. Imagine a husband, who has just discovered his new bride's infidelity, taking his wedding ring (the symbol of the covenant) and throwing it across the room in anger shouting, "It's over!" That scene gives perhaps a hint of what was happening here. The emotions were raw. The words were strong. Perhaps once emotions simmered down, a way of reconciliation could be found, but, in the moment, all seemed to be lost.

How could Israel commit such wickedness? Not only was her infidelity with a bull sinful, it was really stupid! What could possibly cause a newly wedded wife to turn away from a perfectly good, loving husband to get in bed with a bull?

WORLDLY CHRISTIANS

The journey to spiritual wholeness shows us that there is more to redemption than getting out of Egypt. That is certainly important and a major first step, but salvation involves more than deliverance from bondage and difficult circumstances. God wants to change our hearts. The story with the golden calf makes it clear that, though the people of Israel were out of Egypt, "Egypt" was not yet out of them!

Though rarely mentioned in the church today, the Bible says it is impossible to love this world (Egypt) and to love God at the same time. The two loves are fundamentally incompatible; one cancels out the other. Only those on the journey to spiritual wholeness have the capacity to understand such a truth. It is only in leaving Egypt that we discover how "Egyptian" we truly are! Thus, the Bible repeatedly commands those embarked on the journey to spiritual wholeness not to love this present world:

- "Do not love the world or the things in the world. If anyone loves the world, the love of the Father is not in him. For all that is in the world—the desires of the flesh and the desires of the eyes and pride of life—is not from the Father but is from the world. And the world is passing away along with its desires, but whoever does the will of God abides forever" (1 Jn 2:15–17).
- "You adulterous people! Do you not know that friendship with the world is enmity with God? Therefore whoever wishes to be a friend of the world makes himself an enemy of God" (Jas 4:4).
- "Do not be conformed to this world, but be transformed by the renewal of your mind, that by testing you may discern what is the will of God, what is good and acceptable and perfect" (Rom 12:2).
- "If you were of the world, the world would love you as its own; but because you are not of the world, but I chose you out of the world, therefore the world hates you" (Jn 15:19).

Though some equate worldliness with the clothes that we wear, the cars that we drive, or the entertainment we enjoy, such an understanding is far too shallow. Worldliness is a mindset that values things that God disdains and disdains that which God values. Worldliness is patterning our lives after the kingdoms of this world rather than the kingdom of God. We are to be *in* the world but not *of* the world. It is a good thing when a boat is in the water. It is a bad thing when water is in the boat! In Exodus 32, water has gotten in the boat—lots of water!

The story of the golden calf records the first time that newly redeemed Israel was unfaithful to the one who loved her. Unfortunately, it would not be the last. We discover here the sobering reality that sin remains in the hearts and lives of the redeemed. Redemption may deliver us from the bondage and guilt of sin, but the sinful nature is still a troubling reality.

Rather than hiding or minimizing the tragic story of the golden calf, the Bible highlights it. God *wants* us to learn from the mistakes and sins of those who have gone before us. He wants us to understand not just *what* happened to Israel, but *why*. A careful study of Exodus 32 reveals that this is not just ancient history. The sin with the golden calf is still with us today, and one can find many examples of "bull" in the contemporary church.[1] Unless we learn to deal with it as Moses did, our entire journey to spiritual wholeness is jeopardized. The story of the golden calf reveals three characteristics that may indicate bull has gotten into the church: if the clergy follow the people rather than lead them, if worshipers make God in their image, and if people think the purpose of redemption is happiness rather than holiness.

---

1   For those who may not readily understand the idiomatic use of the term "bull," a look in the English dictionary includes the following secondary definitions: nonsense, absurdity, insanity, stupidity, baloney, hypocrisy, hogwash, balderdash, and flap doodle—plus some words my mother taught me never to use!

If the Clergy Follow the People Rather than Lead Them

The story of Israel's apostasy began when Pastor Aaron felt that it was his job to reflect public opinion rather than shape it:

> When the people saw that Moses delayed to come down from the mountain, the people gathered themselves together to Aaron and said to him, "Up, make us gods who shall go before us. As for this Moses, the man who brought us up out of the land of Egypt, we do not know what has become of him." So Aaron said to them, "Take off the rings of gold that are in the ears of your wives, your sons, and your daughters, and bring them to me." So all the people took off the rings of gold that were in their ears and brought them to Aaron. And he received the gold from their hand and fashioned it with a graving tool and made a golden calf. And they said, "These are your gods, O Israel, who brought you up out of the land of Egypt!" (Exodus 32:1–4)

One of the ways to know if there is bull in one's church is if the pastor follows public trends and conforms to cultural pressures rather than leading the way in a distinctively godly direction. It is one thing for a congregation to think that their pastor ought to do what they want him to do, but it is another thing when the pastor agrees! God calls pastors to be thermostats. He expects them to be leaders who regulate the temperature around them. When pastors are thermometers that merely reflect their environment, we have a sure indication of bull in church. Aaron operated as a thermometer when God had called him to be a thermostat. He followed his flock rather than leading them. He felt it was his job to give the people what they wanted rather than to lead them toward what they needed. Woe to the church that has a pastor who thinks it is his (or her) job to reflect public opinion rather than to shape it!

It's easy to imagine how it happened. I picture Pastor Aaron sitting in his clergy office, dressed in clergy robes, surrounded by shelves of clergy books, with clergy diplomas and credentials hanging on the wall. In my mind, I see him reading the latest issue of *Clergy Today* magazine. His attention is captured by the lead article entitled "How to Grow Your Church" written by a megachurch pastor from a nearby city. The article begins like this:

> According to the most recent polling data, people today want a religious experience that is warm, positive, and in sync with culture. They are turned off by a God who lives in fire and smoke on a mountain, dispensing laws and obligations, who is always talking about sin. People today want a more approachable deity who is user-friendly and seeker-sensitive. They want styles of worship that are in tune with trends of modern culture. They want an experience that builds up their self-image, one that is positive, uplifting, and fun. Many churches today are discovering that installing a bull in your Worship Center is the key to building a dynamic and successful church. You may even find that Canaanites and Egyptians will flock to your services. Yes, this innovative and culturally sensitive approach to worship will enable you to win the world!

Sound familiar? "Come on, Pastor Aaron," the people said. "We're tired of the frightening God that Moses worships up on the mountain. We want a warmer, friendlier deity. We want a bull... please!" And rather than warning them of the error inherent in their request, Pastor Aaron gave his congregation what they wanted—and led his church into apostasy in the process!

> **" Pastors should stop trying to entertain the goats and get back to the basic task of feeding the sheep!**

Undoubtedly, the people bore a large measure of blame for what happened, but Moses held Aaron *fully* responsible for the catastrophic situation. "What did this people do to you that *you* have brought such a great sin upon them?" he asked (Ex 32:21, emphasis added). When confronted, Aaron made a feeble attempt to evade blame by pretending that he wasn't really responsible. In what must be one of the greatest clergy quotes in human history, Aaron weakly said:

> You know the people, that they are set on evil. For they said to me, "Make us gods who shall go before us. As for

this Moses, the man who brought us up out of the land of Egypt, we do not know what has become of him." So I said to them, "Let any who have gold take it off." So they gave it to me, and I threw it into the fire, and out came this calf. (Exodus 32:22–24)

God would not let Aaron off the hook. While he might not have been to blame for all that happened, as the pastor in charge, he was fully responsible. God had placed him over the flock in the hopes that he would act like a thermostat and shape the environment around him. Instead, Pastor Aaron failed in his calling and assumed the passive role of a thermometer.

To be candid, I feel a measure of sympathy for Pastor Aaron. As a pastor myself, I know well how hard it can be to stand firm against the majority. I know how seductive it can be to listen to pollsters and marketing experts who urge forms of worship that are culturally relevant so that the church can be more effective in reaching Egyptians and Canaanites. I know how important it is to be responsive to peoples' felt needs and have worship experiences that are in sync with the times and the culture around us. However, I also know the very real and present danger of apostasy and false worship that is present whenever I take my cues from the culture or from the congregation rather than from God. There have been times when I, too, have been guilty of bringing bull into church. One of the great lessons of this tragic story is that pastors should stop trying to entertain the goats and get back to the basic task of feeding the sheep!

If Worshipers Make God in Their Image

For many years, I assumed that the sin with the golden calf involved a violation of the first commandment: "You shall have no other gods before me" (Ex 20:3). As I continued to study the text, however, I began to realize that this wasn't the problem at all. Neither the people nor Aaron were trying to worship another god. The bull was not an attempt to import some foreign deity into Israel such as the Egyptian Apis or the Canaanite Baal. The text is clear. As they worshiped the bull the people said, "These are your gods [Hebrew,

Elohim], O Israel, *who brought you up out of the land of Egypt*" (Ex 32:4, emphasis added). They were not worshiping some foreign idol. They were seeking to worship the one true God, the God who had redeemed them from bondage. They just wanted to worship him in the form of a golden calf.

Aaron was even more clear about who he intended to worship. The bull was a representation not just of the generic Elohim (God, or gods). It was, in fact, a representation of Yahweh, the God who had revealed his personal name to Moses at the burning bush. Aaron built an altar before the calf and said, "Tomorrow shall be a feast to the LORD [Hebrew, *Yahweh*]" (Ex 32:5). Aaron was urging the people to worship the one true God, Yahweh, who had redeemed them, but to worship him in the form of a bull. The great sin committed in worshiping the golden calf was not a violation of the first commandment but of the second:

> You shall not make for yourself a carved image, or any likeness of anything that is in heaven above, or that is in the earth beneath, or that is in the water under the earth. You shall not bow down to them or serve them, for I the LORD your God am a jealous God, visiting the iniquity of the fathers on the children to the third and the fourth generation of those who hate me, but showing steadfast love to thousands of those who love me and keep my commandments. (Exodus 20:4–6)

Do not make an image of Yahweh. Do not make him into a shape that conforms to *your* ideas of what *you* think he is like. Whether your image is a golden calf, a mental picture, or a theological system of thought, beware of shaping God into the form that *you* think he should be. The reason God's people are commanded *not* to make an image of God is because when we try to imagine God (who he is, what he is like, how he acts, etc.), *we get it wrong every time!* The only way to have an accurate knowledge of God is for God to reveal himself, to tell us and to show us who he is and what he is like. This is why God brought his people to Mount Sinai in the first place. He wanted to reveal himself. However, to know him, his people had to humbly look, listen, and learn as he revealed himself. They had to first put away their preconceived notions of who he was and how he performed.

With all the emphasis on worship in the church today, one wonders who people are actually bowing before on Sunday mornings in corporate worship. Are they worshiping God as he is truly is? Or are they perhaps worshiping God as they imagine him to be? Is it possible that someone placed a bull in the sanctuary? The difference between worshiping God as he is and worshiping God as we imagine him to be is comparable to the difference between a lightning bolt and a lightning bug!

The first chapter of the Bible teaches us that God created us in his image (see Gn 1:26–27). He is the prototype; we are the copy. When we break the second commandment, we reverse what God has ordained. Whereas the original purpose of worship is that we would become more and more like God, we sometimes get it backward so that the purpose is to make God become more and more like us. This is the ultimate perversion in worship, because to worship the God who looks like us is to worship ourselves!

The incident with the golden calf is one of the earliest examples of what Robert Bellah calls "Sheilaism." The sociologist from the University of California, in his book, *Habits of the Heart* (1985), noted how Americans want their religion *à la carte*. They want the freedom to create their individual brand of spirituality much like we make our own pastas at Macaroni Grill. We pick and choose. He named this "new religion" after Sheila, one of the people he studied in his research. She had explained to the researchers how she had put together bits and pieces from various religions to construct her own, unique blend. She was fine with the fact that this personal religion she had created for herself would not likely work for anyone else. It made sense to her. She liked it.

O Lord, deliver us! The story of the golden calf reminds us that trying to worship God on our terms just won't work. It didn't work for the Hebrews over 3,000 years ago, and it won't work for us today.

To have a relationship with God, we must meet him on his terms—or not at all!

If People Think the Purpose of Redemption Is Happiness Rather than Holiness

A third way to determine if there is bull in one's church is to discover whether the goal of worship is to make people happy or to make them holy. Those who bowed before the golden calf were passionately engaged in the worship experience. There was loud music, singing, dancing, and feasting (see Ex 32:17–19). In describing the occasion, the Scripture tells us that "the people sat down to eat and drink and rose up to play" (Ex 32:6). The word "play" in Hebrew can have a sexual connotation. The worship experience that day was rather like a wild party, perhaps a drunken orgy. I'm sure when the service ended many shook Aaron's hand warmly and said, "Great worship today, Pastor. Thanks!"

When people measure their worship experience by how it makes them *feel*, we have a pretty good indication that

> **66 We simply cannot worship the Holy One and continue to live an unholy life. We become like what we worship.**

someone has brought bull into church. Assuming that the presence of emotional intensity (tears, joy, goose bumps, etc.) means that genuine worship is happening is a sure indication that the purpose of redemption has been lost. Tragically, many today seem to believe that God's great purpose in bringing us out of Egypt is so that we can be healthy, wealthy, and happy. Thus, our worship of him should emphasize these self-oriented realities. True worship is something different entirely. It is meant to remind us of who God truly is and what he really wants. God's great purpose in salvation is clearly stated in these words: "You shall be holy, for I the LORD your God am holy" (Lv 19:2).

Exodus 32 alerts us to the fact that bad theology always results in bad behavior. If we worship a bull, we soon will begin to act like one! We become like what we worship (see Ps 115:8). If we worship the money god, we will become greedy and worldly. If we worship the sex god, we will become promiscuous. If we worship the God who is holy, we will become holy. We simply cannot worship the Holy One and continue to live an unholy life. We become like what we worship.

WHO IS ON THE LORD'S SIDE?

What should we do if we discover bull in church? How should we respond if we wake up to the frightening reality that rather than worshiping God as he is, we are actually worshiping God as we imagine him to be? Thankfully, Exodus 32 not only describes the problem but also points us to the answer.

First, the idol must be destroyed. Moses knew that it would be impossible to restore true worship until false worship was thoroughly demolished. So "he took the calf that they had made and burned it with fire and ground it to powder and scattered it on the water and made the people of Israel drink it" (Ex 32:20). When it comes to false worship, there can be no compromise, no half-measures, no delay. The idol must be destroyed thoroughly.

Second, atonement must be sought. Moses said to the people, "You have sinned a great sin. And now I will go up to the LORD; perhaps I can make atonement for your sin" (Ex 32:30). Great sins need great forgiveness. Until sin is named, confessed, and repented of, there can be no forgiveness. Until there is forgiveness, we remain stuck in our dysfunctional apostasy, suspended in a state of a ruptured relationship with God. God is ready to forgive and restore us to a right relationship, but we must first come in humble contrition.

Third, a decision is called for. As the drama of reconciliation reached a crescendo, Moses stood in the camp and shouted so that everyone could hear, "Who is on the LORD's side? Come to me" (Ex 32:26). It was only as the Levites stepped forward in bold obedience to God's call that disaster was averted and the future was preserved.

Perhaps the best way to close a chapter such as this is to call us to prayer. Is it possible there is a "bull" in our churches? in our hearts? The words of an old gospel hymn by James Nicholson (1872) provide words to help us pray:

> Lord Jesus, I long to be perfectly whole;
> I want Thee forever to live in my soul.
> Break down every idol, cast out every foe:
> Now wash me, and I shall be whiter than snow.

11
Living with the Holy One
(Leviticus)

"You shall be holy, for I the Lord *your God am holy." (Leviticus 19:2)*

The book of Leviticus is the grave yard for countless numbers of people who make a New Year's resolution to read through the Bible in a year. After enjoying the book of Genesis in January and then savoring most of Exodus, the zealous disciple typically hits Leviticus in mid-February. It takes only a day or two for him to discover that he is facing twenty-seven chapters of rules concerning sacrifice, ordination, liturgy, skin disease, dietary regulations, and how to rid one's house of mildew. At this point, many would-be Bible readers give up in dismay and conclude that the Bible is impossibly difficult to understand.

To be honest, Leviticus is indeed a difficult book. It is full of detailed instructions about what appear to be obscure rituals and ceremonies. One needs a dictionary as well as a thorough knowledge of Jewish history and worship to understand what is going on. For many, the mental effort to understand this book is just too great.

Not only is Leviticus difficult, many find it offensive. No book in the Bible contains more blood and gore. The instructions given for animal sacrifice are detailed and graphic: slitting the throat, skinning the animal, removing the inner organs, burning the carcass, etc. The book also speaks of persons with tattoos and physical deformities in a way that many in our world today find derogatory.

Beyond the book's difficulty and offensive character is the fact that much of what it says is, frankly, embarrassing. It takes great courage just to read aloud some parts of this book in a public worship service. The passages about sexual behavior are graphic and blunt, and there is an entire chapter devoted to the topic of bodily discharges. How did *that* get in the Bible?

When one finds the right approach, however, the book of Leviticus is a wealth of information and blessing for the traveler on the journey to spiritual wholeness. It's not really about why Jews couldn't eat pork, why women were considered unclean during their menstrual cycle, or how to discern between leprosy and acne. The book is really about holiness. Specifically, Leviticus is a manual of instructions to help unholy people know how to live with the holy God who has come to live in their midst.

The book of Exodus ends with the construction of the tabernacle, which God filled with his holy presence. God's arrival in fire was so glorious in holiness that not even Moses was able to enter the tent (see Ex 40:34–35). Though God had come down to dwell in the midst of his people, as yet he had not opened a way for men and women to safely enter his presence and enjoy his fellowship. If Moses wasn't able to enter in God's presence, who could? The book of Exodus ends with this question. The book of Leviticus supplies the answer. The third book of the Pentateuch is written to show travelers on the journey to spiritual wholeness not only how they can have the assurance that God is in their midst but also how they can enter into his holy presence and know him personally and intimately. The book answers the question: How can unholy people live with the Holy One? The journey to spiritual wholeness will never reach its destination until this question is answered.

> " Leviticus is a manual of instructions to help unholy people know how to live with the holy God.

Holiness is so much more than an abstract theological concept. Understanding holiness is a matter of life and death. Leviticus warns us in a manner impossible to forget about the dangers of misunderstanding holiness. The tragic story of Nadab and Abihu, two of Aaron's sons, is a sober reminder of what happens when God's people neglect to come into his presence in the proper way:

> Now Nadab and Abihu, the sons of Aaron, each took his censer and put fire in it and laid incense on it and offered unauthorized fire before the LORD, which he had not commanded them. And fire came out from before the LORD and consumed them, and they died before the LORD. (Leviticus 10:1–3)

It appears that Nadab and Abihu, ignoring the instructions that had been given, attempted to enter into God's holy presence by going behind the veil into the Most Holy Place. With no fear of God, these arrogant priests felt they could approach him in a manner that God had not authorized. Their deaths underscore the boundaries that God has established between that which is holy and that which is not. The only way for the redeemed to have fellowship with the Holy One is by approaching him through the ways he has made known to them. To approach the Holy One, one must be holy and come in a holy manner. Failure to do so can have deadly consequences.

At the risk of oversimplification, we might suggest that holiness is somewhat like radioactive material. When used properly and handled correctly, radioactivity is a very good thing. It can provide energy to light cities and power submarines. However, when radioactive materials are mishandled, great damage can result, and people can be seriously hurt. The book of Leviticus is somewhat analogous to a manual of operations for workers in a nuclear power plant. Such a book of instructions tells all the wonderful things that nuclear power can do as well as warns of the dangers involved when protocols are not strictly followed. So it is with the holiness of God. The book of Leviticus tells us all about the beauty of holiness and what a blessing it is meant to be to all people everywhere. At the same time, it warns of the danger involved in misunderstanding the nature of the power that dwells in our midst.

One can consider that the first half of Leviticus (Chapters 1–15) describes *the way to approach* the Holy One: through sacrifice, a mediatory priesthood, and discerning the difference between what is clean and unclean. The second half of the book (Chapters 17–27) emphasizes *how to live* in God's presence. In these chapters, the focus is on personal holiness: diet, sexual purity, love of neighbor, Sabbath observance, feasts, etc. Chapter 16 serves as a sort of hinge for the entire book.

YOM KIPPUR

At the literary center of the book of Leviticus and at the heart of Israel's faith, Chapter 16 describes the liturgy to be followed in celebrating the Day of Atonement (*Yom Kippur*). In outlining the rituals involved, this chapter both sums up the sacrificial system of the first half of the book and introduces the call to holiness that sums up the last half of the book. The opening verses show the crucial importance of what the Day of Atonement represents:

> The LORD spoke to Moses after the death of the two sons
> of Aaron, when they drew near before the LORD and died,
> and the LORD said to Moses, "Tell Aaron your brother not to
> come at any time into the Holy Place inside the veil, before
> the mercy seat that is on the ark, so that he may not die. For
> I will appear in the cloud over the mercy seat. But in this way
> Aaron shall come into the Holy Place . . . ." (Leviticus 16:1–3)

What follows is a description of how Aaron should enter behind the veil into the Most Holy Place and have intimate fellowship with the Holy One. The theological truth that makes possible this entrance into the presence of God is the doctrine of atonement. This theological truth lies at the very core of Israel's faith and describes how it is possible for sinners to be reconciled to God, how unholy people can have fellowship with the Holy One. Michael Morales, in his excellent book on the theology of Leviticus, states it well:

> Atonement is a *means* to an end, a means to Israel's fellowship and communion with God. This goal is discernible in the English term itself, "at-one-ment", indicating reconciliation between God and humanity. While the precise understanding of the Hebrew verb *kipper*, typically translated "atone," has been complicated by its possible roots and cognates, its scriptural usage implies a twofold meaning: ransom from death and purification from pollution—both functions being involved by varying degrees in atonement.[1]

It is beyond the scope of this chapter to discuss the theological meaning of the various ceremonies involved in the Day of Atonement. Suffice it to say that the narrative of Leviticus 16 makes it clear that God has opened a way for humanity to enter into his holy presence and experience intimate fellowship with him. This intimacy is possible only through a priesthood that is qualified to serve as mediator between an unholy people and a holy God. Further, it requires a sacrifice that both pays the penalty for sin (ransoms from death) and removes that sin from our lives (purification from pollution).

WHAT IS HOLINESS?

The word "holy" and its cognate terms ("sanctify", "holiness", etc.) occur over 150 times in the book of Leviticus. Obviously, it is a term that is of central importance to the book. For those on the journey to spiritual wholeness, this word must be properly understood. Even more than that, it is of critical importance that the term points to something that has been *experienced personally* in the life of the believer.

The word "holy" has two essential aspects. First, it describes something or someone that has been "set apart." To say that God is holy is to say that he is *other than* the created order. He is not a part of nature, but transcends it. He is *set apart*. Interestingly, beyond the

---

1   Michael Morales, *Who Shall Ascend the Mountain of the Lord? A Biblical Theology of the Book of Leviticus* (New York: InterVarsity Press, 2015), 125.

reality of God being holy, Scripture tells of a wide range of objects that also can be considered holy. For example, the Sabbath day is holy because it is different from the other six days of the week. To sanctify (make holy) the Sabbath simply means to *set it apart* for God and his purposes. Similarly, pots and pans in the Tabernacle are called holy not because they are of higher quality than other pots and pans or because they are flawless. They are holy because they have been *set apart* to be used uniquely in the service of God.

Second, the word "holy" indicates moral purity, uprightness, righteousness. To say that God is holy means not only that he is *set apart* but also that he is of absolute moral purity. The apostle John states it succinctly when he says, "In him is no darkness at all" (1 Jn 1:5). Indeed, God is so holy, so pure, that he cannot even "look at wrong" (Hb 1:13). Nothing impure can enter his presence. To call something or someone holy is to indicate that it is clean, pure, and unpolluted by sin or corruption. Our grandparents spoke truth when they told us that "cleanliness is next to godliness."

> **Holiness is not a suggestion. The call to be holy is a command directed to all of God's people.**

The great point that the book of Leviticus makes is this: Because God is holy, those who worship him must be holy, too. God's holiness is meant to cause our holiness. The reason worship and liturgical instructions are so important in Leviticus is because we become like what we worship. If we worship the Holy One as we are instructed to do in this book, then we, too, will become holy. In fact, we can't worship the Holy One and not become holy. To be in his presence is to be transformed into his image. Over and over again, this is the resounding emphasis of the book of Leviticus:

- "I am the LORD your God. Consecrate [sanctify] yourselves therefore, and be holy, for I am holy. . . . For I am the LORD who brought you up out of the land of Egypt to be your God. You shall therefore be holy, for I am holy" (Lv 11:44–45).

- "And the LORD spoke to Moses, saying, 'Speak to all the congregation of the people of Israel and say to them, You shall be holy, for I the LORD your God am holy'" (Lv 19:1–2).

- "Consecrate [sanctify] yourselves, therefore, and be holy, for I am the LORD your God. Keep my statutes and do them; I am the LORD who sanctifies you" (Lv 20:7–8).

- "You shall be holy to me, for I the LORD am holy and have separated you from the peoples, that you should be mine" (Lv 20:26).

- "And you shall not profane my holy name, that I may be sanctified among the people of Israel. I am the LORD who sanctifies you, who brought you out of the land of Egypt to be your God: I am the LORD" (Lv 22:32–33).

Peter obviously was thinking of this central theme that runs through the book of Leviticus when he wrote to Christians in the first century, urging them to "be holy in all your conduct, since it is written, 'You shall be holy, for I am holy'" (1 Pt 1:15–16). Reflecting on this gospel mandate leads to three simple observations: this is a *command*, this a command *addressed to the redeemed*, and this is a command to *be* something not to *do* something.

This Is a Command

Being holy is not optional. It is not something reserved for spiritual giants and super-saints. Holiness is not a suggestion. The call to be holy is a command directed to all of God's people: men and women, young and old, clergy and laity. To be unholy is to be in a state of flagrant disobedience to a clear commandment of God. To ignore this directive or pretend it doesn't apply to us is to place our very souls in mortal peril. The author to Hebrews underscores the seriousness of the matter when he reminds us that without holiness "no one will see the Lord" (Heb 12:14). We are either holy or we perish.

This kind of talk is troubling. In a day when many in the evangelical church have been taught to believe that we will continue to live in our sins till we die, the call to holy living sounds strange and threatening. Yet this is clearly what Scripture commands. To water down God's standards or to twist the Scriptures to mean something they don't is to do precisely what Nadab and Abihu tried to do. The results of such an attitude are always catastrophic.

Though the command to be holy sounds preposterous, we must remember who it is that is issuing the challenge. If God demands it, he will surely help us to do it. God's commands are veiled promises. C. S. Lewis spoke to this reality when he said:

> [God] never talked vague, idealistic gas. When He said, "Be perfect," He meant it. He meant that we must go in for the full treatment. It is hard; but the sort of compromise we are all hankering after is harder—in fact, it is impossible. It may be hard for an egg to turn into a bird: it would be a jolly sight harder for it to learn to fly while remaining an egg. We are like eggs at present. And you cannot go on indefinitely being just an ordinary decent egg. We must be hatched or go bad.[2]

This Is a Command Addressed to the Redeemed

The call to holiness was given not to pagans and those who were lost but to those who had been redeemed by the blood of the Passover Lamb and brought to liberty through the baptismal waters of the Red Sea. The command to be holy was addressed first to the Hebrews at Mount Sinai; however, it applies to the ransomed church of God today. Similarly, in the New Testament, when Peter issues the call to be holy, he is speaking to those who are "born again to a living hope" (1 Pt 1:3, 15–16). Although those who have been born again have experienced God's grace in redemption, there is still something missing in their faith. There is a gap between where they currently are in their spiritual lives and where they ought to be. This gap is not necessarily the result of sin or disobedience. It is simply the recognition that the work of

---

2   C. S. Lewis, *Mere Christianity* (New York: HarperCollins, 1952), 154f.

grace that God wants to do in their hearts is not yet complete. As Paul wrote to the believers in Thessalonica:

> For what thanksgiving can we return to God for you, for all the joy that we feel for your sake before our God, as we pray most earnestly night and day that we may see you face to face and supply what is lacking in your faith? (1 Thessalonians 3:9–10)

The call to holiness is not a command to fix something that is broken. It is rather an invitation to finish something that is incomplete. At the risk of oversimplification, the command to "be holy" is the invitation to bridge the gap between these two columns:

Table 11.1: Bridging the Gap—Holiness

I Am...	But I Am Not Yet...
Redeemed	Holy
Forgiven	Pure
Delivered from sin's guilt	Delivered from sin's power
In God's family	In God's image
Justified	Sanctified

The book of Leviticus is of vital importance for those on the journey to spiritual wholeness, because it reminds us that redemption involves so much more than alleviating our difficult circumstances and changing our behaviors. God wants to get us out of sin. Yes! But he also intends to get sin out of us! Leviticus boldly proclaims that God wants to do more with sin than forgive it; he wants to break its power.

A humorous story is told of a farmer who once tried to find a way to keep his pigs clean. He felt that if they would just stop wallowing in the mud, he could produce a superior breed of pig and thus make more money at the market. He tried hosing them down only to discover that as soon as he turned his back they went back in the mud. He offered seminars to the pigs on the importance of cleanliness, but shortly after the course ended, they went back to their former ways. He put the pigs in a pen with sheep, hoping that association with clean animals would have a moral influence on their behavior. He even taught the pigs to sing worship choruses with titles like "Whiter than Snow" but it was all to no avail. Finally, the farmer said to himself, "Behavior modification doesn't work when you are dealing with pigs. The only way to keep pigs out of the mud is if someone could change their pig nature."

Precisely! Holiness is not behavior modification. It is not a command to try harder. The command to be holy is an invitation to allow God, through his sanctifying Spirit, to come on the inside and change our very nature. "If anyone is in Christ, he is a new creation. The old has passed away; behold, the new has come." (2 Cor 5:17).

This Is a Command to Be Something, Not to Do Something

Whenever holiness is understood as a list of behaviors that God's people are supposed to do or not do, it becomes something toxic. This is how the Pharisees in Jesus' day understood holiness, as conformity to a codified set of rules and behaviors. For them, its presence or absence could be detected by litmus test issues such as clothing, diet, morality, vocabulary, doctrinal precision, and the company one keeps. The book of Leviticus emphasizes the fact that holiness is first and foremost something we *are* before it is something we *do*. Our inner character matters more than our outward behavior. Holiness is a matter of the heart.

> **66 Holiness is not so much a demand for perfect performance as it is an invitation to perfect love.**

Although holiness certainly has huge implications for outward behaviors, it must never be defined only in those terms. When holiness becomes performance-driven, it becomes something God never intended it to be. At its core, to be holy means to be totally devoted to God, set apart completely for him. It means to be cleansed on the inside of moral pollution and the tyranny of self-interest. Seen in this way, holiness describes not a religion but a relationship, an intimacy with the Holy One that makes disobedience unthinkable. Holiness is not so much a demand for perfect performance as it is an invitation to perfect love.

There is a heresy circulating in the church today. Though few preachers would state the matter is these words, the message that often gets communicated from the pulpit is this: We are justified by grace but sanctified (made holy) by works. Those on the pews hear a wonderful message of good news that offers the free gift of salvation to all who believe. However, when these new believers discover areas in their hearts and lives that are still sinful, worldly, unloving, egotistical, and proud, they often hear the preacher point to a solution that is based in works and human performance. "Try harder," the weary pilgrims are told. "The problems in your spiritual walk are an indication that you are obviously not trying hard enough." People on the pew then hear a sermon exhorting them to be more diligent in daily devotions, to pray longer, to memorize Scripture, to begin tithing, to join a small group, to go on a missions trip, to help in the nursery, to go to seminary, etc. Rather than hearing an invitation to allow God to transform their hearts so that they can *be* holy, these dear souls hear an order that commands them to *do* more holy activities.

While the evangelical church has been successful in chasing the doctrine of "works righteousness" out the front door, it has found its way back into the church through the back door. When God's people believe that holiness is the result of human efforts, the results are never pretty. Some become like the Pharisees and look down their spiritual noses at those around them who just don't measure up to their behavioral standards. Others give up all together on the gospel in frustration and despair, concluding that the call to holiness is an impossible delusion.

Here's the Good News. When a person discovers the impossibility of holiness based in human effort, he is actually in a very good place! "What is impossible with men is possible with God" (Lk 18:27). The book of Leviticus very clearly states: "I am the LORD who sanctifies you [makes you holy]" (Lv 22:32). Holiness is *his* work, not ours! What the people couldn't do for themselves, he could do for them. The New Testament makes this point even more emphatically:

> Now may the God of peace himself sanctify you
> completely, and may your whole spirit and soul and
> body be kept blameless at the coming of our Lord Jesus
> Christ. He who calls you is faithful; he will surely do it.
> (1 Thessalonians 5:23–24)

Holiness is not just a command. It is a sacred promise, a promise from God himself. He will do what we can't.

> I will sprinkle clean water on you, and you shall be clean
> from all your uncleannesses, and from all your idols I will
> cleanse you. And I will give you a new heart, and a new spirit
> I will put within you. And I will remove the heart of stone
> from your flesh and give you a heart of flesh. And I will put
> my Spirit within you, and cause you to walk in my statutes
> and be careful to obey my rules. (Ezekiel 36:25–27)

Once we realize that the command to be holy is really a call to whole-hearted love for God, a purity of intention more than a perfection of performance, we are finally in a posture to understand the work of grace that God longs to do in the hearts of the redeemed. Redemption is about so much more than delivering us from painful circumstances and educating us so that we can modify our behavior. Through the blood of the Lamb and the gift of the Holy Spirit, God wants to transform our hearts so that we can become new creations. His Spirit is called the *Holy* Spirit for a reason! Not only does the adjective describe the nature of the Spirit, more to the point, it describes the sanctifying work that the Spirit intends to do in us! He is the *sanctifying* Spirit, poured into our hearts to make us holy.

As the redeemed traveled from Egypt to Canaan, God made his people aware of their need of a new heart. He wanted them to understand that this work of inner cleansing and transformation of character was something that could not be accomplished by human effort. Receiving a new nature is something that can only be accomplished by the grace and power of God!

When holiness is seen as a demand to try harder, it doesn't take long for weary travelers to conclude the endeavor is impossible. Deep within the human heart there is a kind of pig nature that no amount of behavior modification or self-improvement can cure. Unless God can change our hearts and give us a new nature, the call to holiness only mocks us.

A Testimony

One of the best ways to understand the call to holiness is to listen to the story of someone who has discovered the reality. Missionary evangelist E. Stanley Jones (1884–1973) described how he stepped out of the frustration of doing laps in the wilderness in his spiritual walk and stepped into a deeper dimension of grace:

> I found myself about a year after my conversion a very divided person. The conscious mind had been converted— radically and gloriously. But the subconscious mind had not been. There the driving instincts of self, sex, and the herd still reigned, driving for their own completion and satisfaction. These urges clashed with the new morality built up in the conscious mind. I was a house divided against myself. My mother remarked: "Stanley, religion isn't designed to make us unhappy." For she saw the drawn look on my face as a result of inner tension. I was like the ship on which Paul was shipwrecked—it was caught at the place "where two seas met" and was battered by the conflicting currents (Acts 27:41). I was puzzled: Was this the best that Christianity could do—leave you divided against yourself?

> At that time I came across a book—a book of destiny to me: "The Christian's Secret to a Happy Life." I read it avidly, for this was telling of the possibility of total victory—victory at the depths. I came to the forty-second page, when the Voice seemed to say: "Now is the time to get it." But I pleaded that I did not know what I wanted, that I would seek when I was through with the book. But the Voice was the more inexorable: "Now is the time to get it." I saw I was in a controversy, closed the book, fell on my knees.

> . . . As I closed the book and dropped upon my knees I said, "Now Lord, what shall I do?" Very quietly the Voice said: "Will you give me your all? All you know, and all you don't

know?" I replied, as simply as a child: "Yes, Lord, I do." Then the Voice: "Then take my ALL."

I arose from my knees saying, "I do." The pact was verbally sealed on both sides: my all, His All. It was sealed by faith. I walked around the room asserting that faith; and after about ten minutes in which I was literally pushing away doubt, the faith turned to fact and the fact to feeling. I was filled—filled to my depths, and to my finger tips, and to the roots of my hair; I was filled with the Spirit. It was all very quiet—just the silent tears of joy rolling down my cheeks. But waves of refining Fire seemed to sweep my being, cleansing, uniting. The Holy Spirit had moved into the center of my being . . . .[3]

No one gets far on the journey to spiritual wholeness without discovering the need for a deeper work of grace, a work that does more than modify behavior, a work that transforms the heart. As God exposes our need, he reveals the cure. Our all for his all! It's that simple. It's that profound.

3   E. Stanley Jones, *The Way to Power and Poise* (New York: Abingdon-Cokesbury, 1949), 323f.

12
The "Grumpies"
(Numbers 11)

*"I have learned in whatever situation I am
to be content." (Philippians 4:11)*

A monk joined a monastic order that required a vow of silence. Every seventh year, however, each monk could say two words. After serving faithfully for seven years, the new monk was called before the leadership of the order and permitted to speak his two words. "Bad food," he said. The abbots nodded and sent him away. Another seven years passed and he was brought back and allowed again to speak. "Cold floors," he said. Nodding piously, the leaders again sent him away. Seven years later, he was once again permitted to speak. "I quit!" The senior abbot scowled and said, "Well, I'm not surprised. You've done nothing but complain ever since you got here."

Grumbling may not be included in the seven deadly sins, yet in the Bible it is clearly one of the most devastating attitudes a follower of Christ can have. As we walk on the journey to spiritual wholeness, pilgrims must learn contentment. Grumbling and complaining make it impossible to reach our destination.

Numbers 10 describes the moment when, after almost two years camped at Mount Sinai, "the cloud lifted from over the tabernacle . . . and the people of Israel set out . . ." (Nm 10:11–12). How exciting it must have been to be finally on the move again, headed toward the Land of Promise! The covenant was sealed, the law was accepted, the tabernacle was constructed, and God was dwelling in the midst of his people. As the pillar of fire led the congregation northward, there must have been a sense of great anticipation.

Strangely, after only three days of travel, the people once again began to grumble about their circumstances: "And the people complained in the hearing of the LORD about their misfortunes" (Nm 11:1). Though the Hebrews probably assumed that they had a right to complain and were only being "emotionally honest" about their feelings, God saw the situation differently: "When the LORD heard it, his anger was kindled, and the fire of the LORD burned among them and consumed some outlying parts of the camp" (Nm 11:1). Having the grumpies is a more serious sin than most of us realize. Numbers 11 helps us determine the cause, the consequences, and the cure for the grumpies.

THE CAUSE

The people of God began to assume that redemption entitled them to a life that was free of problems and pains. "We deserve better than this," they seemed to say.

> **It was not their hunger that was the problem, but what they were hungry for.**

> Now the rabble that was among them had a strong craving. And the people of Israel also wept again and said, "Oh that we had meat to eat! We remember the fish we ate in Egypt that cost nothing, the cucumbers, the melons, the leeks, the onions, and the garlic. But now our strength is dried up, and there is nothing at all but this manna to look at." (Numbers 11:4–6)

One can discern four different causes of grumbling in this short paragraph: misplaced appetites, arrogance, amnesia, and comparison.

Misplaced Appetites

Some of the people had a "strong craving." Literally, they "desired a desire," or perhaps, "craved a craving." The problem was not that

God's people wanted something with passionate intensity. God created us with appetites and cravings. These, in fact, are part of what constitute the image of God. The issue was not the craving itself, but rather *what* they were craving. It was not their hunger that was the problem, but what they were hungry *for*. The people of God were hungry for the wrong things. No longer content with the wonder bread (manna) that fell freely from heaven each day, the people craved the food they ate back in Egypt when they were slaves. Their appetites were misplaced.

One of the primary things that God wants to accomplish in our lives on the journey to spiritual wholeness is the cleansing of our palates. As we learned in Chapter 4, changing our appetites from the leaks and onions of Egypt to the milk and honey of Canaan doesn't happen overnight. It takes time. The bland taste of manna makes possible the reeducation of our taste buds. No one reaches Canaan until the craving for milk and honey is stronger than the craving for leaks and onions. Grumbling is often an unmistakable signal that our appetites have become fixated on the wrong things. We want something we don't have and this makes us irritable. Until this situation is corrected and our hunger for the things of God is stronger than our hunger for the things of this world, we will continue to whine and complain while we do laps in the wilderness.

Arrogance

Though not explicitly mentioned in the text, we can see the arrogance and pride in the hearts of the people that caused them to shake their fists at God and complain about their circumstances. Think about it. Only a few months earlier, these same people had been slaves in Egypt, making bricks without straw. Then, in what was the greatest display of divine grace in the history of the world, God stepped in and set the Hebrews free. These people whining in the desert knew the story first-hand. They were there when the ten plagues fell on Egypt and the waters of the Red Sea parted. They were there when God turned the bitter water sweet at Marah, defeated the Amalekites, and brought water out of the rock. They saw with their own eyes God descend on Mount Sinai in fire and smoke. That very morning, they had gathered their daily bread that God had rained down freely upon them from heaven. If they needed further evidence of God's goodness and faithfulness, all they needed to do was glance up toward the north end of camp where the Pillar of Fire hovered in transcendent glory. Despite all this, the people dared to whine. It would be hard to find a more brazen example of arrogance in all human history! When we whine and complain about the way God is managing the universe, we reveal only the breadth of our ignorance and the depth of our pride.

Amnesia

A third cause of grumbling is when our memory plays tricks on us. In the desert, the redeemed people of God began to fantasize about "the good ole' days" when they were slaves in Egypt. They remembered when they had fish "that cost nothing" plus the melons and garlic and onions (Nm 11:5). Life was good then, they recalled. How quickly they forgot that the food was free only because they were slaves! How easy it was to romanticize the past so that they forgot the cruel task masters, the bricks without straw, and the babies thrown into the Nile.

I sometimes get nostalgic for "the good ole' days" when I was a student at Westover High School. Life was great back in the late 60s and early 70s. The music was good, the cars were fast, the friends were many, and the activities were all fun. Life was a beach. Or was it? What about the social cliques and the acne? What about drugs and sexual promiscuity? What about peer pressure? What about Vietnam and Watergate? What about political assassinations and desegregation? In my nostalgia, it is easy to forget the unpleasantries of the past.

On the journey to spiritual wholeness, when circumstances get hard, many of us may be tempted to fantasize about the past and long for "the good ole' days." Wise travelers will take their cue from the grumblers in Numbers 11 and doubt the accuracy of their memories. One of the lessons God intends us to learn on the journey to spiritual wholeness is that we can't go back. The past is gone forever and cannot be recovered. Our destiny is determined not by our past but by our future! It is not where we've been that defines who we are, but where we are going. Thank God the Pillar of Fire leads us forward, ever forward.

Comparison

It was when God's people compared themselves to others that we see the final cause of their grumbling. In the minds of the Hebrews, it was the Egyptians, the Midianites, and the Canaanites who seemed to be healthy, wealthy, and happy while they groveled around in the desert, homeless, eating wafers that fell out of the sky. They were indulging in a national pity party.

When I allow comparison in my life, it looks something like this:

- I'm happy with my 7-year-old clunker automobile that has 161,000 miles *until* I pull into the church parking lot on Sunday morning and park next to a late model Lexus owned by one of the Sunday school teachers. Suddenly, I have a bad case of the grumpies.
- I love the church I pastor. The facility is great, my salary is generous, and the people are wonderful *until* I visit that megachurch across town. Inexplicably, our facility begins to feel small, my salary modest, our media capabilities antiquated, and our congregation so unresponsive.
- I think my kids are terrific and my marriage is great *until* I read that Christmas letter from the guy I went to school with years ago. His wife looks like a model, his kids all got scholarships to Ivy League schools, and the happy family has just returned from a mission trip to the Ukraine. Irritably, I wonder what's wrong with the people I live with.

Comparison rarely makes us feel anything other than grumpy. So, the next time we are tempted to compare our situation with someone else's, let's take a moment to notice *who* we are choosing to compare ourselves with. Normally, we compare ourselves with those who are better off than we are: the ones with the larger house, the newer car, the bigger ministry. Rather than comparing ourselves with those who are better off, let's try comparing ourselves with those who have it worse. I think one of the reasons God has sent me repeatedly on trips to Africa and India is so that he can cure me forever of the grumpies! An old proverb puts it succinctly: I once complained I had no shoes, until I met a man who had no feet.

THE CONSEQUENCES

What are the consequences of grumbling and whining? What happens to people when they catch a bad case of the gripes? The first consequence emphasized in Numbers 11 relates to God. When we get the grumpies, God gets angry. In this story, God gets *very* angry. He is so upset that he consumes some of them with fire (see Nm 11:1)!

Every parent can identify with God's reaction. Mother spends hours at the grocery store shopping, spending money that is in short supply. **When we get the grumpies, God gets angry.** She then sweats in a hot kitchen preparing a meal that is nutritious and tasty. Anticipating a joyful moment of family interaction around the dining room table, she invites everyone to dinner only to discover that her twelve-year-old son has arrived with an attitude. With arms folded across his chest and bottom lip protruding, he whines, "Do I have to eat this? Can't I just fix a peanut butter and jelly sandwich and go watch television?" That hurts. It really hurts.

Our Father in heaven understands exactly how that mother feels, because he feels the same way on many occasions. I can only imagine how he felt when his children whined and complained about the manna he showered on them freely every single day. I can only imagine how he felt when no one thanked him for his guidance, provision, and protection. How it must have hurt when the people said, in effect, "We deserve better than this!" No wonder God got angry.

God may have been angry that day, but his servant Moses went into depression, the second consequence of the grumpies. As senior pastor of a congregation of whiny cry-babies, Moses tumbled into a deep pit of despair.

> Moses heard the people weeping throughout their clans, everyone at the door of his tent. And the anger of the LORD blazed hotly, and Moses was displeased. Moses said to the LORD, "Why have you dealt ill with your servant? And why have I not found favor in your sight, that you lay the burden of all this people on me? Did I conceive all this people? Did I give them birth, that you should say to me, 'Carry them in your bosom, as a nurse carries a nursing child,' to the land that you swore to give their fathers? Where am I to get meat to give to all this people? For they weep before me and say, 'Give us meat, that we may eat.' I am not able to carry all this people alone; the burden is too heavy for me. If you will treat me like this, kill me at once, if I find favor in your sight, that I may not see my wretchedness." (Numbers 11:10–15)

As a pastor myself, I must admit that I have a lot of sympathy for Moses. Few things are more discouraging than a congregation of grumbling saints. For Moses, the situation was so disheartening that he prayed that God would kill him at once! The burden of pastoring a congregation of whiners was just more than he could bear. His situation was simply impossible, so Moses wanted to resign. He wanted to lie down and die.

The Scripture tells us that the consequences of grumbling affect not only God and Moses but also the grumblers. Those who are brazen enough to complain about how God is running the universe quickly discover that the consequences for such an attitude are very serious indeed. Grumbling brings on one's own head the very judgment of God, and God's judgment comes in a form that no one could have anticipated: God judges the whiners by giving them what they crave!

THE CURE

Before considering the surprising cure God had for the grumpies, let's first look at how he took care of his servant Moses. Because

Moses was so heavily impacted by the whines and complaints of the congregation he pastored, God responded by bringing Moses both relief and encouragement. As with so many things God does, the relief was not what Moses expected.

> Then the LORD said to Moses, "Gather for me seventy men of the elders of Israel, whom you know to be the elders of the people and officers over them, and bring them to the tent of meeting, and let them take their stand there with you. And I will come down and talk with you there. And I will take some of the Spirit that is on you and put it on them, and they shall bear the burden of the people with you, so that you may not bear it yourself alone. (Numbers 11:16–17)

I don't think this was the answer Moses wanted. Crushed under the weight of the burden of a congregation made up of grumblers, Moses probably hoped that God would either remove the burden or accept his resignation. However, God wasn't about to let Moses resign. The call on Moses to lead these people was greater than ever! Never is leadership more crucial than when an epidemic of grumbling has broken out, infecting everyone and everything.

Rather than removing the burden from Moses' shoulders, God chose to redistribute it. Yes, the burden of ministry was great, far too great for one man to carry alone, but the burden had to be borne. This meant that the burden had to be shared. God raised up seventy men and equipped them for ministry by filling them with his Spirit, so that the burden of the congregation could be shared. As a result, Moses continued to lead, and the needs of the congregation were addressed effectively.

One of the great lessons of this story is learning how God responds when the burdens of life are more than we can bear. While we often pray that God will either remove the burden or accept our resignation, he has a better way. Instead of taking the burden away, he strengthens us by sending reinforcements.

Dave Dravecky was a star pitcher for the San Francisco Giants in the late 1980s and a strong Christian. At the height of his career, he developed cancer in his pitching arm. What could possibly be worse for a pitcher than that? He prayed for healing and sought the help of doctors, but eventually his arm and shoulder had to be amputated. Reflecting on his journey of pain and suffering, Dravecky said:

> Someone once said that the difference between American Christianity and Christianity as it is practiced in the rest of the world has to do with how each views suffering. In America, Christians pray for the burden of suffering to be lifted from their backs. In the rest of the world, Christians pray for stronger backs . . . .[1]

Rather than removing the burden from Moses' back, God gave him stronger shoulders. He gave him seventy Spirit-filled men to share the weight of leadership. This was God's response to Moses' depression. God did not take the problem away or allow Moses to resign. He enabled Moses to handle it.

It is in how God dealt with the whiners, however, that we discover God's most ingenious cure for the grumpies. He could have destroyed them in judgment or zapped them with the Holy Spirit so that they were miraculously transformed into praising saints, but God did something that only he could have thought up:

> And say to the people, "Consecrate yourselves for tomorrow, and you shall eat meat, for you have wept in the hearing of the LORD, saying, 'Who will give us meat to eat? For it was better for us in Egypt.' Therefore the LORD will give you meat, and you shall eat. You shall not eat just one day, or two days, or five days, or ten days, or twenty days, but a whole month, until it comes out at your nostrils and becomes loathsome to you, because you have rejected the LORD who is among you and have wept before him, saying, 'Why did we come out of Egypt?'" (Numbers 11:18–20)

"You want meat? I'll give you meat!" Obviously, God was upset, but though his anger was strong, his powers of rationality were

---

1   "Quoteworthy," *Servant*, November 1992, 8. Quoting from his book, *When You Can't Come Back.*

spectacular. He cured the grumpies by giving the people what they were demanding!

> Then a wind from the LORD sprang up, and it brought quail
> from the sea and let them fall beside the camp, about a day's
> journey [say, ten miles] on this side and a day's journey
> on the other side, around the camp, and about two cubits
> [about 3 feet] above the ground. And the people rose all
> that day and all night and all the next day, and gathered the
> quail. Those who gathered least gathered ten homers [fifty–
> sixty bushels]. And they spread them out for themselves
> all around the camp. While the meat was yet between their
> teeth, before it was consumed, the anger of the LORD was
> kindled against the people, and the LORD struck down the
> people with a very great plague. (Numbers 11:31–33)

God solved the problem of grumbling by giving the people exactly what they wanted. The results were disastrous. Years later, the Psalmist, in speaking of this incident, summed up the matter succinctly: God "gave them what they asked, but sent a wasting disease among them" (Ps 106:15).

The moral of the story is this: Be very careful how you grumble and what you ask God to do; he may just give you what you crave! When you stop and think about it, this is a very good description of hell: a place God has designed for people who insist on having their own way.

The More Excellent Way

We can avoid the tragedy that happened to the Hebrews by allowing the Spirit of holiness to help us examine our desires so that we want only what he wants. God understands how challenging and difficult the journey to spiritual wholeness is, and he stands ready to help when the way is hard. Paul shows us the more excellent way in Philippians 4. Sitting in a Roman prison cell awaiting probable execution under evil emperor Nero, he wrote:

> I have learned in whatever situation I am to be content. I
> know how to be brought low, and I know how to abound.
> In any and every circumstance, I have learned the secret

of facing plenty and hunger, abundance and need. I
can do all things through him who strengthens me.
(Philippians 4:11–13)

The real cure for the grumpies is learning the art of contentment.
Don't expect contentment to come in a flash of spiritual ecstasy,
however. Paul said that it is something to be learned. Though he called
it a "secret," it is an open secret, available to all. True joy in life is not
dependent on the absence of unpleasant circumstances but rather on
the presence of God. It is not the result of having what we crave but
rather of craving what we have.

In his classic allegory, *Pilgrim's Progress*, John Bunyan describes
how Matthew fell ill because he had eaten some green plums from
Beelzebub's orchard.[2] He was "much pained in his bowels, so that
he was with it at times pulled as 'twere both ends together." A godly
physician, named Mr. Skill, examined him and diagnosed the problem:
he had "the gripes." Taking some of the body and blood of Christ, Mr.
Skill formed tablets that would act as a purge (a laxative); adding some
salt, a promise or two, and a dose of the tears of repentance. Though
Matthew feared that the strong medicine would make him worse, he
took it in faith and was immediately cured of the gripes.

---

2   For the full account, see *Pilgrim's Progress, Part 2: The Pilgrimage of
Christiana* (London: Penguin, 1965), 279.

If You Will Only Let God Guide You

By Georg Neumark (1621–1681)

Translated from German to English by Catherine Winkworth

If you will only let God guide you,
And hope in Him through all your ways,
Whatever comes, He'll stand beside you,
To bear you through the evil days;
Who trusts in God's unchanging love
Builds on the Rock that cannot move.

Only be still, and wait His leisure
In cheerful hope, with heart content
To take whate'er the Father's pleasure
And all discerning love have sent;
Nor doubt our inmost wants are known
To Him Who chose us for His own.

Sing, pray, and keep His ways unswerving,
So do thine own part faithfully.
And trust His word, though undeserving,
Thou yet shalt find it true for thee.
God never yet forsook in need
The soul that trusted Him indeed.

13
The Moment of Truth
(Numbers 13–14)

"Therefore, while the promise of entering his rest still stands, let us fear lest any of you should seem to have failed to reach it." (Hebrews 4:1)

As a boy in Sunday School, I learned how it took forty years for the Hebrews to travel across the desert from Egypt to Canaan. I remember thinking, "Wow, that must have been one gigantic desert!" When I imagined the people traveling ten miles a day, six days a week, fifty weeks a year, for forty years, I calculated that the desert must have been thousands of miles across. I still remember the shock I experienced when I looked at a map and discovered that the Sinai Peninsula was actually quite small. The distance from the border of Egypt to the border of Canaan was just over 100 miles. I recall scratching my head in bewilderment: Why did it take them forty years to travel 100 miles? This is the question we are *supposed* to ask as we study the Hebrews' journey. Discerning the answer takes us to the heart of God's purposes in redemption.

Rather than glossing over this traveling nightmare, the Bible actually highlights it. The book of Deuteronomy begins by explaining that "it is an eleven days' journey from Horeb [Mount Sinai] by the way of Mount Seir to Kadesh-barnea [an oasis on the southern border of Canaan]" (Dt 1:2). In other words, the Hebrew people could have reached the Land of Promise in under two weeks. The very next verse emphasizes the tragic fact that they finally reached their destination "in the fortieth year" (Dt 1:3).

Putting the pieces of their journey together, we come up with a picture that looks something like this:

- It took *three months* to travel from the Red Sea to Mount Sinai (see Ex 19:1).
- The people camped at Mount Sinai for *12–18 months* until the Pillar of Fire began to move northward, leading them toward Canaan (see Nm 10:11–12).
- The journey from Sinai to the southern border of Canaan (Kadesh-barnea) covered about 120 miles and typically took only 11 days, as we have noted. For the Hebrews, however, it probably took *several weeks or even months*, as noted in the many stops recorded along the way (see Nm 10:11–36; 33:16–37).

When they arrived at Kadesh-barnea (see Nm 13:1ff), the people had reached the border of Canaan. They received the command to enter the land and possess their inheritance. Thus, the entire journey from Egypt to the Land of Promise had taken them just over *two years*.

This chapter explores what happened at Kadesh-barnea that caused a two-year journey to be turned into a forty-year nightmare.

OGRES IN THE LAND OF PROMISE

It had been 400 years since God first promised to give the land of Canaan to Abraham and his descendants. The people of God had arrived at last on the very border of their promised inheritance. This was the moment for which they had been waiting, dreaming, and praying.

At Kadesh-barnea, Moses appointed a twelve-man fact-finding mission to spy out the land and bring back a report. One man from each tribe was chosen. Before embarking on their reconnaissance mission, Moses gave the men these instructions:

> Go up into the Negeb and go up into the hill country, and see what the land is, and whether the people who dwell in it are strong or weak, whether they are few or many, and whether the land that they dwell in is good or bad, and whether the cities that they dwell in are camps or strongholds, and whether the land is rich or poor, and whether there are trees in it or not. Be of good courage and bring some of the fruit of the land. . . . (Numbers 13:17–20)

For forty days the spies conducted their clandestine operation, gathering information about the region that God had promised to give them. It is easy to imagine the excitement in the camp when the twelve spies finally returned to report on what they had learned. The impact of their arrival was made unforgettable by the cluster of grapes they brought with them. The grapes were so large it took two men to carry a single cluster on a pole between them! Yes, Canaan was an amazing place, a land that flowed with milk and honey. The words of the apostle Paul describe what the people of God experienced that memorable day: "Eye has not seen, nor ear heard, nor have entered into the heart of man the things which God has prepared for those who love Him" (1 Cor 2:9 NKJV).

This is where the plot thickens. The spies reported on the amazing blessings of Canaan, but they emphasized the troubling fact that the Land of Promise already was inhabited by other people:

> We came to the land to which you sent us. It flows with milk and honey, and this is its fruit. However, the people who dwell in the land are strong, and the cities are fortified and very large. And besides, we saw the descendants of Anak there. The Amalekites dwell in the land of the Negeb. The Hittites, the Jebusites, and the Amorites dwell in the hill country. And the Canaanites dwell by the sea, and along the Jordan. (Numbers 13:27–29)

Suddenly, the joy and elation in the camp turned into pessimism and despair. What had at first felt like a celebration now seemed more like a funeral. The descendants of Anak were a legendary race of giants. In some ways similar to modern-day terrorists, the Anakim inspired fear whenever their name was mentioned. It seemed that no one in Israel had anticipated this. Why hadn't God told them about the cruel and blood-thirsty ogres that were camping on their inheritance? In only a moment, the Land of Promise began to resemble Death Valley.

When In Doubt, Vote

Moses consulted with the spies about how to respond to the situation, but he soon discovered that the twelve-man committee was divided. Joshua and Caleb believed that they should advance into Canaan immediately: "Let us go up at once and occupy it, for we are well able to overcome it" (Nm 13:30). This prompted a strong reaction from the other ten members of the committee who felt that any advance into this land of giants would be a suicide mission:

> Then the men who had gone up with him said, "We are not able to go up against the people, for they are stronger than we are." So they brought to the people of Israel a bad report of the land that they had spied out, saying, "The land, through which we have gone to spy it out, is a land that devours its inhabitants, and all the people that we saw in it are of great height. And there we saw the Nephilim (the sons of Anak, who come from the Nephilim), and we seemed to ourselves like grasshoppers, and so we seemed to them." (Numbers 13:31–33)

For anyone who has ever served on a church committee, this kind of situation may sound eerily familiar: When confronted with a difficult situation, let's vote! At Kadesh-barnea, such a solution seemed to provide a clear way forward. I can imagine it happening. The chair of the committee says:

> All in favor of moving forward into Canaan, please raise your right hand. Thanks, Joshua, I see your hand. And yes, Caleb, I see your hand as well. Now, all opposed. One, two, three . . . eight, nine, ten. That's two who vote *for* moving forward, ten

opposed. Gentlemen, it looks like we have solid consensus. We are *not* going into Canaan. Meeting adjourned.

For the watching congregation, the situation could not be more devastating. Obviously influenced by the majority report coming from the twelve-member committee, the people concluded that the situation was hopeless:

> Then all the congregation raised a loud cry, and the people wept that night. And all the people of Israel grumbled against Moses and Aaron. The whole congregation said to them, "Would that we had died in the land of Egypt! Or would that we had died in this wilderness! Why is the LORD bringing us into this land, to fall by the sword? Our wives and our little ones will become a prey. Would it not be better for us to go back to Egypt?" And they said to one another, "Let us choose a leader and go back to Egypt."
>
> Then Moses and Aaron fell on their faces before all the assembly of the congregation of the people of Israel. And Joshua the son of Nun and Caleb the son of Jephunneh, who were among those who had spied out the land, tore their clothes and said to all the congregation of the people of Israel, "The land, which we passed through to spy it out, is an exceedingly good land. If the LORD delights in us, he will bring us into this land and give it to us, a land that flows with milk and honey. Only do not rebel against the LORD. And do not fear the people of the land, for they are bread for us. Their protection is removed from them, and the LORD is with us; do not fear them." Then all the congregation said to stone them with stones. . . . (Numbers 14:1–10)

The situation had become a major crisis. The entire future of Israel was hanging in the balance. The whole purpose of redemption was suddenly called into question. God had been watching all that was happening and stepped in. His response was firm and definitive:

> And the LORD said to Moses, "How long will this people despise me? And how long will they not believe in me, in spite of all the signs that I have done among them? I will strike them with the pestilence and disinherit them, and I will make of you a nation greater and mightier than they." (Numbers 14:11–12)

In a response similar to when Israel sinned with the golden calf (see Ex 32), God was so upset by the rebellious unbelief of his people that he was ready to disinherit them. Once again, Moses acted as an intercessor, and the nation was saved from destruction. Stepping into the gap between a holy God and a sinful people, Moses prayed, "Please pardon the iniquity of this people, according to the greatness of your steadfast love, just as you have forgiven this people, from Egypt until now" (Nm 14:19).

Moses' plea for mercy reached the heart of God, and the people were forgiven once again. This time, however, the results carried a sting. The sin at Kadesh-barnea is a sober reminder that even forgiven sin can carry bitter consequences:

> Then the LORD said, "I have pardoned, according to your word. But truly, as I live, and as all the earth shall be filled with the glory of the LORD, none of the men who have seen my glory and my signs that I did in Egypt and in the wilderness, and yet have put me to the test these ten times and have not obeyed my voice, shall see the land that I swore to give to their fathers. And none of those who despised me shall see it. . . . Turn tomorrow and set out for the wilderness by the way to the Red Sea." (Numbers 14:20–23, 25)

" What should have been Israel's finest hour became her moment of everlasting shame.

God was sending his people back into the desert, where they would spend the next thirty-eight years walking in circles. Though God did not disinherit them, he did deprive them of the ability to reach their promised inheritance. This generation would spend their lives in the land of in-between, between the bondage of Egypt and the freedom of Canaan. They would fall short of the glory that God had prepared for them. They would waste their lives doing laps in a barren wilderness. The Land of Promise would be given to a future generation.

> "'But as for you, your dead bodies shall fall in this wilderness. And your children shall be shepherds in the wilderness forty years and shall suffer for your faithlessness, until the last of your dead bodies lies in the wilderness. According to the number of the days in which you spied out the land, forty days, a year for each day, you shall bear your iniquity forty years, and you shall know my displeasure.' I, the LORD, have spoken. Surely this will I do to all this wicked congregation who are gathered together against me: in this wilderness they shall come to a full end, and there they shall die." (Numbers 14:32–35)

POST MORTEM

We have seen *what* went wrong. The real question is *why*? What caused the redeemed people of God to rebel in unbelief and refuse to move forward to possess their inheritance? They were like a rocket sitting on a launch pad. The final count-down had begun: 4-3-2-1 . . . . At the last minute, the launch was aborted. What should have been Israel's finest hour became her moment of everlasting shame.

Not all moments in time are created equal. On the journey to spiritual wholeness, God leads his people to places and moments when a window of opportunity is open before them. If the opportunity is missed, the window is closed, and the mission is aborted. At Kadesh-barnea, when the people realized the gravity of their sin and its terrible consequences, they tried to salvage the situation by a noble act of delayed obedience: "Here we are. We will go up to the place that the LORD has promised, for we have sinned" (Nm 14:40). Moses warned them that advancing into a land of giants without a clear command of God would be suicidal. They refused to listen, however, and attempted to possess their inheritance in their own strength:

> But they presumed to go up to the heights of the hill country, although neither the ark of the covenant of the LORD nor Moses departed out of the camp. Then the Amalekites and the Canaanites who lived in that hill country came down

and defeated them and pursued them, even to Hormah.
(Numbers 14:44–45)

When God says "move forward," we must move. If we delay, we may find ourselves doing laps in the wilderness. James Russell Lowell (1819–1891) wrote a poem that captures this reality well:

Once to every man and nation,
Comes the moment to decide,
In the strife of truth with false-hood,
For the good or evil side;
Some great cause, some great decision,
Offering each the bloom or blight,
And the choice goes by forever,
Twixt that darkness and that light.

At Kadesh-barnea, Israel faced her moment of truth. There are at least four reasons she failed to make the right choice: fear, peer pressure, double-mindedness, and unbelief. These issues continue to trouble pilgrims today, causing many to make the wrong decision when God brings them to a moment of truth.

Fear

I wonder how many people miss God's best for their lives because of fear. They start out well. In fact, they may have covered many miles on their spiritual journey already. They may have faithfully followed the Pillar of Fire for months, even years. Then, God leads them one day to a place where a decision must be made: their moment of truth. For different pilgrims, the crisis comes in different ways: Should I go back to school and further my education? Should I go on that missions trip? Should I teach that Sunday School class? Should I get married? Should I tithe my income? Should I witness to my boss? In the providence of God, everything seems to hinge on how the question is answered.

Many pilgrims, like those at Kadesh-barnea, make a decision rooted in fear. They look at the size of the obstacle rather than the size of their God. Fear causes paralysis. They hesitate, and the window of opportunity closes, perhaps forever. Many Christians today look back with deep regret on a moment when God was asking them to step forward in faith, but they hesitated and pulled back, because they were afraid.

At Kadesh-barnea, the people of God were controlled by their fears. "We can't go into Canaan," they seemed to say. "There are big scary giants over there and we might get hurt." What a different spirit we see in Caleb and Joshua. Rather than focusing on the size of the Anakim, they focused on the size of their God! They had seen God send ten plagues on Egypt, divide the waters of the Red Sea, provide bread from heaven every day, and make water come out of a rock. They had seen him descend in thunder and fire on Mount Sinai. Caleb and Joshua believed the God they served was able to handle the giants of Canaan, so they pleaded with the people, "Do not fear the people of the land, for they are bread for us. Their protection is removed from them, and the LORD is with us; do not fear them" (Nm 14:9).

When I was in college, I was paralyzed by the fear of speaking in public. While taking the required speech class, I lived in trauma. I somehow managed to give the required ten-minute speech, but I spent the entire semester worrying about it. When I began to sense a call into pastoral ministry, I remember well how I panicked. "No way, Lord!" I shouted. "I can't go into the ministry, because I can't speak. You'd better choose someone else." Looking back, I tremble to think how close I came to missing God's will for my life. Oswald Chambers gives a profound insight about fear when he writes, "The remarkable thing about fearing God is that when you fear God you fear nothing else, whereas if you do not fear God you fear everything else."[1]

Jesus knew the power fear has to derail God's people, causing them to miss the blessings God has prepared for them. Speaking to those he loved the most, he urged them to put their fears in proper perspective:

I tell you, my friends, do not fear those who kill the body, and after that have nothing more that they can do. But I will warn you whom to fear: fear him who, after he has killed,

---

1   Oswald Chambers, *The Complete Works of Oswald Chambers* (Grand Rapids: Discovery House, 2000), 537.

has authority to cast into hell. Yes, I tell you, fear him!
(Luke 12:4–5)

How different the history of Israel would have been if at Kadesh-barnea they had feared God more than the giants!

Peer Pressure

A second reason the children of Israel failed miserably at Kadesh-barnea was because they assumed they could discern the will of God by taking a poll. When the going got tough, they made a decision based on what the majority thought they should do. While democratic principles may work fairly well in human governments, they are not helpful at all when it comes to discerning the will of God. The kingdom of God is *not* a democracy!

How many times do we miss God's will because we listen to the majority rather than to God? When we care more about the opinions of our friends and family than we do about the opinion of God, we are in danger of finding ourselves wasting our lives doing laps in the wilderness. Whether it concerns business practices, relationships, politics, financial decisions, or sexual ethics, many miss God's plan for their lives because they make decisions based on public opinion rather than divine direction.

> **"How different the history of Israel would have been if at Kadesh-barnea they had feared God more than the giants!**

Thank God for the men and women in history who have dared to obey the will of God even when it meant standing alone. As with Joshua and Caleb, the cost of making such a decision may be great, but the influence of such a life is incalculable. The rewards for doing the right thing are great indeed. Consider the blessings that have come to the world through those who have dared to stand alone against the majority:

- Noah built an ark on dry ground while his neighbors mocked and laughed. His courageous example of going against the grain still inspires us today.
- Early in his life as a Christian, Paul made a firm decision about which voice he wanted to listen to and who he wanted to please: "For am I now seeking the approval of man, or of God? Or am I trying to please man? If I were still trying to please man, I would not be a servant of Christ" (Gal 1:10). No wonder he became the greatest missionary in history!
- When Martin Luther nailed his ninety-five theses to the door of the church in Wittenberg, he must have felt so very alone. However, the reformation that came to the global church because of his courageous stand changed our world for the better.
- William Wilberforce spoke out against slavery and the slave trade when virtually everyone else in the British Empire saw no problem with things that were obviously so good for the economy. Thanks largely to his efforts, slavery was abolished in Great Britain.
- Dietrich Bonhoeffer was a Lutheran pastor in Nazi Germany who refused to sign a loyalty oath to Adolf Hitler when it seemed that every other pastor believed it was the right thing to do. His courage reminds us never to give in to peer pressure when determining the will of God, even in the face of death.

A number of years ago on a visit to London, Katy and I had the privilege of visiting Bunhill Fields, a non-conformist cemetery that is nestled amid tall buildings and busy city streets. In this four-acre plot of ground, considered unconsecrated by the official Anglican Church, are buried men and women from the seventeenth and eighteenth centuries who simply did not conform to the majority view. As we walked through the shaded cemetery, pausing to read the names and epitaphs of the dead, Katy and I realized that we were indeed on holy ground. These social misfits changed the world. Their lives impacted history precisely because they refused to conform to the majority. In this tiny piece of real estate, we stood with reverent awe at the graves of:

- John Bunyan, Baptist pastor and author of *Pilgrim's Progress*.
- Daniel Defoe, author of *Robinson Crusoe*.
- George Fox, founder of the Quaker movement.
- Susannah Wesley, the mother of John and Charles Wesley.
- Isaac Watts, one of the greatest English hymn writers in the history of the church.
- John Owen, one of the greatest Puritan preachers and theologians.

I remember saying to Katy as we left, "I want to be a non-conformist, too."

No one knew better than Jesus that the call to follow him was a call to go against the crowd and be willing to stand alone.

> Enter by the narrow gate. For the gate is wide and the way is easy that leads to destruction, and those who enter by it are many. For the gate is narrow and the way is hard that leads to life, and those who find it are few. (Matthew 7:13–14)

We caution our young teens about the dangers of peer pressure regarding drugs and alcohol abuse. It is of far greater importance that we caution our teens—and ourselves—to remember the eternal dangers of allowing peer pressure to wrongly influence our obedience to God.

Double-mindedness

A third reason that explains why the Hebrews turned back in unbelief at Kadesh-barnea and failed to possess their inheritance is double-mindedness. In the spiritual no-man's land between Egypt and Canaan, the people of God simply could not make up their minds which direction they wanted to go. Should they move forward toward Canaan or should they choose a new leader and go back toward Egypt? Their hearts were torn. They were double-minded.

Of course, this was not the first time the children of Israel showed signs of spiritual bi-polar disorder. On numerous occasions during their journey, we have seen this instability manifested in their unpredictable behaviors, their off-the-cuff decisions, and their mercurial devotion. On the one hand, they had an appetite for the milk and honey of Canaan and wanted to travel toward the kingdom of God. On the other hand, they still had an appetite for the leaks and onions of Egypt. They simply couldn't make up their minds in which direction they wanted to go! Their double-mindedness caused them to be "unstable in all [their] ways" (Jas 1:8). One might classify their problem as a type of spiritual schizophrenia characterized by doubt, confusion, inner turmoil, and being out of touch with reality. Such people have enough faith to get out of Egypt but not enough to get in to Canaan. They spend their lives doing laps in the wilderness.

In many ways, the spiritual experience of the Hebrews resembles that described by the apostle Paul in the seventh chapter of Romans:

> For I do not understand my own actions. For I do not do what I want, but I do the very thing I hate. . . . For I have the desire to do what is right, but not the ability to carry it out. For I do not do the good I want, but the evil I do not want is what I keep on doing. Now if I do what I do not want, it is no longer I who do it, but sin that dwells within me. . . . For I delight in the law of God, in my inner being, but I see in my members another law waging war against the law of my mind and making me captive to the law of sin that dwells in my members. Wretched man that I am! Who will deliver me from this body of death? (Romans 7:15–24)

Untold thousands of believers have set out on the journey to spiritual wholeness in the hopes of one day reaching the land of victory only to find themselves plagued by a type of spiritual bi-polar disorder. As a result, they wander in circles in the desert with no hope of deliverance. At one moment pulled toward the kingdom of God and the next pulled toward the kingdoms of this world, these double-minded pilgrims, like Paul, cry out, "Who will deliver me from this body of death?"

No one reaches the Land of Promise without first finding a cure for double-mindedness. God offers a solution that cleanses the heart of inner division and makes the mind single in its devotion. Joshua and Caleb knew such an inner work of grace, and the gospel invites others to know it as well. Paul bore witness to such a work in his own heart when he wrote:

> But one thing I do: forgetting what lies behind and straining forward to what lies ahead, I press on toward the goal for the prize of the upward call of God in Christ Jesus. Let those of us who are mature think this way, and if in anything you think otherwise, God will reveal that also to you. (Philippians 3:13–15)

Soren Kierkegaard summed it up succinctly in the title to a little book he wrote about the human heart: *Purity of Heart Is to Will One Thing.*

> " **The root cause of missing God's purpose for their lives was simply that they did not believe that God was able to do what he had promised.**

Unbelief

A final reason for the debacle at Kadesh-barnea is actually the underlying cause of all the other issues: unbelief. The root cause of missing God's purpose for their lives was simply that they did not believe that God was able to do what he had promised. From God's perspective, this was the core issue: "How long will they not believe in me, in spite of all the signs that I have done among them?" (Nm 14:11).

The problem was not that they *couldn't* believe but that they *wouldn't!* Ultimately, unbelief is a choice. More than fear, more than peer pressure, and more than double-mindedness, the real sin at Kadesh-barnea was unbelief. Though some may pretend that sins such as murder and adultery are much more serious, the Bible makes it clear that unbelief is deadly: "Whoever does not believe is condemned already," Jesus said (Jn 3:18). The book of Hebrews makes it clear that "without faith, it is impossible to please God" (Heb 11:6). Unbelief keeps us out of Canaan forever. Ultimately, it will be the sole explanation for every sinner's damnation in hell.

At Kadesh-barnea, the sin of unbelief is the ultimate reason why the people wasted their lives doing laps in the wilderness. They fell short of God's purpose for them and died in the land of in-between, out of Egypt but not in Canaan. People often ask: "But what happens to those who die in the land of in-between? For those who have enough faith to get out of Egypt but not enough to get in to Canaan, what happens at the final judgment? Are they saved? Will God let them in heaven?" After years of reflection, I've finally come to the conclusion that God doesn't intend to give a definitive answer. It's certainly a good thing to be out of Egypt, a *very* good thing. However, it is certainly a bad thing to fall short of our inheritance, a *very* bad thing. For those doing laps in the wilderness, the fear of the Lord should be the beginning of wisdom.

A Message to Those in the Land of In-between

As a minister of the gospel, I never want to be guilty of reassuring people in their double-mindedness and unbelief. If they are wandering in circles in the wilderness or turning back in unbelief and fear, I want to do all that I can to scare the hell out of them—literally! I want to urge people forward, using fear of falling from grace as a motivator when necessary. No one has ever stated this better than the author of the book of Hebrews. Using the story of what happened at Kadesh-barnea as his text, he wrote strong words to Christian believers, warning them of the danger of falling from grace:

> Take care, brothers, lest there be in any of you an evil, unbelieving heart, leading you to fall away from the living God. But exhort one another every day, as long as it is called "today," that none of you may be hardened by the deceitfulness of sin. For we have come to share in Christ, if

indeed we hold our original confidence firm to the end. As it is said,

"Today, if you hear his voice, do not harden your hearts as in the rebellion."

For who were those who heard and yet rebelled? Was it not all those who left Egypt led by Moses? And with whom was he provoked for forty years? Was it not with those who sinned, whose bodies fell in the wilderness? And to whom did he swear that they would not enter his rest, but to those who were disobedient? So we see that they were unable to enter because of unbelief.

Therefore, while the promise of entering his rest still stands, let us fear lest any of you should seem to have failed to reach it. . . . For if Joshua had given them rest, God would not have spoken of another day later on. So then, there remains a Sabbath rest for the people of God, for whoever has entered God's rest has also rested from his works as God did from his. Let us therefore strive to enter that rest, so that no one may fall by the same sort of disobedience. (Hebrews 3:12–19, 4:1, 8–11)

The author of Hebrews makes it clear that what happened at Kadesh-barnea is not just history. It has a gospel application for all those who have embarked on the journey to spiritual wholeness. The promise is real, but so is the warning. What happened to them could happen to you. Therefore, today, if *you* hear his voice, do not turn back in unbelief.

14
The Land of In-Between
(Numbers 15–36)

"How foolish can you be? After starting your new lives in the Spirit, why are you now trying to become perfect by your own human effort?" (Galatians 3:3 NLT)

After the rebellion at Kadesh-barnea, the remainder of the book of Numbers (Chapters 15–36) recounts the long, sad saga of thirty-eight years of aimless wandering in the desert. These were the wasted years, notable in large part for their tedious boredom and inconsequentiality. The English title "Numbers" comes from the two censuses that are included in the book, but the primary emphasis in this fourth book of the Pentateuch is not so much on numbering the population as it is on describing the meandering journey of a people who had lost their way. The Hebrew title of the book better captures what the narrative is really all about: "In the Wilderness."

Tragically, like the Hebrews of long ago, many Christians today spend their lives walking in circles in a barren land. They have enough faith to get out of Egypt but don't seem to have the faith needed to cross over into the land of victory, abundance, and rest. For the most part, their spiritual lives are unfruitful and marked by mediocrity.

For the people of God who started on the original journey to spiritual wholeness from Egypt to Canaan, Numbers 15–36 highlights the most notable events that occurred during this thirty-eight-year period. For the Christian, these stories are of more than historical interest. They typify and illustrate the kinds of experiences followers of Christ may expect to encounter as they walk their own journey to spiritual wholeness. This chapter touches on only a few highlights from these years in the land of in-between.

An Important Lesson to Learn

Discerning a clear structure for the book of Numbers is not easy. Rules and regulations seem to be inserted almost randomly into the text. However, the placement of Chapter 15 seems intended to teach a very important lesson for travelers on the journey to spiritual wholeness.

After the tragedy at Kadesh-barnea, God's people needed to pause and think deeply about sin. Most importantly, they needed to understand that, though all sin is serious, not all sins are equal. Some sins are far worse than others.[1]

Some sins are *unintentional*. Whether committed by the congregation as a corporate whole or by an individual, these are mistakes of judgment, unintended wrongs and errors made because of ignorance. These misdeeds are indeed sins and without atonement they can bring judgment and tragic consequences. However, their unintentionality means that, once recognized as a violation of God's law, the sinner responds with an immediate effort to rectify the wrong (e.g., confession, apology, correction, restitution, etc.). Typically, the issue is handled quickly and easily. Moses stated the matter in these terms:

> But if you sin unintentionally [by mistake], and do not observe all these commandments that the LORD has spoken . . . then if it was done unintentionally without the knowledge of the congregation, all the congregation shall offer one bull from the herd for a burnt offering, a pleasing aroma to the LORD . . . . And the priest shall make atonement for all the congregation of the people of Israel,

---

1   The Roman Catholic Church distinguishes between mortal and venial sins. Though the practical application of this teaching has been greatly abused, the attempt to recognize that all sins are not equal has biblical support.

and they shall be forgiven, because it was a mistake. . . .
(Numbers 15:22–25)

What happened at Kadesh-barnea, however, was no mistake. The refusal to cross over into Canaan was a willful and intentional decision to say "No" to a clear command from God. This kind of sin demanded a different approach in seeking forgiveness and making atonement. God wanted his people to understand that this kind of "high-handed" sin falls into a different category.

> But the person who does anything with a high hand, whether he is native or a sojourner, reviles the LORD, and that person shall be cut off from among his people. Because he has despised the word of the LORD and has broken his commandment, that person shall be utterly cut off; his iniquity shall be on him. (Numbers 15:30–31)

High-handed sins refer to those actions and attitudes that are brazen, willful, and premeditated. The sinner knows very well that such actions are wrong and yet, like a rebellious teenager, does them anyway. The text explains that this type of sin "reviles the LORD" and "despises" his Word. In effect, these sinners are shaking their fists at God in defiance. They know what God requires and have made a willful choice not to do it. The larger context of Scripture indicates that this sin also can be forgiven, but the depth of the sin requires a parallel depth of confession and repentance. Without true contrition for one's blasphemous, rebellious spirit, God wants his people to know that high-handed sinners will be "utterly cut off." Without a sacrificial lamb to bear the penalty for sin, the rebel will bear his own sin— forever: "His iniquity shall be on him" (Nm 15:31).

On the journey to spiritual wholeness, it is so important to understand that not all sins are equal. All cancer is serious and potentially deadly, but some cancers are more dangerous than others. In a similar way, all sin is serious and needs atonement, but some sins are deadlier than others. We must learn to discern the difference in these two types of sin. Our very salvation depends on it!

Life in the Land of In-Between

Four incidents during this part of the Hebrews' journey serve as warnings for four different types of temptation that come to those struggling to make sense of the land of in-between:

- Korah's rebellion—the issue of submitting to spiritual authority (see Nm 16:1–14).
- The bronze serpent—the issue of grumbling about one's circumstances (see Nm 21:4–9).
- Baal worship at Peor—the issue of sexual immorality (see Nm 25:1–3).
- Settling in the land of Gilead—the almost Christian (see Nm 32).

Korah's Rebellion: Spiritual Authority

The first temptation recorded in this portion of Scripture relates to spiritual authority. Every traveler on the journey to spiritual wholeness must learn how to submit to God-ordained authority.

> **How do we determine who has rightful spiritual authority over the people of God?**

Refusing to submit to the right leader or choosing to submit to the wrong leader are both recipes for disaster. How can one learn to discern the difference between those who are called by God to lead and those who are self-appointed pretenders? The sad story of Korah's rebellion helps us answer this question.

Now Korah . . . and Dathan and Abiram . . . took men. And they rose up before Moses, with a number of the people of Israel, 250 chiefs of the congregation, chosen from the assembly, well-known men. They assembled themselves together against Moses and against Aaron and said to them, "You have gone too far! For all in the congregation are holy, every one of them, and the LORD is among them. Why then do you exalt yourselves above the assembly of the LORD?" When Moses heard it, he fell on his face, and he said to Korah and all his company, "In the morning the LORD will

show who is his, and who is holy, and will bring him near to
him. The one whom he chooses he will bring near to him.
Do this: take censers, Korah and all his company; put fire in
them and put incense on them before the LORD tomorrow,
and the man whom the LORD chooses shall be the holy one.
You have gone too far, sons of Levi! . . . Therefore it is against
the LORD that you and all your company have gathered
together. What is Aaron that you grumble against him?"
(Numbers 16:1–7, 11)

Korah and his supporters thought that Moses and Aaron had
"gone too far" (Nm 16:3). In their eyes, Moses and Aaron were nothing
more than self-appointed tyrants who thought they were holier than
everyone else. They also were quick to point out that Moses and
Aaron had failed to deliver on their promises (see Nm 16:12–14). Such
perceived short-comings in leadership were Korah's excuse for leading
an insurrection.

How *do* we determine who has rightful spiritual authority over the
people of God? This is a question of great importance on the journey to
spiritual wholeness. A wrong answer keeps one in the desert forever. A
right answer leads to one's God-ordained inheritance.

Many among the Hebrews that day believed that Korah was right
and should be followed as a legitimate leader. The situation reached
such a level of crisis that the entire mission of God once again was
placed in jeopardy. This text is written so we never ever forget what
happens to those who follow the wrong spiritual leader. Korah was
the one who had "gone too far" (Nm 16:7). In challenging the spiritual
authority of Moses, he and his followers were in open rebellion against
God himself. This was no unintentional sin. This was no mistake. This
was shaking one's fist at God in a brazen refusal to submit to his will.
God's response to Korah's high-handed rebellion was quick, firm, and
terrifying:

And Moses said, "Hereby you shall know that the LORD has
sent me to do all these works, and that it has not been of
my own accord. If these men die as all men die, or if they
are visited by the fate of all mankind, then the LORD has not
sent me. But if the LORD creates something new, and the

ground opens its mouth and swallows them up with all that belongs to them, and they go down alive into Sheol, then you shall know that these men have despised the LORD." And as soon as he had finished speaking all these words, the ground under them split apart. And the earth opened its mouth and swallowed them up, with their households and all the people who belonged to Korah and all their goods. So they and all that belonged to them went down alive into Sheol, and the earth closed over them, and they perished from the midst of the assembly. And all Israel who were around them fled at their cry, for they said, "Lest the earth swallow us up!" And fire came out from the LORD and consumed the 250 men offering the incense. (Numbers 16:28–35)

For those traveling on the journey to spiritual wholeness, the lesson is clear: Be discerning in your choice of spiritual leadership. Trust only those who are placed in authority by God himself. Those who are self-appointed will be judged severely, as will those who follow them. The writer of the book of Hebrews speaks clearly about the importance of a divine call to spiritual leadership: "No one takes this honor for himself, but only when called by God, just as Aaron was" (Heb 5:4).

> " God's remedy for the grumpies, therefore, was something that could be applied quickly and easily: look and live.

The Bronze Serpent: A Cure for Grumbling

The story of the bronze serpent on a pole reminds us of another temptation that often comes to those on the journey to spiritual wholeness who find themselves in the land of in-between: grumbling. In previous chapters, we already have seen the importance of this recurring theme in the desert wanderings, but here we see not only the problem but also the ultimate solution.

From Mount Hor they set out by the way to the Red Sea, to go around the land of Edom. And the people became impatient on the way. And the people spoke against God and against Moses, "Why have you brought us up out of Egypt to die in the wilderness? For there is no food and no water, and we loathe this worthless food." Then the LORD sent fiery serpents among the people, and they bit the people, so that many people of Israel died. And the people came to Moses and said, "We have sinned, for we have spoken against the LORD and against you. Pray to the LORD, that he take away the serpents from us." So Moses prayed for the people. And the LORD said to Moses, "Make a fiery serpent and set it on a pole, and everyone who is bitten, when he sees it, shall live." So Moses made a bronze serpent and set it on a pole. And if a serpent bit anyone, he would look at the bronze serpent and live. (Numbers 21:4–9)

This was not the first time the people had grumbled and complained about their circumstances. This time, however, God seemed intent upon bringing a final and definitive cure. He sent poisonous snakes to cure his people of the grumpies. Then, he told Moses to make a bronze serpent and set it on a pole. The cure for the snake that bit them was the snake that healed them. Amazingly, no magic formulas, expensive fees, or religious liturgies were required. Healing came freely to all who simply would look in faith to the bronze snake on the pole.

Though complaining about their circumstances was obviously a serious offense, it is doubtful that these grumblers were guilty of a high-handed sin. Belly-aching is typically something we do unintentionally when frustrations reach a boiling point. To grumble against God is clearly wrong and a whiny spirit can keep one in the desert for a long time, but this kind of sin is not in the category of willful blasphemy and rebellious unbelief. In fact, when confronted, the people were quick to confess, "We have sinned" (Nm 21:7). God's remedy for the grumpies, therefore, was something that could be applied quickly and easily: look and live.

Admittedly, the snake on the pole was a strange way to deal with a murmuring spirit. The New Testament sheds additional light on this story, helping us to more fully understand the lesson it teaches. Jesus himself spoke about this incident, indicating that the snake on the pole was an allusion to himself and to the mission he was to accomplish. In a conversation with a Pharisee named Nicodemus, who seemed to be stuck doing laps in the wilderness, Jesus gave one of the most important statements on salvation in the entire Bible:

> And as Moses lifted up the serpent in the wilderness, so must the Son of Man be lifted up, that whoever believes in him may have eternal life. For God so loved the world, that he gave his only Son, that whoever believes in him should not perish but have eternal life. (John 3:14–16)

Basing his remarks on the story of the snake on the pole, Jesus gave Nicodemus the essential core of what it means to be a child of God, what it means to be saved. Salvation is:

- Initiated by God, not man. We cannot save ourselves.
- Motivated by love. God loves us more than we can ever imagine.
- Grounded in the death of God's own Son, lifted up (on a cross) for the poison of sin that has infected us all.
- Appropriated through faith: look and live.
- Available for the whole world. No one is excluded from the invitation.

Perhaps the most important thing to remember about the snake on the pole is that this healing for the poison of sin was offered to those who *already* were redeemed. The invitation to look and live was offered to those who already were engaged in the journey to spiritual wholeness, making their way from Egyptian bondage to the Land of Promise. The sin problem is not just an issue for pagans and unbelievers. It is a recurring problem in the life of the redeemed. The story reminds every traveler on the journey to spiritual wholeness of the problem of sin's poison and the promise of sin's cure: look and live!

Baal Worship: Sexual Immorality

A third temptation that frequently comes to those journeying through the land of in-between is sexual immorality. The story of what happened with the Moabite women at Peor is one that God hoped his people would never forget.

> While Israel lived in Shittim, the people began to whore with the daughters of Moab. These invited the people to the sacrifices of their gods, and the people ate and bowed down to their gods. So Israel yoked himself to Baal of Peor. And the anger of the Lord was kindled against Israel. (Numbers 25:1–3)

The most glaring truth that jumps off the page in this tragic story is the linkage between idolatry and immorality. The brief account does not make clear whether the worship of Baal led the Hebrews into sexual immorality or whether the sexual immorality with the Moabite women led the Hebrews to worship Baal. Which comes first: the chicken or the egg? Does bad theology result in immoral behavior or does immoral behavior result in bad theology? This story may not give a definitive answer to the question, but it does remind us that the two sins (immorality and idolatry) usually come together.

Earlier, the Hebrews had sought to worship their own God in the form of a bull (see Ex 32), but in this incident at Peor it seems they were worshiping Baal himself, typically represented in the form of a bull. This was a serious sin. Worshiping other gods was a capital offense in Israel. Likely, it was the enticements of the Moabite women who invited the Hebrew men to join them in their carnal festivals that led the people of God into both pagan worship and sexual perversions. In the ancient Near East, the worship of Baal, a fertility god, was often a full-blown orgy involving food, drink, dancing, and sex. While God's intent for his people was holiness, the worship of Baal had another outcome entirely.

Thankfully, there were a few in Israel who had the spiritual discernment and the moral courage to realize what was happening and to do something about it. Phinehas is the real hero of this story. When a Jewish man named Zimri and his Midianite girlfriend named Cozbi brazenly engaged in immoral behavior "in the sight of Moses and the entire congregation" (Nm 25:6), Phinehas drove his spear through them both! This action both stopped the plague of judgment that already had killed 24,000 people and brought a strong word of approval from God himself:

> And the LORD said to Moses, "Phinehas the son of Eleazar, son of Aaron the priest, has turned back my wrath from the people of Israel, in that he was jealous with my jealousy among them, so that I did not consume the people of Israel in my jealousy. Therefore say, 'Behold, I give to him my covenant of peace, and it shall be to him and to his descendants after him the covenant of a perpetual priesthood, because he was jealous for his God and made atonement for the people of Israel.'" (Numbers 25:10–13)

Over a thousand years later, writing to the church in Corinth, a city famous for its sexual immorality and idol worship, Paul used this incident from Numbers 25 to warn a congregation of new believers about the dangers of sexual temptation:

> **Sexual immorality has been the ruin of many as they have sought to find their way through the land of in-between.**

> We must not indulge in sexual immorality as some of them did, and twenty-three thousand fell in a single day. . . . Now these things happened to them as an example, but they were written down for our instruction, on whom the end of the ages has come. Therefore let anyone who thinks that he stands take heed lest he fall. (1 Corinthians 10:8–12)

Sexual immorality has been the ruin of many as they have sought to find their way through the land of in-between. The Bible tells how sexual sin caused the downfall of the strongest man (Samson), the wisest man (Solomon), and the godliest man (David). Reader beware: No one is immune from these kinds of temptations! Both the Old and the New Testaments are full of warnings about the danger of being seduced by the carnal pleasures of this world. Whether the lure comes through sexual sin or through bad theology, travelers on the journey to spiritual wholeness must be both discerning and courageous. As Paul warned of the dangers, however, he also spoke of the glorious promise God gives to those who seek his help when temptation comes:

> No temptation has overtaken you that is not common to man. God is faithful, and he will not let you be tempted beyond your ability, but with the temptation he will also provide the way of escape, that you may be able to endure it. (1 Corinthians 10:13)

The Land of Gilead: the Almost Christian

Perhaps the most shocking story of all comes toward the end of the book of Numbers when we learn of three tribes of Israel who decided to make the land of in-between their permanent home. After traveling for forty years toward their inheritance, Reuben, Gad, and the half-tribe of Manasseh asked if they could make their home in Gilead, on the *eastern* shore of the Jordan River:

> Now the people of Reuben and the people of Gad had a very great number of livestock. And they saw the land of Jazer and the land of Gilead, and behold, the place was a place for livestock. So the people of Gad and the people of Reuben came and said to Moses and to Eleazar the priest and to the chiefs of the congregation . . . . "If we have found favor in your sight, let this land be given to your servants for a possession. Do not take us across the Jordan." (Numbers 32:1–2, 5)

The request to settle down permanently *outside* of Canaan is staggering. These people had traveled for decades, dreaming of the inheritance that God had prepared for them. After coming so far and traveling for so long, when they were on the very borders of Canaan, they decided to stop short of their destination. It is one thing to miss the Land of Promise because of battles, obstacles, failures, and sin. It is another to fall short of Canaan because of a willful, conscious choice to settle for something less than God intends!

The surface explanation given in Numbers 32 for such a shocking decision is simply that Gilead was a good place to raise livestock: "The land [Gilead] is a land for livestock, and your servants have livestock" (Nm 32:4). What could be more rational and self-evident than that? There is always a logic to sin and disobedience. People who choose to stop short of God's best always think they have a good reason for making such a bad decision.

These tribes also believed their decision would not have negative implications for anyone else. In fact, they made a solemn promise that, after unpacking their luggage in the land of in-between, the men would cross the Jordan with the other nine tribes and help fight the battles necessary so that their kinsmen could obtain their inheritance in Canaan:

> We will build sheepfolds here [in Gilead] for our livestock,
> and cities for our little ones, but we will take up arms, ready
> to go before the people of Israel, until we have brought them
> to their place. . . . We will not return to our homes until each
> of the people of Israel has gained his inheritance. For we will
> not inherit with them on the other side of the Jordan and
> beyond, because our inheritance has come to us on this side
> of the Jordan to the east. (Numbers 32:16–19)

The people were tired and weary. They had been traveling for forty long years, and they'd grown accustomed to the land of in-between. It felt like home. They thought settling *close* to the Land of Promise was enough. Though they could see their inheritance from Gilead and perhaps even could smell the fruit, they were content with being *almost* there. Like these three tribes, many Christians think it is enough to give God ninety-eight percent obedience. God will still love us, right?

Remembering what had happened at Kadesh-barnea some thirty-eight years earlier, Moses equated their stopping short of their inheritance as a sign of high-handed rebellious apostasy. His initial response was harsh:

> Why will you discourage the heart of the people of Israel
> from going over into the land that the LORD has given them?
> Your fathers did this, when I sent them from Kadesh-barnea

to see the land. For when they went up to the Valley of Eshcol and saw the land, they discouraged the heart of the people of Israel from going into the land that the LORD had given them. . . . And behold, you have risen in your fathers' place, a brood of sinful men, to increase still more the fierce anger of the LORD against Israel! For if you turn away from following him, he will again abandon them in the wilderness, and you will destroy all this people." (Numbers 32:7–9, 14–15)

The three tribes, however, were persistent. They did not give up in their demand to settle east of the Jordan River. Amazingly, God reluctantly gave them what they wanted. He allowed them to settle for a future he never intended them to have, and they fell short of the glory of God. Years later, when enemies attack, these tribes were the first to be destroyed and lost to history.

John Wesley preached a famous sermon in 1741 at Oxford University entitled "The Almost Christian." His text was Acts 26:28 where King Agrippa says to Paul, "You almost persuade me to become a Christian" (NKJV). Wesley explained that an "almost Christian" is someone who has the outward form of godliness. He doesn't take God's name in vain, commit adultery, or live in debauchery. He attends church and uses the means of grace. Sharing his own testimony, Wesley admitted that for many years he, too, was an "almost Christian."

Coming to the heart of his message, Wesley told the faculty and students of Oxford what it means to be an "altogether Christian": to love God with all your heart, soul, mind, and strength, to love your neighbor as yourself, and to live by faith—not a mere intellectual acceptance of certain doctrines but a faith that brings repentance and obedience. He concluded his sermon with these strong words:

The God and Father of our Lord Jesus Christ, who now stands in the midst of us, knows that if any man die without this faith and this love, good it were for him that he had never been born. Awake, then, you who sleep, and call upon your God . . . . Let no man persuade you by vain words to rest short of this prize of your high calling . . . . May we all thus experience what it is to be, not almost only; but altogether Christian. . . .

Many Christians today are essentially doing laps in the wilderness, a tragic existence that God never intended anyone to live. Whether they are following the wrong spiritual leader—or perhaps not following the right one—grumbling about their circumstances, ensnared by sexual immorality, or settling for being almost in the center of God's will, there is still hope for them. It is not too late. When asked, God will help them to deal with what is threatening to keep them in the land of in-between forever. Then, they, too, can enter into the joy of their inheritance.

15
The Heart of the Matter
(Deuteronomy)

"Love is the fulfilling of the law." (Romans 13:10)

After a short historical introduction, the book of Deuteronomy opens with words from God that must have sounded like music in the ears of the weary travelers: "You have been traveling around this mountain country long enough. Turn northward" (Dt 2:2). The time had come for them to cease walking in circles, to cross over into the Land of Promise, and to possess their inheritance.

The book of Deuteronomy (the word literally means, "second law") describes the renewal of the covenant God made with his people at Mount Sinai almost forty years earlier. God gave Israel a second chance to enter the land of their inheritance. Set in the Plains of Moab, on the eastern shore of the Jordan River, the book recounts God's final instructions to his people as they prepared to enter their inheritance. They had arrived at the border of Canaan. They could see the Land of Promise just across the river. This was the moment they had been waiting for.

Before they could cross over and begin the conquest, however, Moses urged the people to pause and reflect on where they'd been and where they were going. He wanted to share a few things from his heart with the congregation he had pastored for forty years. Moses was 120 years old, and he knew he was about to die and would not enter the Land of Promise himself. This was his final chance to speak his mind and share his heart with the people he loved so dearly.

Last words are important. When someone is facing death, their final thoughts, when spoken, have great significance. This is especially true when the one saying goodbye has been a person of influence. The American patriot Nathan Hale, for example, just before he was hung by the British in 1776, famously said, "I only regret that I have but one life to give for my country." As he lay dying from wounds received during the battle of Trafalgar (1805), Admiral Nelson summed up his life with the words, "Thank God, I have done my duty." Those at the side of Mother Teresa as she breathed her last (1997) heard her say, "Jesus, I love you; Jesus, I love you."

The book of Deuteronomy contains the last words of Moses. It takes thirty-four chapters for Moses to express his final thoughts. Because he knew these people so well and because he knew God so intimately, Moses had a lot to say. In these amazing chapters, he reveals his deepest longings, greatest fears, and brightest hopes for his people.

Moses' final words are really a series of sermons. We can picture him, old and feeble, leaning on his staff as he

> **66 The choices they make today will have a profound influence on what they experience tomorrow.**

delivered his deepest thoughts about God, redemption, and the future. One way to understand the structure of Deuteronomy is to see three major sermons:

- Chapters 1–11 focus on *the past*. The key word is "remember." If God's people forget from where they have come and what they have learned and experienced on the journey to spiritual wholeness, they will surely fail when they cross the Jordan and enter the land of Canaan.
- Chapters 12–26 focus on *the present*. The key word is "obey." Though they are commanded to love the Lord with all their being, Moses explains that obedience will be the evidence of their love.

- Chapters 27–34 focus on *the future*. The key word is "choose." Moses' final words are a ringing call for God's redeemed people to choose life. He wants the people to understand that the choices they make today will have a profound influence on what they experience tomorrow.

Interestingly, the writers of the New Testament love the book of Deuteronomy and quote from it over eighty times. The book covers many themes and subjects: a rehearsal of history, a summation of the law, an exhortation to loving obedience and a warning of the dangers and temptations that lie ahead. Mostly, it summarizes the essence of God's purpose in redemption. Moses insists that the heart of the matter is the matter of the heart.

At the risk of oversimplification, Moses' final message can be organized around three questions:

1. *What does God really want?* Answering this question clarifies the purpose of salvation.
2. *What hinders me from doing what God really wants?* Answering this question diagnoses the fundamental human problem.
3. *Can God fix me so that I can do what he really wants?* Answering this question introduces us to what God's grace can do in a receptive human heart.

What Does God Really Want?

Moses had delivered some 613 different laws to the people of God. These commands related to all manner of human activity and religious observance. There were instructions for worship, property disputes, clothing, marriage, Sabbath observance, diet, ritual cleanliness, and much more. With so many laws covering so many different topics, it could be very confusing! Discerning which laws were primary and which were secondary was difficult. How easy it would be to major on minors and to minor on majors! As Moses prepared the people for his departure, he wanted to make sure that they fully understood the essential core of what God *really* wanted from his people. Perhaps his greatest fear was that they would become so obsessed with outward conformity to legal obligations of minor significance that they would miss the one thing God really wanted. His dying prayer was that the people would always keep the main thing the main thing.

Nowhere in all of Scripture is the main thing more clearly and succinctly stated than in the sixth chapter of Deuteronomy. These words express the most fundamental confession of the Jewish faith.[1] For Christians, it is noteworthy that Jesus quoted this passage when asked by a teacher of the law which commandment was the most important of all (see Mt 22:35–40).

> Hear, O Israel: The LORD our God, the LORD is one. You shall love the LORD your God with all your heart and with all your soul and with all your might. And these words that I command you today shall be on your heart. You shall teach them diligently to your children, and shall talk of them when you sit in your house, and when you walk by the way, and when you lie down, and when you rise. You shall bind them as a sign on your hand, and they shall be as frontlets between your eyes. You shall write them on the doorposts of your house and on your gates. (Deuteronomy 6:4–9)

" God wanted a relationship, not just religious performance.

Moses knew that the main thing was (and is) love, whole-hearted love. Though ritual sacrifice, ethical performance, and doctrinal precision all have their place, what God *really* wanted from his people was whole-hearted love. Obedience was important only as it was the natural overflow of love. God wanted a relationship, not just religious performance. Jesus understood this truth better than anyone who has ever lived. "If you love me, you will keep my commandments," he said

---

1   Called the Shema (from the first Hebrew word in the text: "Hear!"), these words are typically regarded as the centerpiece of Jewish doctrine and faith. They are meant to be recited daily.

in John 14:15. What does God really want? Whole-hearted love. The heart of the matter is the matter of the heart.

Moses knew how many different possible motivations there were that potentially influenced those walking the journey to spiritual wholeness. We share many of them still today:

- Fear: I don't want to end up in hell.
- Need: My marriage is a mess and my finances are in trouble. God, can you help?
- Guilt: I've done some really bad stuff and my conscience is killing me.
- Reward: I'd love to experience some of that milk and honey. If I follow God's path for my life, then I can be healthy, wealthy, and happy.
- Loneliness: I'm isolated and alone, but the folks at church seem so nice.

Though any of these motivations may be acceptable as a reason for *beginning* the journey, none will sustain us in a healthy manner for the long haul. As in marriage, the only thing that provides a solid foundation for the journey of life is whole-hearted love. On the Plains of Moab, after forty years of traveling together, God wanted to know: Israel, do you love me with all your heart? He was not asking about their performance but about their love.

It is interesting to note the final conversation that Jesus had with Peter in the Gospel of John. After living and walking together for three years through both joys and sorrows, victories and defeats, Jesus turned to ask Peter one final question:

> "Simon, son of John, do you love me more than these?" He said to him, "Yes, Lord; you know that I love you." He said to him, "Feed my lambs." He said to him a second time, "Simon, son of John, do you love me?" He said to him, "Yes, Lord; you know that I love you." He said to him, "Tend my sheep." He said to him the third time, "Simon, son of John, do you love me?" Peter was grieved because he said to him the third time, "Do you love me?" and he said to him, "Lord,

you know everything; you know that I love you." Jesus said to him, "Feed my sheep." . . . And after saying this he said to him, "Follow me." (John 21:15–17, 19)

This is what salvation is all about. This is the main thing. This is the purpose of redemption: whole-hearted love.

I'm reminded of a scene from the movie version of the musical *Fiddler on the Roof*. Tevia and Golda, an elderly Russian couple, watch as their daughters, one after another, fall in love and get married. Because theirs was an arranged marriage, romance and love had little to do with the union they made decades earlier. In fact, Tevia and Golda met face to face for the first time on their wedding day! Struggling to make sense of it all, Tevia looks at his wife and asks, "Golda, do you love me?" What follows is one of the most emotionally powerful scenes in the movie.

> Golda: With our daughters getting married, and this trouble in the town, you're upset. You're worn out. Go inside. Go lie down. Maybe it's indigestion.
>
> Tevia: Ah, no, Golda, I'm asking you a question. Do *you love me?*
>
> Golda: You're a fool, Tevia.
>
> Tevia: I know, but *do you love me?*
>
> Golda: Do I love you?
>
> Tevia: Well?
>
> Golda: For years I've washed your clothes, cooked your meals, cleaned your house, given you children, milked your cow. After all these years, why talk about love right now?
>
> Tevia: Golda, the first time I met you was on our wedding day. I was scared. I was shy. I was nervous.
>
> Golda: So was I.
>
> Tevia: But my father and my mother said we'd learn to love each other and now I'm asking: Golda, *do you love me?*
>
> Golda: I'm your wife.
>
> Tevia: I know, but *do you love me?*

Golda: (aside) Do I love him?... For years I've lived with him, fought with him, starved with him. For years my bed is his. If that's not love, what is?

Tevia: Then you love me?

Golda: I suppose I do.

Tevia: And I suppose I love you too. . . .

The analogy is imperfect, but God is something like Tevia. After years of living together with the people he had redeemed, there was something he really wanted to know: *Did they love him with whole-hearted love?*

When we realize that what God really wants is *not* our performance and obedience but our whole-hearted love, we typically have two equal, and opposite, reactions. On the one hand, we are overwhelmed with relief. What good news it is to learn that God is not a policeman in the sky, constantly measuring our performance! What freedom comes in the discovery that God does not demand perfect conformity to all his rules.

On the other hand, the realization that what God really wants is whole-hearted love causes us to shudder in terror. Suddenly, we are reminded of all the twisted lusts, divided loyalties, and misplaced affections that lurk deep within. We love God—we really do!—but we love other things as well. When we think of the true condition of the inner, hidden world of our hearts, we may agree with the words C. S. Lewis used to describe what he discovered when he first began to honestly look inside his heart: "And there I found what appalled me: a zoo of lusts, a bedlam of ambitions, a nursery of fears, a harem of fondled hatreds. My name was legion."[2]

An honest assessment of the true condition of our hearts leads to a sobering conclusion: The one thing God really wants is the one thing we really can't do! God wants perfect love from an undivided heart, but our hearts are sick, divided and tormented by the tyranny of self-interest. This leads to the second great question that Moses asked.

---

2   C. S. Lewis, *Surprised by Joy* (New York: Harcourt, 1955), 226.

What Hinders Me from Doing What God Really Wants?

As he said farewell to his congregation, Moses emphasized not only the fundamental purpose of salvation (whole-hearted love) but also the fundamental *problem*. Like a wise doctor dealing with a patient struggling to understand the nature of his disease, Moses knew that an accurate diagnosis was essential for finding a cure. Thus, Moses clarified the problem:

> And now, Israel, what does the LORD your God require of you, but to fear the LORD your God, to walk in all his ways, to love him, to serve the LORD your God with all your heart and with all your soul, and to keep the commandments and statutes of the LORD, which I am commanding you today for your good? Behold, to the LORD your God belong heaven and the heaven of heavens, the earth with all that is in it. Yet the LORD set his heart in love on your fathers and chose their offspring after them, you above all peoples, as you are this day. Circumcise therefore the foreskin of your heart, and be no longer stubborn. (Deuteronomy 10:12–16)

The reason we are unable to love God whole-heartedly is because we suffer from a form of heart disease. The words Moses used are interesting. He told the people that their hearts were "uncircumcised" and "stubborn" (Dt 10:16). The people of God knew all about circumcision of the body as the outward sign of their membership in the family of God, but this was the first time they learned of their need for a circumcision "of the foreskin of [their] heart." Moses was telling the redeemed people of God that whole-hearted love is possible only when there has been a surgical work of grace deep within. Such an operation makes the heart undivided and pure and addresses the "stubbornness" that remains even in the hearts of those who have been redeemed. The word "stubborn" is sometimes translated "stiff-necked," referring to an ox that resists the master while plowing a field, stiffening its neck in obstinate disobedience. When Moses described the heart as "stubborn," he was helping the redeemed to become aware of their willful refusal to submit to God's plan for their lives. The problem is not one of outward behavior but of inward attitude. In the hearts of those who have experienced redemption and have followed God on the journey to spiritual wholeness for years, there often remains an obstinate stubbornness deep inside where ego-centrism and selfish ambition compete with God for control. This kind of spiritual arteriosclerosis can keep people doing laps in the desert forever. On the Plains of Moab, *this* was the problem that Moses addressed.

Moses explained to the people that God's work of grace thus far in their lives had mainly dealt only with surface issues and behaviors. True, God's grace had been powerful enough to get them out of bondage and through the desert. Yet there was more to salvation than getting them out of Egypt. God intended to get Egypt out of them! Before entering the land of Canaan, Moses insisted that the people of God recognize that the appetites, attitudes, and ways of thinking that they learned in Egypt must cease to define and control their hearts. Until this heart disease was addressed and cured, the people would never escape the desert, cross the Jordan, and begin to possess the land of their inheritance.

Spiritual arteriosclerosis is serious. Indeed, left untreated, hardening of the heart is typically deadly! The only way to love God with whole-hearted devotion is to submit to heart surgery so that the inner division and impurity is finally and decisively cured.

A personal experience made the reality of heart disease very real for me. On May 17, 2015, I suffered a heart attack. With no previous history of heart disease, the attack was a complete surprise. The Lord helped me get to the Emergency Room in time so that a surgical procedure at midnight could insert a stent into a clogged artery, both saving my life and fixing the problem. Today, I'm healthy and strong, thank the Lord, but the experience taught me three important lessons about heart disease, both physical and spiritual.

First, heart disease typically happens to those who are older. I was sixty-two when I suffered my heart attack and had no symptoms prior to this that indicated there was a problem. In a similar manner, it was years after they began the journey that the Hebrews became aware of their heart disease. In the beginning, their youthful vigor and enthusiasm caused them to believe they were healthy and strong, able to handle everything that came their way. On the Plains of Moab, like a divine cardiologist, Moses helped them to look deep within at the true condition of their hearts. He wanted them to understand that an uncircumcised, stubborn heart would keep them wandering in the desert forever. They would have been incapable of understanding this lesson earlier in the journey.

Second, those who have heart disease typically don't know they have heart disease. In my case, on May 16, I felt fine. There were no symptoms that indicated something was wrong, which is precisely why heart disease is so serious! What is true physically is equally true spiritually. Those on the verge of a spiritual disaster often have no clue of the danger they are in. "I feel fine," they will tell you. It requires someone like Moses, someone trained and mature, to assess the true condition of our hearts and give us a spiritual EKG that reveals what is really going on inside.

 Those who have heart disease typically don't know they have heart disease.

Third, the person with heart disease cannot cure himself. Lying on the table in the emergency room, I knew the problem was much bigger than I was! Unless a trained doctor surgically went inside my heart to deal with the problem, I would probably die. So it is with spiritual arteriosclerosis. The problem can't be fixed by interventions that are self-administered. We need a Divine Cardiologist to cut us open and do what we can't do for ourselves.

This awareness of the need for circumcision of the heart leads naturally to the third and final question that Moses asked the people as he prepared to say goodbye.

CAN GOD FIX ME SO THAT I CAN DO WHAT GOD REALLY WANTS?

Moses' last words to the people of Israel reminded them that what God really wanted (whole-hearted love) was the one thing they really could not do. Their uncircumcised hearts would bring only ruin and death unless the problem could be fixed. This sets the stage for the climax of Moses' sermon. As he concluded, Moses made clear that God could do a work in the human heart to bring healing to the inner division and purity to the inner pollution so that God's people could love him with whole-hearted devotion:

> And the LORD your God will circumcise your heart and the heart of your offspring, so that you will love the LORD your God with all your heart and with all your soul, that you may live. (Deuteronomy 30:6)

The cure for heart disease is not some heightened form of behavior modification. The remedy is not to try harder. The amazing promise is that God himself wants to heal our wounded hearts! The salvation God offers will transform our very natures so that we can indeed love him with whole-hearted affection. Notice that this is something that God alone can do. We are not justified by grace and sanctified by works. God circumcises our hearts in the very same way that he delivered us out of Egypt: by grace through faith. The New Testament is equally emphatic on this important point:

> Now may the God of peace himself sanctify you completely, and may your whole spirit and soul and body be kept blameless at the coming of our Lord Jesus Christ. He who calls you is faithful; he will surely do it. (1 Thessalonians 5:23–24)

Those who have had their hearts circumcised by the transforming power of God's grace discover that they are able to keep God's law and do what he asks them to do:

> For this commandment that I command you today is not too hard for you, neither is it far off. . . . But the word is very near you. It is in your mouth and in your heart, so that you can do it. . . . I call heaven and earth to witness against you today, that I have set before you life and death, blessing and curse. Therefore choose life, that you and your offspring may live, loving the LORD your God, obeying his voice and holding fast to him, for he is your life and length of days, that you may dwell in the land that the LORD swore to your fathers, to Abraham, to Isaac, and to Jacob, to give them. (Deuteronomy 30:11, 14, 19–20)

THE UN-DRAGONNING OF EUSTACE CLARENCE SCRUBB

Sometimes an illustration helps to capture a doctrinal truth in a way that abstract teaching can't quite achieve. In *The Chronicles of Narnia*, C. S. Lewis paints an unforgettable picture of heart transformation that conveys many of the truths in this chapter. In *The Voyage of the Dawn Treader*, Lewis describes the transformation of an egotistical, self-centered, pompous brat named Eustace Clarence Scrubb. While visiting a deserted island, Eustace discovers a cave full of treasure. Wanting to hoard the wealth all for himself, his greed turns him into a dragon. This sets the stage for his life-changing encounter with the lion Aslan (the Christ-figure in the Narnia stories). Lewis' description of what happens next is a fitting conclusion to this chapter devoted to the subject of the circumcision of the heart. Eustace tells the story:

> Well, I looked up and saw the very last thing I expected: a huge lion coming slowly towards me. . . . I was terribly afraid of it. You may think that, being a dragon, I could have knocked any lion out easily enough. But it wasn't that kind of fear. I wasn't afraid of it eating me, I was just afraid of it—if you can understand. Well, it came close up to me and looked

straight into my eyes. And I shut my eyes tight. But that wasn't any good because it told me to follow it. . . .

At last we came to the top of a mountain I'd never seen before and on the top of this mountain there was a garden— trees and fruit and everything. In the middle of it there was a well.... The water was as clear as anything and I thought if I could get in there and bathe it would ease the pain in my leg. But the lion told me I must undress first.

I was just going to say that I couldn't undress because I hadn't any clothes on when I suddenly thought that dragons are snaky sort of things and snakes can cast their skins. Oh, of course, thought I, that's what the lion means. So I started scratching myself and my scales began coming off all over the place. And then I scratched a little deeper and instead of just scales coming off here and there, my whole skin started peeling off beautifully, like it does after an illness, or as if I was a banana. In a minute or two I just stepped out of it. I could see it lying there beside me, looking rather nasty. It was a most lovely feeling. So I started to go down into the well for my bathe.

But just as I was going to put my feet into the water I looked down and saw that they were all hard and rough and wrinkled and scaly just as they had been before. Oh, that's all right, said I, it only means I had another smaller suit on underneath the first one, and I'll have to get out of it too. So I scratched and tore again and this under skin peeled off beautifully and out I stepped and left it lying beside the other one and went down to the well for my bathe.

Well, exactly the same thing happened again. And I thought to myself, oh dear, how ever many skins have I got to take off? So I scratched away for the third time and got off a third skin, just like the two others, and stepped out of it. But as soon as I looked at myself in the water I knew it had been no good.

Then the lion said—but I don't know if it spoke—"You will have to let me undress you." I was afraid of his claws, I can tell you, but I was pretty nearly desperate now. So I just lay flat down on my back to let him do it.

The very first tear he made was so deep that I thought it had gone right into my heart. And when he began pulling the skin off, it hurt worse than anything I've ever felt. The only thing that made me able to bear it was just the pleasure of feeling the stuff peel off. You know—if you've ever picked the scab off a sore place. It hurts like billy-oh but it is such fun to see it coming away.

Well, he peeled the beastly stuff right off—just as I thought I'd done it myself the other three times, only they hadn't hurt—and there it was lying on the grass: only ever so much thicker, and darker, and more knobbly-looking than the others had been. And there was I as smooth and soft as a peeled switch and smaller than I had been. Then he caught hold of me—I didn't like that much for I was very tender underneath now that I'd no skin on—and threw me into the water. It smarted like anything but only for a moment. After that it became perfectly delicious and as soon as I started swimming and splashing I found that all the pain had gone from my arm. And then I saw why. I'd turned into a boy again. . . .

"I think you've seen Aslan," said Edmund.

Moving to the end of the chapter, the narrator takes up the story and concludes with these words:

> 66 No one gets out of the desert and into the land of victory without heart surgery.

It would be nice, and fairly nearly true, to say that "from that time forth Eustace was a different boy." To be strictly accurate, he began to be a different boy. He had relapses. There were still many days when he could be very tiresome. But most of those I shall not notice. The cure had begun.[3]

No one gets out of the desert and into the land of victory without heart surgery. What God really wants (whole-hearted love) is the one thing we cannot do—until we cease striving and let him do it. The Divine Cardiologist wants to circumcise our hearts. We must let him.

3   C. S. Lewis, *The Chronicles of Narnia: The Voyage of the Dawn Treader (Book Five)* (New York: HarperCollins, 1952), 106–112.

ICU (I See You)

By Stan Key

I thought that I was doing fine
And in control of what was mine
When suddenly, I'm on my back
Suffering from a heart attack.

The monitor above my bed
Puts fear and panic in my head.
They tell me I will lose my life
If I refuse the surgeon's knife.

"Lord, I'm almost in despair
Lying in Intensive Care;
The sickness of my heart is such
I need more than human touch!"

The Great Physician took my hand
And spoke so I could understand;
"Your options here are only two:
But the choice remains with you.

If the fear of my incision
Leads you to the wrong decision
You may spare yourself some pain
Yet your sickness will remain.

But if you submit to me
Trusting my ability,
You will find the operation
Causes inward transformation!"

As he spoke, his loving Voice
Gave me power to make the choice:
"Doctor, please! I'm in your care,
Cut me open, strip me bare."

16
Crossing Jordan
(Joshua 1–5)

"You have not passed this way before." (Joshua 3:4)

In the year 40 BC, Julius Caesar led his army across a river in northeastern Italy named the Rubicon. Though the river itself was small, its significance rested in the fact that it marked the northern boundary of what was then known as Italy, the territory under the jurisdiction of Rome. For armed forces to enter these lands without a clear invitation was a capital offense. To cross the Rubicon was tantamount to an attack upon Rome, an armed invasion. Julius Caesar clearly understood the symbolic significance of what he was doing, as did the leaders in Rome. Crossing the Rubicon was a declaration of war. Once across, nothing would ever be the same again. The die was cast. The phrase "crossing the Rubicon" has thus come to refer to that moment in time when a person commits himself irrevocably to a certain course of action. The point of no return has been reached. From this moment forward, there is no turning back.

When the people of God finally reached the banks of the Jordan River, they faced a moment of eternal significance. Crossing over to the other side meant leaving the desert and the years of spiritual mediocrity and entering an unknown land filled with danger and adventure. Once across the Jordan, they could never turn back. From this point forward, they would either possess their inheritance—or die trying.

Just as crossing the Red Sea at the beginning of the Exodus was a moment of critical importance that would be celebrated for centuries to come, so too the crossing of the Jordan River marked a moment that would be remembered forever in the history of Israel. However, before we look at the events of that momentous day, let's pause for a short lesson in theology.

TWO STAGES OF THE CHRISTIAN LIFE

Even a cursory look at the map of the Exodus introduces us to the importance of two bodies of water. The Red Sea marks the border between Egypt and the desert. Similarly, the Jordan River defines the boundary between the desert and Canaan. Crossing the Red Sea describes that crisis moment when Israel was once and for all redeemed from bondage and set free to become all that God intended her to be. Although their redemption was a free gift of grace, it required a step of faith to make it a reality. In a similar way, crossing the Jordan River marked another important passage in the life of the redeemed. Getting across

> **He brought us out that he might bring us in.**

this body of water marked a second crisis experience for the people of God, and a miracle of grace was necessary to make the passage possible. At the Jordan River, the people once again had to step out in faith if they were to leave the desert and begin to possess their inheritance in the Land of Promise.

These crossings mark two similar and yet distinct moments in the journey to spiritual wholeness. The first crisis got the people out of bondage. The Exodus journey reminds us that, though they were fully redeemed and completely free, they were not yet in their promised inheritance. They were in the Sinai Peninsula, not Canaan. A second crisis moment was needed to get the people of God out of the desert and into the abundance of life God had prepared for them in the Land of Promise. Moses spoke of these two stages of the journey to spiritual wholeness in these terms:

> When your son asks you in time to come, "What is the meaning of the testimonies and the statutes and the rules that the LORD our God has commanded you?" then you shall say to your son, "We were Pharaoh's slaves in Egypt. And the LORD brought us out of Egypt with a mighty hand. And the LORD showed signs and wonders, great and grievous, against Egypt and against Pharaoh and all his household, before our eyes. And *he brought us out* from there, *that he might bring us in* and give us the land that he swore to give to our fathers." (Deuteronomy 6:20–23, emphasis added)

He brought us out that he might bring us in. Getting out of Egypt is the first challenge of the journey. Getting in to Canaan is the second. The map has a pedagogical value that is impossible to miss. God's purpose in salvation is to get us:

- Out of bondage and into freedom.
- Out of a life of barrenness and into a life of fruitfulness.
- Out of defeat and into victory.
- Out of a diet of leaks and onions and into a diet of milk and honey.
- Out a life of sin and into a life of holiness.

Getting out demands one set of spiritual realities. *Getting in* demands another. What could be clearer than this?[1]

Many have misunderstood God's purposes in redemption because they have been led to believe that Canaan is a metaphor of heaven and the Jordan River is a picture of death. In other words, one must *die* to possess the inheritance God has prepared for you. Many gospel songs and choruses employ this imagery. For example, William

---

[1] The New Testament has its own way of talking about the "two stages" of the Christian life. In broad terms, it presents the work Jesus did on the cross and in rising from the dead as the work that sets us free from the bondage to sin. Then the gift of the Spirit at Pentecost marks that moment when God's redeemed people are purified and empowered for service.

Williams writes these words in his great hymn, *Guide Me, O Thou Great Jehovah*:

When I tread the verge of Jordan,
Bid my anxious fears subside:
Death of death, and hell's destruction,
Land me safe on Canaan's side.

Another writer who pictures Canaan as heaven is Samuel Stennett. In his old gospel song, *On Jordan's Story Banks I Stand*, we read these words:

No chilling winds nor poisonous breath
Can reach that healthful shore;
Sickness, sorrow, pain and death,
Are felt and feared no more.

Though many have been blessed and inspired by songs such as these, it is difficult to find support for such an understanding in the pages of Holy Scripture. There is simply no solid biblical evidence that the Jordan River is intended to be understood as a picture of death. Rather, the thrust of Scripture is to view Canaan as a picture of the abundant life that God intends for all the redeemed now, in this life. Crossing the Jordan River is the crisis of faith that makes entrance into such a reality possible. Both Paul (see 1 Cor 10:1–13) and the author of Hebrews (see Heb 3–4) made use of the map of the Exodus to preach the gospel of Jesus Christ. When they urged believers to push beyond the desert of spiritual mediocrity and to press on to the promised rest God has in store, it seems clear they were *not* talking about heaven. Rather, they were exhorting travelers on the journey to spiritual wholeness to step forward by faith and possess the fullness of God's blessing now: victory over sin, fruitfulness, and rest.

For those traveling the journey to spiritual wholeness, how we understand Canaan has weighty implications. When one's mental map indicates that the Jordan River represents death, then one begins to assume that victorious living is possible only *after* we die. The desert then becomes normative for defining the Christian life. Living in sin and spiritual defeat, bearing little or no fruit, wandering aimlessly in circles, experiencing double-mindedness and spiritual mediocrity are all we should ever really expect in this life. When we die, God will finally fix our problems and heal our wounds. In the meantime, we just trudge the weary road in this land of in-between. Hopefully, we can experience a measure of growth toward maturity, but we can never really expect to live a life of victory here in this world.

When the desert becomes normative, Romans 7 becomes the basic text to define the journey to spiritual wholeness:

> For I know that nothing good dwells in me, that is, in my flesh. For I have the desire to do what is right, but not the ability to carry it out. For I do not do the good I want, but the evil I do not want is what I keep on doing. . . . Wretched man that I am! . . . (Romans 7:18–19, 24)

Many in the church today apparently believe that what Paul describes in Romans 7 is as good as it gets. Dr. Alexander Whyte, a famous Scottish Presbyterian preacher of the nineteenth century, famously thundered at his Edinburgh congregation, "You'll never get out of the seventh of Romans while I'm your minister."[2]

Rediscovering the map of the Exodus and learning how to preach the map may well be one of the most important things a pastor can do to help his congregation experience the fullness of salvation that Jesus died to make possible. God is raising up fresh voices to help Christians in this generation see the great promise of God contained in the map of salvation. For example, Dallas Willard speaks of the journey to spiritual wholeness in his book, *Renovation of the Heart:*

> The work of spiritual formation in Christlikeness is the work of claiming the land of milk and honey in which we are, individually and collectively, to dwell with God. The old hymn rings out:
>
> *On Jordan's stormy banks I stand*
> *And cast a wistful eye*

<hr>

2   Quoted in J. I. Packer's book *A Quest for Godliness* (Wheaton: Crossway, 2010), 197f.

> *To Canaan's fair and happy land,*
> *Where my possessions lie.*

> But the real Jordan, the spiritual "Jordan," is not physical
> death, as has usually been supposed. We need not and must
> not wait until we die to live in the land of milk and honey;
> and if we will only move to that land now, the passage in
> physical death will be but one more day in the endless life we
> have long since begun.[3]

No one enters the abundant life until they have a theology that proclaims such a reality is possible here, now, in this life! When the Jordan River is seen as a metaphor of death, then victorious living becomes possible only after we die! This book is written to propose a better, more biblical way to think—and live.

GETTING FROM HERE TO THERE

So, what's involved in crossing the spiritual Jordan? What does it take to get out of the desert of spiritual mediocrity and into the abundance of life that God wants us to experience? How do we get from where we are to where we ought to be? Joshua 1–5 suggests there are at least five things that are essential:

1. Determine who you are going to follow.
2. Clarify the objective.
3. Prepare for the transition.
4. Put your feet in the water.
5. Explain to your children what you have done.

Determine Who You Are Going to Follow

No one reaches their God-ordained potential if they are following the wrong leader. To reach our destination on the journey to spiritual wholeness we must learn to be very selective about the voices we heed and the books that we read. Often it takes one type of leadership to get us out of Egypt and another type to get us in to Canaan. Determining

---

3   Dallas Willard, *Renovation of the Heart* (Colorado Springs: Navpress, 2002), 43.

who we will trust to guide us in our spiritual journey is one of the most important questions in all of life. Our eternal destiny hangs in the balance.

The book of Joshua begins by making it clear that Joshua was God's designated choice to lead the people into their promised inheritance:

> After the death of Moses the servant of the LORD, the LORD said to Joshua the son of Nun, Moses' assistant, "Moses my servant is dead. Now therefore arise, go over this Jordan, you and all this people, into the land that I am giving to them, to the people of Israel. . . . Just as I was with Moses, so I will be with you. I will not leave you or forsake you. Be strong and courageous, for you shall cause this people to inherit the land that I swore to their fathers to give them. Only be strong and very courageous, being careful to do according to all the law that Moses my servant commanded you. Do not turn from it to the right hand or to the left, that you may have good success wherever you go." (Joshua 1:1–2, 5–7)

Reaching the land of milk and honey requires a God-called, Spirit-anointed, biblically-grounded guide. To follow the wrong leader is a recipe for disaster. It is important to remember that the name Joshua means "Yahweh is salvation." It later took the form of "Yeshua" and finally "Jesus." In ultimate terms, only Jesus can lead us out of the desert, across the Jordan, and into our inheritance. In fact, the book of Joshua highlights the reality that it wasn't really Joshua at all who was leading Israel. Joshua got his orders from Someone infinitely more highly placed. Just as Israel followed Joshua, Joshua followed the Commander of the Army of the Lord (see Jos 5:13–15). Human leaders are effective only as they take their cues from the Lord himself. Paul stated it succinctly: "Be imitators of me, as I am of Christ" (1 Cor 11:1).

Clarify the Objective

What is Canaan like? After crossing the Jordan, what is life going to be like in the Land of Promise? This is a question of huge significance. The history of the church is full of tragic examples of Christians who believed that crossing over into a deeper experience with God meant receiving a certain spiritual gift or having an intense emotional experience. Others have had the expectation that, when they reached their inheritance, their lives would be characterized by health, wealth, and happiness. Still others have tried to define the abundant life in terms of missionary service or social action. Such misconceptions about what the deeper life entails only lead to frustration and discouragement.

The Scriptures we have been examining concerning the Exodus teach us three important realities about the inheritance God has prepared for his people once they cross over into the Land of Promise.

First, it will be a place of warfare. Perhaps the strongest argument against those who claim the Jordan River is a metaphor of death and Canaan is a picture of heaven is here. When God's people reached the Land of Promise, they immediately encountered those who were hostile to their presence and who did all they could either to push them back into the desert or to destroy them. Canaan was full of enemies of God! This certainly cannot be true of heaven. Violent people living in fortified cities were occupying the very territories that God had promised the tribes of Israel. Though their inheritance was a gift of grace, the ransomed church of God was about to discover that they had to fight to possess it.

> " Crossing the Jordan and entering our inheritance means that we become fertile people.

The next chapter examines the battle of Jericho and discovers that it is meant to serve as a model for how warfare is to be conducted in Canaan. The redeemed must realize that they are not to wage war as the world wages war. Their tactics are to be different as are their strategic objectives. The victory at Jericho will teach Israel that trumpets are more important than swords in the battle of the Lord. Christians are called to be soldiers of the cross on a crusade of love (see 2 Cor 10:3–5).

Second, it will be a place of abundance and fruitfulness. For forty years, the children of Israel had experienced the barren sterility of the desert. Nothing grew in the Sinai Peninsula. On the other side of the Jordan River, however, the land was lusher and more fertile than anything they had ever experienced.

> For the LORD your God is bringing you into a good land, a land of brooks of water, of fountains and springs, flowing out in the valleys and hills, a land of wheat and barley, of vines and fig trees and pomegranates, a land of olive trees and honey, a land in which you will eat bread without scarcity, in which you will lack nothing . . . . And you shall eat and be full, and you shall bless the LORD your God for the good land he has given you. (Deuteronomy 8:7–10)

Crossing the Jordan and entering our inheritance means that we become fertile people. Our lives bear fruit and the shame of our barrenness is forever taken away. The sterility that defined the long years of wandering in the desert is finally over. It is no accident that the New Testament speaks of the ministry of the Holy Spirit as one of making God's people fruitful. Whether that fertility is seen in the fruit of the Spirit that develops godly character (see Gal 5:22–23) or in the fruit of ministry and evangelism (see Jn 15:5; Acts 1:8), the deeper life is characterized by amazing fertility and growth.

Once in Canaan, God's people discover that they have been blessed so that they can be a blessing. Far from being a place to relax and enjoy the perks of salvation, Canaan is where the redeemed discover that the purpose of spiritual wholeness is to spread the Good News of the kingdom to the ends of the earth. In Canaan, God finally is able to share with his people the real burden that weighs so heavily on his heart: the tribes and nations and peoples of the world who do not yet know his name. Canaan thus becomes a launching pad for the Lord's redemptive plan for the entire world. Speaking to Abraham of his future descendants who would live in the Land of Promise, God said, "in you all the families of the earth shall be blessed" (Gn 12:3). God brought his redeemed people to Canaan not just for their sake but for the sake of the world.

Citizenship in the Land of Promise means that one lives for those who are not yet citizens of the Land of Promise. God calls his people into abundant living so that *through them* he can reach a lost and suffering world. The prayer of Psalm 67 expresses well what should be the desire of all those who dwell in Canaan:

> May God be gracious to us and bless us
> and make his face to shine upon us,
> that your way may be known on earth,
> your saving power among all nations. (Psalm 67:1–2)

Third, it will be a place of rest. Though many different terms are used in the Bible to describe Canaan, perhaps the most interesting is the word "rest." Repeatedly, the Land of Promise is called a place of rest:

- "My presence will go with you and I will give you rest" (Ex 33:14).
- "For you have not as yet come to the rest and to the inheritance that the LORD your God is giving you" (Dt 12:9).
- "The LORD your God is providing you a place of rest and will give you this land" (Jos 1:13).
- "And the LORD gave them rest on every side . . ." (Jos 21:44).
- "So then, there remains a Sabbath rest for the people of God, for whoever has entered God's rest has also rested from his works as God did from his. Let us therefore strive to enter that rest . . ." (Heb 4:9–11).

The word "rest," for many people, conjures up a picture of inactivity. One might imagine that crossing into Canaan means a hammock and a glass of cold lemonade. There is nothing to do but sit and relax now that we are here in the land of milk and honey, right? Nothing could be further from the truth! Once on the western shore of the Jordan River, the people were confronted with a life of very intense activity. There were cities to construct, crops to plant, and battles to fight. They had a nation to build. How could the Land of Promise be a place of rest when there was so much work to do? Answering this question takes us to the heart of what the deeper life is all about.

To cross over into a deeper experience of God's saving grace means a level of surrender and trust that one has never experienced before.

To enter Canaan means that our hearts are no longer divided and our trust in the promises of God is total. We are his, completely his. This means that serving God no longer feels like a duty or obligation. It is all privilege. We obey God not because we *have to* but because we *want to*. We keep his commandments because we love him (see Jn 14:15), and his commandments "are not burdensome" (1 Jn 5:3). Our lives are no longer dominated by the ego-centric, self-serving, world-pleasing agenda that once controlled our hearts. The battles we now fight are not ours; they are his, and when victory is won, all the glory is his as well. Our lives in Canaan will be as busy and demanding as ever—maybe more—but the stress and anxiety will be gone. In the land of abundant living we discover the paradoxical truth that our work is no longer laborious toil. The curse has been reversed (see Gen3:17–19). No one stated this surprising reality better than Jesus:

> Come to me, all who labor and are heavy laden, and I will
> give you rest. Take my yoke upon you, and learn from me,
> for I am gentle and lowly in heart, and you will find rest
> for your souls. For my yoke is easy, and my burden is light.
> (Matthew 11:28–30)

Prepare for the Transition

Just as crossing the Red Sea demanded a time of preparation (teachings, plagues on Egypt, the Passover, etc.), so crossing the Jordan River was preceded by some very specific instructions. The preparations are especially spelled out in the Joshua 3:1–6.

Wait for a Divine Signal

On the eastern shore of the Jordan River, the people could clearly see Canaan on the other side, but they dared not cross over without a clear signal from God. Besides, God had not yet made it clear how the people were supposed to get through the water. As the people meditated on the obstacle that stood in their way, they received a clear command: "As soon as you see the ark of the covenant of the LORD your God being carried by the Levitical priests, then you shall set out from your place and follow it" (Joshua 3:3). In pivotal spiritual moments like this, timing is crucial. Wait for God. He will show you what to do and when to do it.

Expect the Unexpected

The people standing on the river bank had a long track record with God in their journey. They had seen him provide bread from heaven and water from rocks. They had experienced both God's protection and his provision. They had seen him get angry and manifest his wrath against rebels and traitors. However, standing there on the eastern shore, they were facing something entirely new. This was a situation they had not yet encountered. God reassured the people by gently reminding them, "You have not passed this way before" (Jos 3:4). In other words, God was telling his people:

> 66 This is the moment to ask God to cleanse the heart and make it single in its intention to love and obey God.

Things are about to change! Once on the other side of the Jordan, life will never again be what it was here in the desert. In Canaan, you will live by the power of the Spirit, not by the power of the flesh. Over there, the logic of Egyptian wisdom will be of little value. You'll need the mind of Christ. In the Sinai Peninsula, you were given a series of tests at the University of the Desert to prepare you for what lies ahead. But tomorrow, when you cross over into the land of promise, you need to understand that this is not a test. This is real life! Everything you have experienced from the Red Sea till now has been a preparation for this moment and for the life that awaits you over there. You're ready. You can do this because I am with you. Welcome to Canaan!

Sanctify Yourselves

We've seen that the book of Leviticus underscores the truth that it is *God* who sanctifies his people (see Lv 20:8). *He* is the one who sets them apart and makes them holy. Yet here, on the banks of the

Jordan, the emphasis is different. "Sanctify *yourselves*," the people are told (see Jos 3:5). Though God was certainly the primary actor in the work of sanctification, the people had to understand that they, too, had a crucial role to play. They were called to set themselves apart for God and his will for their lives. They were to purify themselves from those behaviors and attitudes that defiled and polluted their souls. To sanctify themselves meant that they were to come to a place of full surrender to God and his purposes for their lives. It meant their trust in God could no longer be partial. From this point forward, they had to trust him completely.

Such an act of self-consecration involved a deeper level of repentance than they had yet experienced. It meant a deep level of sorrow not just for what they had done but for who they were. Entering a deeper dimension of salvation meant becoming aware that the problem of sin was not just in their hands, but in their hearts. The hymn writer Robert Robinson stated it so powerfully in *Come Thou Fount of Every Blessing*:

> *O to grace how great a debtor*
> *Daily I'm constrained to be!*
> *Let Thy goodness, like a fetter,*
> *Bind my wandering heart to Thee:*
> *Prone to wander, Lord, I feel it,*
> *Prone to leave the God I love.*
> *Here's my heart, O take and seal it;*
> *Seal it for Thy courts above.*

Only those keenly aware of the bent to sinning that resides deep in every heart will be able to cross the Jordan and possess their inheritance. Entering into a life of holiness requires believers to repent of the ego-centric self-absorption and love of the world that has characterized their hearts until now. This is the moment to ask God to cleanse the heart and make it single in its intention to love and obey God. It is time to trust that God can indeed do what he has promised. "He who calls you is faithful; he will surely do it" (1 Thes 5:24).

Put Your Feet in the Water

Normally, the Jordan was a small river flowing gently from Galilee down toward the Dead Sea. In many places, it was quite narrow, perhaps only 100 feet wide, and somewhat shallow. Typically, crossing the Jordan was no big deal. However, when the Israelites arrived, it was spring, and the melting snow in the north would have caused the little river to become a raging torrent. It would have been deep, wide, and swift. Crossing such a river would have been a risky undertaking. To get to the other side demanded supernatural help. God had to open the way.

We tend to say: If God parts the waters *then* I'll march forward; if God opens a door, *then* I'll walk through it; or if God provides, *then* I'll step out in faith. At the Jordan River, God wanted his people to understand that the journey to spiritual wholeness doesn't work like that. To walk by faith means that *first*, we must step out in faith, and *then,* God will make a way. The world thinks that seeing is believing. In the kingdom of God, it is just the opposite. *First*, we believe in God. *Then*, we see him act.

> And Joshua said, "Here is how you shall know that the living God is among you and that he will without fail drive out from before you the Canaanites, the Hittites, the Hivites, the Perizzites, the Girgashites, the Amorites, and the Jebusites. Behold, the ark of the covenant of the Lord of all the earth is passing over before you into the Jordan. Now therefore take twelve men from the tribes of Israel, from each tribe a man. And when the soles of the feet of the priests bearing the ark of the LORD, the Lord of all the earth, shall rest in the waters of the Jordan, the waters of the Jordan shall be cut off from flowing, and the waters coming down from above shall stand in one heap." (Joshua 3: 10–13)

Did you notice how God explained that the waters of the Jordan would be cut off from flowing only *after* the soles of the feet of the priests entered the river? "Did I not tell you that if you *believed* you would *see* the glory of God?" (Jn 11:40, emphasis added). No one enters the land of abundant living without a similar step of faith.

Explain to Your Children What You Have Done

Crossing the Jordan is a big deal. These kinds of moments don't come around often in life, and when they do, we must make sure that the significance of what has happened is not forgotten. It is especially important that our children know the story of how God led us out of the desert of spiritual mediocrity and into the blessings of Canaan. Future generations need to know what happened at the Jordan River.

Joshua's instructions were clear: Twelve men, one from each tribe, were to take twelve large stones and put them on their shoulders as they walked through the river bed of the Jordan. On the western shore, at a place named Gilgal, in Canaan, the men were then to build a monument from the stones they had chosen. Joshua was insistent that the people understand the reason for this pile of stones:

> And he said to the people of Israel, "When your children ask their fathers in times to come, 'What do these stones mean?' then you shall let your children know, 'Israel passed over this Jordan on dry ground.' For the LORD your God dried up the waters of the Jordan for you until you passed over, as the LORD your God did to the Red Sea, which he dried up for us until we passed over, so that all the peoples of the earth may know that the hand of the LORD is mighty, that you may fear the LORD your God forever." (Joshua 4:21–24)

Failure to remember moments of spiritual significance can be deadly, not only for us but also for our children. The twelve stones at Gilgal were to be a "sign" (Jos 4:6) and "a memorial forever" (Jos 4:7). We must remember how God brought his people out so that he could bring them in!

Lord, I Believe a Rest Remains

Charles Wesley (1707–1788)

*Lord, I believe a rest remains
To all thy people known,
A rest where pure enjoyment reigns,
And thou art loved alone:*

*A rest, where all our souls desire
Is fixed on things above;
Where fear, and sin, and grief expire,
Cast out by perfect love.*

*O that I now the rest might know,
Believe, and enter in!
Now, Saviour, now the power bestow,
And let me cease from sin.*

*Remove this hardness from my heart,
This unbelief remove:
To me the rest of faith impart,
The Sabbath of thy love.*

*Thy name to me, thy nature grant!
This, only this be given:
Nothing beside my God I want,
Nothing in earth or heaven.*

*Come, Father, Son, and Holy Ghost,
And seal me thine abode!
Let all I am in thee be lost,
Let all be lost in God.*

17
Soldiers of Christ, Arise!
(Joshua 5:13–6:27)

"Fight the good fight of faith." (1 Timothy 6:12)

As far back as I can remember, I loved playing war. While my two sisters were inside having a tea party with their dolls and stuffed animals, I was out in the back yard digging a fox hole to fight off evil invaders and save the world. Every stick was a potential rifle and every clod of dirt a hand grenade. It seemed that I was hard-wired so that I wanted to hit something, shoot something, or blow something up! I had no greater aspiration than to die heroically on a field of battle, giving my life for some great cause. Modern psychologists might suggest a pathological disorder to explain such behaviors, but I'm not so sure. The Scriptures tell us that the Lord himself is "a man of war" (Ex 15:3). If we are created in his image, then it stands to reason that we are born for battle. To be sure, when the heart is selfishly wicked, the urge to fight is a sinful tendency that needs to be quelled. The countless wars and interpersonal conflicts that mark human existence give eloquent expression to the fact that the warrior instinct can have tragic consequences.

The call to holiness teaches us that God does not want to eradicate our desire to fight; he wants to sanctify it. The Scriptures are full of exhortations to the saints to put on the full armor of God and fight the good fight of faith (see Eph 6:10–20; 1 Tm 6:12; etc.). While a deeper work of grace does indeed aim to cure us forever of the desire to hurt other people and take what is theirs, its goal is certainly not to turn us into wimps and pacifists. Our very survival in the Land of Promise hinges upon our learning how to fight the *right* battles, for the *right* reasons, using the *right* weapons.

This final chapter in *Journey to Spiritual Wholeness* is a call to battle. Just as the people of Israel discovered the necessity of combat the moment they crossed over the Jordan, Christians today who desire to live a life of complete devotion to Jesus Christ must learn how to practice sanctified warfare. Their very survival depends on it.

MISSION JERICHO

At long last, the people of God had reached their inheritance! Their years of fruitless wandering in the desert were over. They had crossed the Jordan and were finally in the land God had promised to give them. They were home. They could now relax and enjoy some milk and honey, right?

The Hebrew people discovered that Canaan was full of cruel and wicked people. To be exact, the land of their inheritance was inhabited by Amalekites, Hittites, Jebusites, Amorites, Canaanites, Perizzites, and Hivites, not to mention the dreaded Nephilim. It took the people only a few days to comprehend that the land of rest was certainly *not* going to be a land of inactivity. The country was full of scary people who lived in fortified cities. They were surrounded by enemies who wanted either to push them back into the desert or to kill them.

> 66 Christians today who desire to live a life of complete devotion to Jesus Christ must learn how to practice sanctified combat. Their very survival depends on it.

Possessing one's inheritance in an environment such as this demands that one think and act like a soldier. Approaching the land of abundant living with the wrong mindset ensures frustration and raises the possibility of experiencing defeat in the very place that God has promised victory. Paul's counsel to young Timothy as he launched forward in his quest to do the will of God is right on target:

> Share in suffering as a good soldier of Christ Jesus. No soldier gets entangled in civilian pursuits, since his aim is to please the one who enlisted him. An athlete is not crowned unless he competes according to the rules. It is the hard-working farmer who ought to have the first share of the crops. Think over what I say, for the Lord will give you understanding in everything. (2 Timothy 2:3–7)

Having crossed the Jordan River, the people paused on the western shore to get their bearings in this strange new land called Canaan. After making sure that the men of the new generation had all experienced the initiatory rite of circumcision (see Jos 5:1–9), the people did something they had not done in almost forty years:

> While the people of Israel were encamped at Gilgal, they kept the Passover on the fourteenth day of the month in the evening on the plains of Jericho. And the day after the Passover, on that very day, they ate of the produce of the land, unleavened cakes and parched grain. And the manna ceased the day after they ate of the produce of the land . . . . (Joshua 5:10–12)

Once these preparations were finished, the people looked around to determine what would be the first order of business in their new home. Almost immediately, they realized that the fortress of Jericho stood in their path, blocking access to the interior. There would be no forward progress until this obstacle was dealt with.

The book of Joshua introduces us to the secret of victorious living by outlining the steps Israel took in fighting the battle of Jericho. For Christians today, this translates into teaching on the art of spiritual warfare. The story of what happened at Jericho (see Jos 5:13–6:27) teaches us that there are four things a soldier of Christ needs to know to experience spiritual victory: know what it means to know, know your commander-in-chief, know your enemy, and know your strategy and weapons.

Know What It Means to Know

Perhaps the most problem-riddled, dysfunctional church in the New Testament was Corinth. The church struggled with divisions, immorality, false doctrine, lawsuits among its members, the misuse of spiritual gifts, and drunkenness at church potluck dinners. Yet the Corinthians saw themselves as spiritually mature! Their problem was that they didn't know what they didn't know, and what they thought they knew only revealed their ignorance. Paul spoke strongly: "If anyone imagines that he knows something, he does not yet know as he ought to know" (1 Cor 8:2). At least part of the problem was that the Corinthians had a very Greek (Western) understanding of knowledge. They thought that knowledge was the result of gaining much information. If they knew *about* something and could define it and analyze it, then they thought they knew it. Because they had lots of information about spiritual gifts, doctrinal definitions, and social relationships, they drew the conclusion that they were knowledgeable and wise, spiritually mature. Paul sought

> 66 **The real question was not if the Lord was on their side—but if they were on his.**

to introduce these Greeks to a more Hebraic way of thinking. For the Hebrew mind, "to know" something means to experience it (see Gn 4:1; Jer 22:16; etc.). True knowledge involves far more than academic facts and information. It involves first-hand experience.

When we apply this concept to what was happening to God's people as they first entered the land of Canaan, we discover that the first thing a soldier of Christ needs to know is that it is not enough to know *about* spiritual warfare. To be victorious in facing the battles ahead, Israel needed to know war, to experience it for themselves. This was not theory; this was life! The book of Judges, written a generation later, also makes this important point:

> Now these are the nations that the LORD left, to test Israel
> by them, that is, all in Israel who had not experienced all the
> wars in Canaan. It was only in order that the generations of

the people of Israel might know war, to teach war to those who had not known it before. (Judges 3:1–2)

The deeper life is all about conflict and battle. Fighting against the world, the flesh, and the devil characterizes life in the Land of Promise. No one will possess their inheritance until they experience "war" first-hand. There are no exceptions. To enter the Land of Promise means that we must take on the mentality of a soldier and engage the forces that fight against the kingdom of God.

KNOW YOUR COMMANDER-IN-CHIEF

The turning point in the battle of Jericho occurred *before* the battle even took place. As General Joshua contemplated the walled city that was before him, a mysterious visitor suddenly confronted him with a drawn sword in his hand. Joshua was about to experience the most important battle of his entire life.

> When Joshua was by Jericho, he lifted up his eyes and looked, and behold, a man was standing before him with his drawn sword in his hand. And Joshua went to him and said to him, "Are you for us, or for our adversaries?" And he said, "No; but I am the commander of the army of the LORD. Now I have come." And Joshua fell on his face to the earth and worshiped and said to him, "What does my lord say to his servant?" And the commander of the LORD's army said to Joshua, "Take off your sandals from your feet, for the place where you are standing is holy." And Joshua did so. (Joshua 5:13–15)

Scholars debate the precise identity of this unnamed military commander who comes to visit Joshua. The circumstances, however, have all the trappings of a divine manifestation of God himself. This seems to have been a pre-incarnate appearance of the Second Person of the Trinity! The lesson Joshua needed to learn was of such magnitude that God himself came to reinforce the lesson.

Who's in charge? *That* is the question that had to be settled *before* the battle for Jericho even began. Prior to this moment, Joshua had assumed that he was the one in charge. He was, after all, the general.

Feeling threatened by this divine visitor holding a drawn sword, Joshua asked, "Are you for us, or for our adversaries?" (Jos 5:13). In other words, Joshua wanted to know which side this guy was on. I love the answer the Lord gave: "No." What kind of an answer is *that*? Apparently, Joshua was asking the wrong question. His thinking about the battle was all wrong. The real question was not if the Lord was on *their* side—but if they were on *his.*

The armed visitor then stated the real purpose for his coming: "I am the commander of the army of the LORD. Now I have come" (Jos 5:14). In other words, the Lord was saying to General Joshua, "I have not come to take sides—I have come to take over!" This was the moment when everything changed for Joshua. This was the moment that defined Israel's future and gave her the assurance of victory. Now, Joshua clearly understood that the battle he was about to fight was not his battle; it was God's. When Joshua fell on his face in worship before his heavenly visitor, he surrendered to the one who was really in charge.

Victory comes through surrender. It is only when we come, like Joshua, to a place of full consecration, where we give all control over to the Lord, that we are ready to fight. A soldier of Christ must come to the place where he realizes he is not in charge. The battle is the Lord's.

KNOW YOUR ENEMY

In spiritual warfare, recognizing who the enemy is may be harder than you think. As Joshua looked out on Jericho, contemplating the battle, he probably thought that everyone living in that wicked city was an enemy of God and should be destroyed. From a distance, it is so easy to categorize and stereotype the people around us, often assuming they are the enemy before we've ever even met them. At Jericho, the Hebrews were in for a surprise. Inside the walls of the city was an ally they did not even know they had. Not every citizen of Jericho was to be considered an enemy.

The story of Rahab (see Jos 2) reminds us that God has loyal followers in the most surprising places. Rahab was not only a citizen of a pagan city hostile to God but also a prostitute! Who could have imagined that someone like this would be on God's side? Though everyone else in the city of Jericho was to be destroyed, the Lord made sure that Rahab was spared because of the faith she had shown in protecting the spies.

> And the city and all that is within it shall be devoted to the
> LORD for destruction. Only Rahab the prostitute and all
> who are with her in her house shall live, because she hid the
> messengers whom we sent. (Joshua 6:17)

As the story of the battle of Jericho was told and retold through Israel's history, Rahab came to be recognized as perhaps the real heroine of the story, and her fame was celebrated down through the centuries as one of the giants of the faith. God even saw fit to include her in the genealogical chain that gave birth to the Messiah (see Mt 1:5), and her name is mentioned among the heroes and heroines of the faith (see Heb 11:31). The book of James names her as someone who illustrates the principle that faith without works is dead (see Jas 2:25).

For those who cross over into the land of abundant living, spiritual warfare will be a constant reality in the quest to possess our inheritance. Success will hinge to a large degree on the ability to discern who the enemy is and who he isn't. Seen in spiritual terms, the real enemy is rarely a person or a group. The real enemies of God are sin, deception, lies, idolatry, hatred, arrogance, worldliness, and the like. God did not hate the citizens of Jericho. In fact, he loved them and longed for their salvation. Paul wrote about the nature of our true enemy:

> For we do not wrestle against flesh and blood, but against
> the rulers, against the authorities, against the cosmic powers
> over this present darkness, against the spiritual forces of evil
> in the heavenly places. (Ephesians 6:12)

Remember who the enemy is: the world, the flesh, and the devil. When we focus on individuals, groups, or nations, assuming *they* are the enemy, we risk being blind to allies God may have placed behind enemy lines. In fighting them, we may be fighting against God.

Know Your Strategy and Weapons

The most amazing thing about the battle of Jericho is the strategy employed and the weapons used. In typical attacks on walled cities, one would expect to see the classic examples of siege warfare: battering rams, ladders, siege towers, catapults, etc. However, in Canaan, the methods of fighting are very different. God's instructions were crystal clear:

> You shall march around the city, all the men of war going around the city once. Thus shall you do for six days. Seven priests shall bear seven trumpets of rams' horns before the ark. On the seventh day you shall march around the city seven times, and the priests shall blow the trumpets. And when they make a long blast with the ram's horn, when you hear the sound of the trumpet, then all the people shall shout with a great shout, and the wall of the city will fall down flat, and the people shall go up, everyone straight before him."
> (Joshua 6:3–5)

Although General Joshua's response to these instructions is not recorded, I can imagine that his first reaction must have been something like this: "You want me to do *what*? You want us to just take some trumpets and walk around the city? Won't we need catapults and ladders? Are these our *only* instructions?" It sounds more like a comedy routine and a recipe for disaster, but Joshua remembered that, just a short time earlier, he had fallen on his face at the feet of the Commander of the army of the Lord in full surrender and worship. In that moment of total consecration, he had decided to trust God and his leadership. Jericho was God's battle, and he had the right to define his strategy and to choose his weapons.

The strategy God wants us to follow and the weapons he wants us to use are just as important as the battle itself. To opt for a strategy of our own using worldly weapons ensures defeat—even if we "win." The history of the church is full of tragic examples of men and women who fought the right battles but used the wrong weapons. Paul was emphatic on this point as he exhorted the believers in Corinth:

> For though we walk in the flesh, we are not waging war according to the flesh. For the weapons of our warfare are not of the flesh but have divine power to destroy strongholds. We destroy arguments and every lofty opinion raised against the knowledge of God, and take every thought captive to obey Christ . . . . (2 Corinthians 10:3–5)

To fight spiritual battles using worldly weapons makes a travesty of the abundant life God has given us. To survive and thrive in the Land of Promise, one must learn to fight the Lord's battles in the Lord's way.

In the garden of Gethsemane, when a large cohort of soldiers came to arrest Jesus, Peter found a sword and attacked. He only succeeded in cutting off the ear of the servant of the High Priest (see Jn 18:10–11). Though Peter undoubtedly felt he had done something heroic, Jesus saw it otherwise. On the one hand, Peter was in the right battle, and he was on the right side. He was even ready to die for his faith. On the other hand, he was using the wrong weapons and following a misguided strategy. Such action threatened to undermine the very mission that Jesus had called him to perform.

Paul clarified any confusion about the weapons we should use in fighting the Lord's battles. In Ephesians 6:10–20, he enumerated the armor a soldier of Christ needs for success in spiritual combat. One simple way to personalize this list so that it becomes a part of our lives in the battles we face is to turn each piece of armor into a prayer. Consider beginning each day and dressing for battle by praying something like this:

1. *The belt of truth.* O Lord, Satan's power comes through the lies that he tells: lies about God; lies about me; lies about others; and lies about the truth. Today, Lord, I put on the belt of truth so that I can stand against those lies and speak the truth that sets us free.
2. *The breastplate of righteousness.* Lord, this piece of armor protects my heart, from which come the issues of life. Forgive the

sins I've committed and cleanse me from the inbred sin that yet remains. My strength in battle today hinges in great measure on the integrity of my character. O Lord, guard my heart.

3. *The shoes of the gospel of peace.* When I meet conflict today, Lord, let my heart be at peace. Lead my steps so that these shoes of the gospel of peace spread your presence everywhere I go.

4. *The shield of faith.* It's dangerous out there, Lord. Protect me today from temptation, discouragement, and doubt. When sin seeks to lure me into its snare, enable me to see the danger and quench the fiery darts of the adversary with the shield of faith.

5. *The helmet of salvation.* Anchor me in your saving grace today, Lord, so that my conscience is clean and my thoughts are pure. Protect my mind so I think only with the mind of Christ.

6. *The sword of the Spirit, which is the word of God.* Help me, Lord, to know when it is time to move from a defensive posture to an offensive one. Give me courage and strength to advance and possess new territory for you.

> " My strength in battle today hinges in great measure on the integrity of my character.

7. *Praying always in the Spirit.* Teach me to pray, Lord. Help me to live in an attitude of praise, thanksgiving, confession, and intercession. Through the day, nudge me, prompt me, call me to prayer.

Notice that there is no armor for the back. Soldiers in the army of the Lord are safest when they press forward, facing the enemy. Those who turn and run are in more danger than those who stand and fight. When we fight, however, we must use spiritual weapons. To use worldly weapons in the Lord's battle is to lose, even if we win.

The story is told about a young lad who was a bugler in one of Napoleon's regiments. He had dutifully learned all the signals related to giving audible commands on the field of battle. One day, the battle was going badly and an officer ran up to the bugle boy and shouted,

"Sound retreat! Sound retreat!" Standing erect and at full attention, the boy shouted back, "Sir, Napoleon's bugle boy doesn't know retreat."

God calls us to cross the Jordan and possess our inheritance. The opposition will be fierce and the battles will be full of danger. However, in the army of the Lord, there is no turning back. We will either win the battle and possess the land or we will die trying.

Soldiers of Christ, Arise

Charles Wesley (1707–1788)

Soldiers of Christ, arise
And put your armor on,
Strong in the strength which God supplies,
Through His eternal Son;
Strong in the Lord of Hosts,
And in His mighty pow'r,
Who in the strength of Jesus trusts
Is more than conqueror.

Stand then in His great might,
With all His strength endued;
And take, to arm you for the fight,
The panoply of God,
That, having all things done,
And all your conflicts past,
Ye may o'ercome through Christ alone,
And stand complete at last.

Leave no unguarded place,
No weakness of the soul,
Take every virtue, every grace,
And fortify the whole.
To keep your armor bright
Attend with constant care,
Still walking in your Captain's sight
And watching unto prayer.

From strength to strength go on;
Wrestle, and fight, and pray;
Tread all the powers of darkness down,
And win the well-fought day:
Still let the Spirit cry
In all His soldiers, "Come!"
Till Christ the Lord descend from high,
And take the conquerors home.

Questions for Discussion

Introduction

1. What are the different metaphors of salvation used in the Bible? Which metaphor best describes your experience?

2. How does thinking of spiritual wholeness as a journey impact the way you think about conversion, sin, assurance, evangelism, perseverance, sanctification, etc.?

3. How did Paul address the issue of spiritual immaturity by preaching the map?

4. The race is determined at the finish line, not in the starting blocks. Discuss this.

5. How does 1 Corinthians 10:13 encourage you to keep pressing on in your own journey?

Chapter 1—Who Am I?

1. Describe a time when you felt like an eagle on a turkey farm.

2. In what way was pain a gift to the Hebrews in Egypt? How has pain been a gift to you?

3. The study claims that you don't discover your identity by looking in the mirror but rather when you lose yourself and find God. Discuss this.

4. How does one get to the place where the appetite for "milk and honey" is stronger than the appetite for "leaks and onions"?

5. Moses' call at the burning bush is illustrative of the call that God offers everyone. How have you experienced such a call?

CHAPTER 2:—REDEEMED

1. In what ways does the Exodus express God's love for the Egyptians and his desire for them to be saved as well as the Hebrews?

2. Describe a time in your life when you discovered that obedience to the will of God seemed to make the situation worse rather than better.

3. Is it possible to believe in the one true God before your false gods have been exposed as frauds?

4. How does the miracle at the Red Sea help you to understand how faith and works go together?

5. Water and blood have great symbolic (sacramental) value in the two primary ordinances of the church: Baptism and Communion. How does the Exodus enrich your understanding of these two sacraments and help you to better understand your own journey to spiritual wholeness?

6. Make it personal: Are you currently between the devil and the deep blue sea in some situation in your life? How has this chapter helped you to face the challenge?

CHAPTER 3—THE BITTER PLACE

1. What experiences in your life have caused you to burst into joyful song like the Hebrews did after their redemption at the Red Sea?

2. What does it mean to have a "theology of the desert"? What happens when followers of Christ have no such theology?

3. Why does God lead his redeemed people to bitter places?

4. Describe a time in your life when God led you to a bitter place. What kind of test was God conducting in your life? Did you pass the test?

5. Think of a bitter reality that you are facing now. Which part of the Creed of Marah is most challenging for you to affirm?

Chapter 4—Wonder Bread

1. How have you reacted when you found yourself in a place of great scarcity and want?

2. Do you agree with the statement, "the Bible is a food-driven book"? Why or why not?

3. Do you ever suffer from the grumpies? What is its cure?

4. How can you recognize someone who has a spiritual eating disorder? What can you do to offer help?

5. Have you learned to feed yourself? What is your daily routine?

6. In what sense is Jesus the "true bread" from heaven? How is he like the manna of Exodus 16? How is he different?

Chapter 5—Spiritual Warfare

1. Describe a time in your life when God gave you a second chance (a re-test) to learn a lesson you failed to learn the first time.

2. What does it mean to test God? Describe a situation when this was happening.

3. What is the primary lesson about spiritual warfare you learned from this chapter?

4. When it comes to spiritual warfare, do you first think about the need to fight or the need to pray? What does this reveal about your journey?

5. Which of the four principles of intercession (identification, unity, agony, and authority) do you need most in your own efforts at intercessory prayer?

Chapter 6—The Stress Test

1. How do you handle times of great stress, when you feel overworked and on the point of burnout? What did you learn in this chapter that might help you in the future?

2. What happens when a pastor or ministry leader reaches a point of burnout? How should the church respond?

3. Does your church have a small group ministry? Is it seen as a "program," or is it viewed as the indispensable expression of the body of Christ?

4. Is there an area in your life where you need organization and administration? How is it hindering your journey? What is God asking you to do about it?

Chapter 7—Dearly Beloved, We Are Gathered Here . . .

1. How has this study changed your perspective of Mount Sinai?

2. What is it like to be married to God, a spouse who is perfect in every way?

3. How is the worship of other gods like adultery?

4. Is divorce possible for someone in a covenant relationship with God?

5. How does marriage help us to better understand the nature and purpose of redemption?

6. What's new about the New Covenant?

Chapter 8—Oh, How I Love Your Law!

1. What behavior typifies someone who believes in antinomianism? Why is it important to recognize this false belief system today?

2. What behavior typifies someone who follows the heresy of legalism? Why is it important to recognize this false belief system today?

3. Is it possible to be genuinely redeemed and still have mistaken notions about who God is and what he wants?

4. What is the role of the moral law in the life of the believer?

5. Do you believe it is possible to keep God's law? Do you believe this is possible for you?

Chapter 9—A House for God

1. What spaces (places, locations, buildings, etc.) have sacred meaning for you? How do you use these spaces?

2. How does the architecture of your church and especially the space where you worship contribute to authentic worship? How does it detract?

3. In Moses' day, God's people are forbidden to make an image of him but they are encouraged to build a beautiful building and fill it with meaningful symbols that help in worship. What principles should we draw from this reality?

4. How does understanding the tabernacle help us prepare our bodies to be temples of God?

Chapter 10—A Lot of Bull

1. How does the story of the golden calf fit into your understanding of the journey to spiritual wholeness?

2. Have you ever been in a church where there was clergy malpractice? Describe what it was like.

3. Have you ever been guilty of shaping God into the form you thought he should be rather than allowing him to reveal himself to you? How did you correct your error?

4. What does true worship look like?

Chapter 11—Living with the Holy One

1. What is your personal history with the book of Leviticus? How has this chapter affected your thinking?

2. Define the word "holy" and describe how it defines God.

3. The author states that "we can't worship the Holy One and not become holy." Do you agree? Discuss this.

4. What happens when holiness is understood as what I *do* rather than who I *am*?

5. Make it personal: Am I holy? How do I become holy?

Chapter 12—The "Grumpies"

1. Do you think of grumbling and complaining as a serious sin? Why does God treat it so seriously?

2. How does one go about changing an appetite (craving) for leeks and onions to an appetite for milk and honey?

3. Have you been critical of how God was leading your life and providing for your needs? What does such an attitude signify? How should it be addressed?

4. If you are a parent, think of a time your children craved something that was bad for them. How did you handle it?

5. Has God ever given you something you asked for—and then you regretted that he did? Discuss this.

Chapter 13—The Moment of Truth

1. What happens to those who have enough faith to get out of Egypt but not enough to get in to Canaan? What happens to those who die in "the desert"?

2. Has God ever brought you to a place like Kadesh-barnea? How did you respond at your "moment of truth"? What did you learn?

3. Have you ever gone against the crowd in determining the will of God? What happened?

4. Which one of the four reasons that caused the Hebrews to turn back (fear, peer pressure, double-mindedness, or unbelief) represents your greatest struggle?

Chapter 14—The Land of In-Between

1. What is the difference between unintentional sins and high-handed sins? Why is this difference important?

2. How do you know if a spiritual leader is ordained by God (like Moses) or self-appointed (like Korah)?

3. Describe the linkage between idolatry (bad theology) and immorality. Which comes first? Why is this connection so important to recognize?

4. Have you been tempted to settle for something less than God's best? What did you do about it?

CHAPTER 15—THE HEART OF THE MATTER

1. What does the statement "the heart of the matter is the matter of the heart" mean?

2. Does the thought that God is much more interested in the state of our hearts than in the quantity of our good works (performance) comfort you or trouble you?

3. Why are we so inclined to focus on outward performance rather than inward love?

4. Do you believe that the gospel is more than behavior modification? Has it transformed you in the very depths of your inward being?

5. Does your church preach justification by faith but sanctification by works?

CHAPTER 16—CROSSING JORDAN

1. How do you respond to the notion of "two crisis experiences" of the Christian life? Does this comfort you or trouble you?

2. What is the theological importance of the question of whether the Jordan River is a symbol for death or whether it marks the introduction to the victorious life?

3. When you think about your own spiritual journey, is Romans 7 or Romans 8 normative? Does your experience reflect your theology or does your theology reflect your experience?

4. If life in Canaan is busy and demanding, how can it possibly be called a place of "rest"?

5. Has there been a time in your own journey when God told you to first "put your feet in the water" and *then* he would open up a way for you?

6. Why do so few Christians seem to be experiencing the abundant, victorious life?

CHAPTER 17—SOLDIERS OF CHRIST, ARISE!

1. Do you tend to think of spiritual warfare as part of the normal Christian life or as an exception to the rule?

2. Describe a situation when you knew you were in the right battle and on the right side but you used the wrong weapons. What was the result?

3. Why is it so important to realize that our real enemy is in the cosmic realm rather than the human realm?

4. Think of a spiritual battle you are currently facing. Look again at the "four things a soldier of Christ must know." What is God saying to you?